Dear Future Exam Success Story

First of all, **THANK YOU** for purchasing Mometrix study materials!

Second, congratulations! You are one of the few determined test-takers who are committed to doing whatever it takes to excel on your exam. **You have come to the right place.** We developed these study materials with one goal in mind: to deliver you the information you need in a format that's concise and easy to use.

In addition to optimizing your guide for the content of the test, we've outlined our recommended steps for breaking down the preparation process into small, attainable goals so you can make sure you stay on track.

We've also analyzed the entire test-taking process, identifying the most common pitfalls and showing how you can overcome them and be ready for any curveball the test throws you.

Standardized testing is one of the biggest obstacles on your road to success, which only increases the importance of doing well in the high-pressure, high-stakes environment of test day. Your results on this test could have a significant impact on your future, and this guide provides the information and practical advice to help you achieve your full potential on test day.

Your success is our success

We would love to hear from you! If you would like to share the story of your exam success or if you have any questions or comments in regard to our products, please contact us at **800-673-8175** or **support@mometrix.com**.

Thanks again for your business and we wish you continued success!

Sincerely,
The Mometrix Test Preparation Team

Need more help? Check out our flashcards at:
http://MometrixFlashcards.com/PraxisII

I0894310

Copyright © 2026 by Mometrix Media LLC. All rights reserved.
Printed in the United States of America

Mometrix
TEST PREPARATION

Praxis® II

Special Education: Teaching Speech to Students with Language Impairments (5881) Exam

Secrets Study Guide

Praxis is a registered trademark of Educational Testing Service, which is not affiliated with Mometrix Test Preparation and does not endorse this product.

TABLE OF CONTENTS

Introduction

Thank you for purchasing this resource! You have made the choice to prepare yourself for a test that could have a huge impact on your future, and this guide is designed to help you be fully ready for test day. Obviously, it's important to have a solid understanding of the test material, but you also need to be prepared for the unique environment and stressors of the test, so that you can perform to the best of your abilities.

For this purpose, the first section that appears in this guide is the **Secret Keys**. We've devoted countless hours to meticulously researching what works and what doesn't, and we've boiled down our findings to the five most impactful steps you can take to improve your performance on the test. We start at the beginning with study planning and move through the preparation process, all the way to the testing strategies that will help you get the most out of what you know when you're finally sitting in front of the test.

We recommend that you start preparing for your test as far in advance as possible. However, if you've bought this guide as a last-minute study resource and only have a few days before your test, we recommend that you skip over the first two Secret Keys since they address a long-term study plan.

If you struggle with **test anxiety**, we strongly encourage you to check out our recommendations for how you can overcome it. Test anxiety is a formidable foe, but it can be beaten, and we want to make sure you have the tools you need to defeat it.

Copyright © Mometrix Media. You have been licensed one copy of this document for personal use only. Any other reproduction or redistribution is strictly prohibited. All rights reserved.
This content is provided for test preparation purposes only and does not imply an endorsement by Mometrix of any particular political, scientific, or religious point of view.

Secret Key #1 – Plan Big, Study Small

There's a lot riding on your performance. If you want to ace this test, you're going to need to keep your skills sharp and the material fresh in your mind. You need a plan that lets you review everything you need to know while still fitting in your schedule. We'll break this strategy down into three categories.

Information Organization

Start with the information you already have: the official test outline. From this, you can make a complete list of all the concepts you need to cover before the test. Organize these concepts into groups that can be studied together, and create a list of any related vocabulary you need to learn so you can brush up on any difficult terms. You'll want to keep this vocabulary list handy once you actually start studying since you may need to add to it along the way.

Time Management

Once you have your set of study concepts, decide how to spread them out over the time you have left before the test. Break your study plan into small, clear goals so you have a manageable task for each day and know exactly what you're doing. Then just focus on one small step at a time. When you manage your time this way, you don't need to spend hours at a time studying. Studying a small block of content for a short period each day helps you retain information better and avoid stressing over how much you have left to do. You can relax knowing that you have a plan to cover everything in time. In order for this strategy to be effective though, you have to start studying early and stick to your schedule. Avoid the exhaustion and futility that comes from last-minute cramming!

Study Environment

The environment you study in has a big impact on your learning. Studying in a coffee shop, while probably more enjoyable, is not likely to be as fruitful as studying in a quiet room. It's important to keep distractions to a minimum. You're only planning to study for a short block of time, so make the most of it. Don't pause to check your phone or get up to find a snack. It's also important to **avoid multitasking**. Research has consistently shown that multitasking will make your studying dramatically less effective. Your study area should also be comfortable and well-lit so you don't have the distraction of straining your eyes or sitting on an uncomfortable chair.

The time of day you study is also important. You want to be rested and alert. Don't wait until just before bedtime. Study when you'll be most likely to comprehend and remember. Even better, if you know what time of day your test will be, set that time aside for study. That way your brain will be used to working on that subject at that specific time and you'll have a better chance of recalling information.

Finally, it can be helpful to team up with others who are studying for the same test. Your actual studying should be done in as isolated an environment as possible, but the work of organizing the information and setting up the study plan can be divided up. In between study sessions, you can discuss with your teammates the concepts that you're all studying and quiz each other on the details. Just be sure that your teammates are as serious about the test as you are. If you find that your study time is being replaced with social time, you might need to find a new team.

Copyright © Mometrix Media. You have been licensed one copy of this document for personal use only. Any other reproduction or redistribution is strictly prohibited. All rights reserved.
This content is provided for test preparation purposes only and does not imply an endorsement by Mometrix of any particular political, scientific, or religious point of view.

Secret Key #2 – Make Your Studying Count

You're devoting a lot of time and effort to preparing for this test, so you want to be absolutely certain it will pay off. This means doing more than just reading the content and hoping you can remember it on test day. It's important to make every minute of study count. There are two main areas you can focus on to make your studying count.

Retention

It doesn't matter how much time you study if you can't remember the material. You need to make sure you are retaining the concepts. To check your retention of the information you're learning, try recalling it at later times with minimal prompting. Try carrying around flashcards and glance at one or two from time to time or ask a friend who's also studying for the test to quiz you.

To enhance your retention, look for ways to put the information into practice so that you can apply it rather than simply recalling it. If you're using the information in practical ways, it will be much easier to remember. Similarly, it helps to solidify a concept in your mind if you're not only reading it to yourself but also explaining it to someone else. Ask a friend to let you teach them about a concept you're a little shaky on (or speak aloud to an imaginary audience if necessary). As you try to summarize, define, give examples, and answer your friend's questions, you'll understand the concepts better and they will stay with you longer. Finally, step back for a big picture view and ask yourself how each piece of information fits with the whole subject. When you link the different concepts together and see them working together as a whole, it's easier to remember the individual components.

Finally, practice showing your work on any multi-step problems, even if you're just studying. Writing out each step you take to solve a problem will help solidify the process in your mind, and you'll be more likely to remember it during the test.

Modality

Modality simply refers to the means or method by which you study. Choosing a study modality that fits your own individual learning style is crucial. No two people learn best in exactly the same way, so it's important to know your strengths and use them to your advantage.

For example, if you learn best by visualization, focus on visualizing a concept in your mind and draw an image or a diagram. Try color-coding your notes, illustrating them, or creating symbols that will trigger your mind to recall a learned concept. If you learn best by hearing or discussing information, find a study partner who learns the same way or read aloud to yourself. Think about how to put the information in your own words. Imagine that you are giving a lecture on the topic and record yourself so you can listen to it later.

For any learning style, flashcards can be helpful. Organize the information so you can take advantage of spare moments to review. Underline key words or phrases. Use different colors for different categories. Mnemonic devices (such as creating a short list in which every item starts with the same letter) can also help with retention. Find what works best for you and use it to store the information in your mind most effectively and easily.

Copyright © Mometrix Media. You have been licensed one copy of this document for personal use only. Any other reproduction or redistribution is strictly prohibited. All rights reserved.
This content is provided for test preparation purposes only and does not imply an endorsement by Mometrix of any particular political, scientific, or religious point of view.

Secret Key #3 – Practice the Right Way

Your success on test day depends not only on how many hours you put into preparing, but also on whether you prepared the right way. It's good to check along the way to see if your studying is paying off. One of the most effective ways to do this is by taking practice tests to evaluate your progress. Practice tests are useful because they show exactly where you need to improve. Every time you take a practice test, pay special attention to these three groups of questions:

- The questions you got wrong
- The questions you had to guess on, even if you guessed right
- The questions you found difficult or slow to work through

This will show you exactly what your weak areas are, and where you need to devote more study time. Ask yourself why each of these questions gave you trouble. Was it because you didn't understand the material? Was it because you didn't remember the vocabulary? Do you need more repetitions on this type of question to build speed and confidence? Dig into those questions and figure out how you can strengthen your weak areas as you go back to review the material.

Additionally, many practice tests have a section explaining the answer choices. It can be tempting to read the explanation and think that you now have a good understanding of the concept. However, an explanation likely only covers part of the question's broader context. Even if the explanation makes perfect sense, **go back and investigate** every concept related to the question until you're positive you have a thorough understanding.

As you go along, keep in mind that the practice test is just that: practice. Memorizing these questions and answers will not be very helpful on the actual test because it is unlikely to have any of the same exact questions. If you only know the right answers to the sample questions, you won't be prepared for the real thing. **Study the concepts** until you understand them fully, and then you'll be able to answer any question that shows up on the test.

It's important to wait on the practice tests until you're ready. If you take a test on your first day of study, you may be overwhelmed by the amount of material covered and how much you need to learn. Work up to it gradually.

On test day, you'll need to be prepared for answering questions, managing your time, and using the test-taking strategies you've learned. It's a lot to balance, like a mental marathon that will have a big impact on your future. Like training for a marathon, you'll need to start slowly and work your way up. When test day arrives, you'll be ready.

Start with the strategies you've read in the first two Secret Keys—plan your course and study in the way that works best for you. If you have time, consider using multiple study resources to get different approaches to the same concepts. It can be helpful to see difficult concepts from more than one angle. Then find a good source for practice tests. Many times, the test website will suggest potential study resources or provide sample tests.

Copyright © Mometrix Media. You have been licensed one copy of this document for personal use only. Any other reproduction or redistribution is strictly prohibited. All rights reserved.
This content is provided for test preparation purposes only and does not imply an endorsement by Mometrix of any particular political, scientific, or religious point of view.

Practice Test Strategy

If you're able to find at least three practice tests, we recommend this strategy:

Untimed and Open-Book Practice

Take the first test with no time constraints and with your notes and study guide handy. Take your time and focus on applying the strategies you've learned.

Timed and Open-Book Practice

Take the second practice test open-book as well, but set a timer and practice pacing yourself to finish in time.

Timed and Closed-Book Practice

Take any other practice tests as if it were test day. Set a timer and put away your study materials. Sit at a table or desk in a quiet room, imagine yourself at the testing center, and answer questions as quickly and accurately as possible.

Keep repeating timed and closed-book tests on a regular basis until you run out of practice tests or it's time for the actual test. Your mind will be ready for the schedule and stress of test day, and you'll be able to focus on recalling the material you've learned.

Copyright © Mometrix Media. You have been licensed one copy of this document for personal use only. Any other reproduction or redistribution is strictly prohibited. All rights reserved.
This content is provided for test preparation purposes only and does not imply an endorsement by Mometrix of any particular political, scientific, or religious point of view.

Secret Key #4 – Pace Yourself

Once you're fully prepared for the material on the test, your biggest challenge on test day will be managing your time. Just knowing that the clock is ticking can make you panic even if you have plenty of time left. Work on pacing yourself so you can build confidence against the time constraints of the exam. Pacing is a difficult skill to master, especially in a high-pressure environment, so **practice is vital**.

Set time expectations for your pace based on how much time is available. For example, if a section has 60 questions and the time limit is 30 minutes, you know you have to average 30 seconds or less per question in order to answer them all. Although 30 seconds is the hard limit, set 25 seconds per question as your goal, so you reserve extra time to spend on harder questions. When you budget extra time for the harder questions, you no longer have any reason to stress when those questions take longer to answer.

Don't let this time expectation distract you from working through the test at a calm, steady pace, but keep it in mind so you don't spend too much time on any one question. Recognize that taking extra time on one question you don't understand may keep you from answering two that you do understand later in the test. If your time limit for a question is up and you're still not sure of the answer, mark it and move on, and come back to it later if the time and the test format allow. If the testing format doesn't allow you to return to earlier questions, just make an educated guess; then put it out of your mind and move on.

On the easier questions, be careful not to rush. It may seem wise to hurry through them so you have more time for the challenging ones, but it's not worth missing one if you know the concept and just didn't take the time to read the question fully. Work efficiently but make sure you understand the question and have looked at all of the answer choices, since more than one may seem right at first.

Even if you're paying attention to the time, you may find yourself a little behind at some point. You should speed up to get back on track, but do so wisely. Don't panic; just take a few seconds less on each question until you're caught up. Don't guess without thinking, but do look through the answer choices and eliminate any you know are wrong. If you can get down to two choices, it is often worthwhile to guess from those. Once you've chosen an answer, move on and don't dwell on any that you skipped or had to hurry through. If a question was taking too long, chances are it was one of the harder ones, so you weren't as likely to get it right anyway.

On the other hand, if you find yourself getting ahead of schedule, it may be beneficial to slow down a little. The more quickly you work, the more likely you are to make a careless mistake that will affect your score. You've budgeted time for each question, so don't be afraid to spend that time. Practice an efficient but careful pace to get the most out of the time you have.

Copyright © Mometrix Media. You have been licensed one copy of this document for personal use only. Any other reproduction or redistribution is strictly prohibited. All rights reserved.
This content is provided for test preparation purposes only and does not imply an endorsement by Mometrix of any particular political, scientific, or religious point of view.

Secret Key #5 – Have a Plan for Guessing

When you're taking the test, you may find yourself stuck on a question. Some of the answer choices seem better than others, but you don't see the one answer choice that is obviously correct. What do you do?

The scenario described above is very common, yet most test takers have not effectively prepared for it. Developing and practicing a plan for guessing may be one of the single most effective uses of your time as you get ready for the exam.

In developing your plan for guessing, there are three questions to address:

- When should you start the guessing process?
- How should you narrow down the choices?
- Which answer should you choose?

When to Start the Guessing Process

Unless your plan for guessing is to select C every time (which, despite its merits, is not what we recommend), you need to leave yourself enough time to apply your answer elimination strategies. Since you have a limited amount of time for each question, that means that if you're going to give yourself the best shot at guessing correctly, you have to decide quickly whether or not you will guess.

Of course, the best-case scenario is that you don't have to guess at all, so first, see if you can answer the question based on your knowledge of the subject and basic reasoning skills. Focus on the key words in the question and try to jog your memory of related topics. Give yourself a chance to bring the knowledge to mind, but once you realize that you don't have (or you can't access) the knowledge you need to answer the question, it's time to start the guessing process.

It's almost always better to start the guessing process too early than too late. It only takes a few seconds to remember something and answer the question from knowledge. Carefully eliminating wrong answer choices takes longer. Plus, going through the process of eliminating answer choices can actually help jog your memory.

Summary: Start the guessing process as soon as you decide that you can't answer the question based on your knowledge.

Copyright © Mometrix Media. You have been licensed one copy of this document for personal use only. Any other reproduction or redistribution is strictly prohibited. All rights reserved.
This content is provided for test preparation purposes only and does not imply an endorsement by Mometrix of any particular political, scientific, or religious point of view.

How to Narrow Down the Choices

The next chapter in this book (**Test-Taking Strategies**) includes a wide range of strategies for how to approach questions and how to look for answer choices to eliminate. You will definitely want to read those carefully, practice them, and figure out which ones work best for you. Here though, we're going to address a mindset rather than a particular strategy.

Your odds of guessing an answer correctly depend on how many options you are choosing from.

Number of options left	5	4	3	2	1
Odds of guessing correctly	20%	25%	33%	50%	100%

You can see from this chart just how valuable it is to be able to eliminate incorrect answers and make an educated guess, but there are two things that many test takers do that cause them to miss out on the benefits of guessing:

- Accidentally eliminating the correct answer
- Selecting an answer based on an impression

We'll look at the first one here, and the second one in the next section.

To avoid accidentally eliminating the correct answer, we recommend a thought exercise called **the $5 challenge**. In this challenge, you only eliminate an answer choice from contention if you are willing to bet $5 on it being wrong. Why $5? Five dollars is a small but not insignificant amount of money. It's an amount you could afford to lose but wouldn't want to throw away. And while losing $5 once might not hurt too much, doing it twenty times will set you back $100. In the same way, each small decision you make—eliminating a choice here, guessing on a question there—won't by itself impact your score very much, but when you put them all together, they can make a big difference. By holding each answer choice elimination decision to a higher standard, you can reduce the risk of accidentally eliminating the correct answer.

The $5 challenge can also be applied in a positive sense: If you are willing to bet $5 that an answer choice *is* correct, go ahead and mark it as correct.

Summary: Only eliminate an answer choice if you are willing to bet $5 that it is wrong.

Copyright © Mometrix Media. You have been licensed one copy of this document for personal use only. Any other reproduction or redistribution is strictly prohibited. All rights reserved.
This content is provided for test preparation purposes only and does not imply an endorsement by Mometrix of any particular political, scientific, or religious point of view.

Which Answer to Choose

You're taking the test. You've run into a hard question and decided you'll have to guess. You've eliminated all the answer choices you're willing to bet $5 on. Now you have to pick an answer. Why do we even need to talk about this? Why can't you just pick whichever one you feel like when the time comes?

The answer to these questions is that if you don't come into the test with a plan, you'll rely on your impression to select an answer choice, and if you do that, you risk falling into a trap. The test writers know that everyone who takes their test will be guessing on some of the questions, so they intentionally write wrong answer choices to seem plausible. You still have to pick an answer though, and if the wrong answer choices are designed to look right, how can you ever be sure that you're not falling for their trap? The best solution we've found to this dilemma is to take the decision out of your hands entirely. Here is the process we recommend:

Once you've eliminated any choices that you are confident (willing to bet $5) are wrong, select the first remaining choice as your answer.

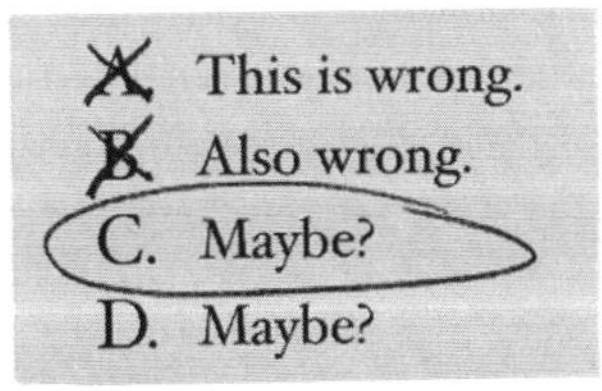

Whether you choose to select the first remaining choice, the second, or the last, the important thing is that you use some preselected standard. Using this approach guarantees that you will not be enticed into selecting an answer choice that looks right, because you are not basing your decision on how the answer choices look.

This is not meant to make you question your knowledge. Instead, it is to help you recognize the difference between your knowledge and your impressions. There's a huge difference between thinking an answer is right because of what you know, and thinking an answer is right because it looks or sounds like it should be right.

Summary: To ensure that your selection is appropriately random, make a predetermined selection from among all answer choices you have not eliminated.

Copyright © Mometrix Media. You have been licensed one copy of this document for personal use only. Any other reproduction or redistribution is strictly prohibited. All rights reserved.
This content is provided for test preparation purposes only and does not imply an endorsement by Mometrix of any particular political, scientific, or religious point of view.

Test-Taking Strategies

This section contains a list of test-taking strategies that you may find helpful as you work through the test. By taking what you know and applying logical thought, you can maximize your chances of answering any question correctly!

It is very important to realize that every question is different and every person is different: no single strategy will work on every question, and no single strategy will work for every person. That's why we've included all of them here, so you can try them out and determine which ones work best for different types of questions and which ones work best for you.

Question Strategies

☑ Read Carefully

Read the question and the answer choices carefully. Don't miss the question because you misread the terms. You have plenty of time to read each question thoroughly and make sure you understand what is being asked. Yet a happy medium must be attained, so don't waste too much time. You must read carefully and efficiently.

☑ Contextual Clues

Look for contextual clues. If the question includes a word you are not familiar with, look at the immediate context for some indication of what the word might mean. Contextual clues can often give you all the information you need to decipher the meaning of an unfamiliar word. Even if you can't determine the meaning, you may be able to narrow down the possibilities enough to make a solid guess at the answer to the question.

☑ Prefixes

If you're having trouble with a word in the question or answer choices, try dissecting it. Take advantage of every clue that the word might include. Prefixes can be a huge help. Usually, they allow you to determine a basic meaning. *Pre-* means before, *post-* means after, *pro-* is positive, *de-* is negative. From prefixes, you can get an idea of the general meaning of the word and try to put it into context.

☑ Hedge Words

Watch out for critical hedge words, such as *likely, may, can, often, almost, mostly, usually, generally, rarely,* and *sometimes.* Question writers insert these hedge phrases to cover every possibility. Often an answer choice will be wrong simply because it leaves no room for exception. Be on guard for answer choices that have definitive words such as *exactly* and *always.*

☑ Switchback Words

Stay alert for *switchbacks.* These are the words and phrases frequently used to alert you to shifts in thought. The most common switchback words are *but, although,* and *however.* Others include *nevertheless, on the other hand, even though, while, in spite of, despite,* and *regardless of.* Switchback words are important to catch because they can change the direction of the question or an answer choice.

Copyright © Mometrix Media. You have been licensed one copy of this document for personal use only. Any other reproduction or redistribution is strictly prohibited. All rights reserved.
This content is provided for test preparation purposes only and does not imply an endorsement by Mometrix of any particular political, scientific, or religious point of view.

⊘ Face Value

When in doubt, use common sense. Accept the situation in the problem at face value. Don't read too much into it. These problems will not require you to make wild assumptions. If you have to go beyond creativity and warp time or space in order to have an answer choice fit the question, then you should move on and consider the other answer choices. These are normal problems rooted in reality. The applicable relationship or explanation may not be readily apparent, but it is there for you to figure out. Use your common sense to interpret anything that isn't clear.

Answer Choice Strategies

⊘ Answer Selection

The most thorough way to pick an answer choice is to identify and eliminate wrong answers until only one is left, then confirm it is the correct answer. Sometimes an answer choice may immediately seem right, but be careful. The test writers will usually put more than one reasonable answer choice on each question, so take a second to read all of them and make sure that the other choices are not equally obvious. As long as you have time left, it is better to read every answer choice than to pick the first one that looks right without checking the others.

⊘ Answer Choice Families

An answer choice family consists of two (in rare cases, three) answer choices that are very similar in construction and cannot all be true at the same time. If you see two answer choices that are direct opposites or parallels, one of them is usually the correct answer. For instance, if one answer choice says that quantity *x* increases and another either says that quantity *x* decreases (opposite) or says that quantity *y* increases (parallel), then those answer choices would fall into the same family. An answer choice that doesn't match the construction of the answer choice family is more likely to be incorrect. Most questions will not have answer choice families, but when they do appear, you should be prepared to recognize them.

⊘ Eliminate Answers

Eliminate answer choices as soon as you realize they are wrong, but make sure you consider all possibilities. If you are eliminating answer choices and realize that the last one you are left with is also wrong, don't panic. Start over and consider each choice again. There may be something you missed the first time that you will realize on the second pass.

⊘ Avoid Fact Traps

Don't be distracted by an answer choice that is factually true but doesn't answer the question. You are looking for the choice that answers the question. Stay focused on what the question is asking for so you don't accidentally pick an answer that is true but incorrect. Always go back to the question and make sure the answer choice you've selected actually answers the question and is not merely a true statement.

⊘ Extreme Statements

In general, you should avoid answers that put forth extreme actions as standard practice or proclaim controversial ideas as established fact. An answer choice that states the "process should be used in certain situations, if..." is much more likely to be correct than one that states the "process should be discontinued completely." The first is a calm rational statement and doesn't even make a definitive, uncompromising stance, using a hedge word *if* to provide wiggle room, whereas the second choice is far more extreme.

Copyright © Mometrix Media. You have been licensed one copy of this document for personal use only. Any other reproduction or redistribution is strictly prohibited. All rights reserved.
This content is provided for test preparation purposes only and does not imply an endorsement by Mometrix of any particular political, scientific, or religious point of view.

Ø Benchmark

As you read through the answer choices and you come across one that seems to answer the question well, mentally select that answer choice. This is not your final answer, but it's the one that will help you evaluate the other answer choices. The one that you selected is your benchmark or standard for judging each of the other answer choices. Every other answer choice must be compared to your benchmark. That choice is correct until proven otherwise by another answer choice beating it. If you find a better answer, then that one becomes your new benchmark. Once you've decided that no other choice answers the question as well as your benchmark, you have your final answer.

Ø Predict the Answer

Before you even start looking at the answer choices, it is often best to try to predict the answer. When you come up with the answer on your own, it is easier to avoid distractions and traps because you will know exactly what to look for. The right answer choice is unlikely to be word-for-word what you came up with, but it should be a close match. Even if you are confident that you have the right answer, you should still take the time to read each option before moving on.

General Strategies

Ø Tough Questions

If you are stumped on a problem or it appears too hard or too difficult, don't waste time. Move on! Remember though, if you can quickly check for obviously incorrect answer choices, your chances of guessing correctly are greatly improved. Before you completely give up, at least try to knock out a couple of possible answers. Eliminate what you can and then guess at the remaining answer choices before moving on.

Ø Check Your Work

Since you will probably not know every term listed and the answer to every question, it is important that you get credit for the ones that you do know. Don't miss any questions through careless mistakes. If at all possible, try to take a second to look back over your answer selection and make sure you've selected the correct answer choice and haven't made a costly careless mistake (such as marking an answer choice that you didn't mean to mark). This quick double check should more than pay for itself in caught mistakes for the time it costs.

Ø Pace Yourself

It's easy to be overwhelmed when you're looking at a page full of questions; your mind is confused and full of random thoughts, and the clock is ticking down faster than you would like. Calm down and maintain the pace that you have set for yourself. Especially as you get down to the last few minutes of the test, don't let the small numbers on the clock make you panic. As long as you are on track by monitoring your pace, you are guaranteed to have time for each question.

Ø Don't Rush

It is very easy to make errors when you are in a hurry. Maintaining a fast pace in answering questions is pointless if it makes you miss questions that you would have gotten right otherwise. Test writers like to include distracting information and wrong answers that seem right. Taking a little extra time to avoid careless mistakes can make all the difference in your test score. Find a pace that allows you to be confident in the answers that you select.

Copyright © Mometrix Media. You have been licensed one copy of this document for personal use only. Any other reproduction or redistribution is strictly prohibited. All rights reserved.
This content is provided for test preparation purposes only and does not imply an endorsement by Mometrix of any particular political, scientific, or religious point of view.

⊘ Keep Moving

Panicking will not help you pass the test, so do your best to stay calm and keep moving. Taking deep breaths and going through the answer elimination steps you practiced can help to break through a stress barrier and keep your pace.

Final Notes

The combination of a solid foundation of content knowledge and the confidence that comes from practicing your plan for applying that knowledge is the key to maximizing your performance on test day. As your foundation of content knowledge is built up and strengthened, you'll find that the strategies included in this chapter become more and more effective in helping you quickly sift through the distractions and traps of the test to isolate the correct answer.

Now that you're preparing to move forward into the test content chapters of this book, be sure to keep your goal in mind. As you read, think about how you will be able to apply this information on the test. If you've already seen sample questions for the test and you have an idea of the question format and style, try to come up with questions of your own that you can answer based on what you're reading. This will give you valuable practice applying your knowledge in the same ways you can expect to on test day.

Good luck and good studying!

Copyright © Mometrix Media. You have been licensed one copy of this document for personal use only. Any other reproduction or redistribution is strictly prohibited. All rights reserved.
This content is provided for test preparation purposes only and does not imply an endorsement by Mometrix of any particular political, scientific, or religious point of view.

Copyright © Mometrix Media. You have been licensed one copy of this document for personal use only. Any other reproduction or redistribution is strictly prohibited. All rights reserved.
This content is provided for test preparation purposes only and does not imply an endorsement by Mometrix of any particular political, scientific, or religious point of view.

Foundations of Speech and Language Development

Foundations

Milestones of Receptive Language Development

Birth to Six or Seven Months

Newborns notice environmental sounds; they wake up, startle, or cry upon hearing loud, unexpected noises; they become still or quiet to attend to new sounds; and they listen to nearby speech. By three months of age, infants turn toward speakers when they hear their voices, smile or stop crying when they hear familiar voices, stop their activity to attend closely to unfamiliar voices, and frequently respond to comforting tones of both familiar and unfamiliar voices. From four to six months, they recognize and respond to the word "no"; they respond to changes in speakers' vocal tones; they respond to nonspeech sounds such as birds singing, dogs barking, and other animals' vocalizations; and they respond to sounds that toys, machines, and other objects make, which often fascinate them. They enjoy hearing music and rhythmic sounds. They display interest or apprehension when looking for the sources of all types of sounds that are new to them. By the age of seven months, typically, babies observably listen to others who speak to them.

Seven Months to Two Years

By the age of seven months, developing babies typically turn and look at the faces of people calling their names and listen to others speaking to them. Between 7 and 12 months, they discover and enjoy playing simple interactive games such as peekaboo, patty-cake, and I see and tickling or finger-play games such as 'round and 'round the garden (went the teddy bear). During this same period, babies begin recognizing nouns/proper nouns naming familiar people/animals/things, e.g., Mommy, Daddy, doggie, kitty, bunny, eyes, phone, or key. They begin to follow simple directions/requests, e.g., "Give that to Mommy," and questions, e.g., "Do you want more milk?" From one to two years of age, children can point to a few of their body parts—e.g., eyes, nose, tummy—when asked and point to pictures in books, given names of animals/objects/people pictured. They can follow simple commands such as "Hot—don't touch!" or "Roll the truck" and understand simple questions, e.g., "Who likes Susie?", "What's in your bag?", and "Where's the kitty?" Toddlers enjoy hearing songs, rhymes, and simple stories, and they want these and simple games repeated over and over.

Ages Two to Five Years

By two years old, toddlers understand two-stage directions, e.g., "Take off your clothes and put them in the laundry hamper." They understand the concept or meaning of opposites or contrasts such as go/stop, hot/cold, yummy/yucky, or on/in. They recognize and attend to nonspeech sounds such as ringing telephones or doorbells; when they hear these, they may get excited, point at the source of the sound, try to answer the phone or door, or urge parents to answer them. By the time they are three to four years old, children typically understand simple questions beginning with who, what, and where. They can hear and recognize when others call them from another room. Any hearing problems often become more apparent in children at these ages. Experts advise parents suspecting hearing deficits to take children for hearing screenings. Children of ages four to five years enjoy hearing simple stories and can answer related questions. They hear and understand almost all of the speech they are exposed to in their home and daycare or preschool environments.

Copyright © Mometrix Media. You have been licensed one copy of this document for personal use only. Any other reproduction or redistribution is strictly prohibited. All rights reserved.
This content is provided for test preparation purposes only and does not imply an endorsement by Mometrix of any particular political, scientific, or religious point of view.

Milestones of Expressive Language Development

Birth to 6 Months

Newborns communicate pain/discomfort and pleasure to others. By three months, infants smile upon seeing parents. They make gooing, cooing sounds expressing contentment and frequently repeat the same sounds. Their crying sounds become differentiated to express different needs such as hunger, pain, fear, or anger. By the time they are four to six months old, babies gurgle and engage in vocal play when they are happily occupying themselves or when parents play with them. Babbling develops and becomes very prominent during the four- to six-month age range, sometimes including intonations that mimic conversational speech, and including multiple speech sounds, particularly the bilabial consonants /b/, /p/, /m/, and /w/ as well as vowels. By the time they reach six months of age, babies can communicate to their parents that they want something or want the parents to do something. They develop the ability to produce very urgent vocal sounds to induce adults to take action on their behalf.

Seven Months to Three Years

From the age of 7 to 12 months, babies' babbling changes in sound due to its including both long and short vowels and larger numbers of consonants. They begin to use other sounds than crying to get and keep parents' attention. By the time they are one year old, most children begin uttering their first words, e.g., "Mama," "night-night," "bye-bye," "no," "kitty," or "doggie," albeit somewhat unclearly. From one to two years old, children acquire more new words with each month; their pronunciation becomes clearer, and they articulate more initial consonants of words. They begin combining two words to form simple sentences and questions, e.g., "More cookie," "Kitty go," "Where ball?", or "What that?" Toddlers at the ages of two to three years typically demonstrate dramatic vocabulary development. They apparently know words to identify/describe nearly everything. They routinely make one-, two-, and three-word utterances, which family members usually understand. They may draw attention to/ask for things by naming them (e.g., "box"), identifying characteristics ("heavy!"); commenting ("wow!"); describing actions ("penguin out!" when removing a stuffed animal from a toy car) or giving directions ("watch this!").

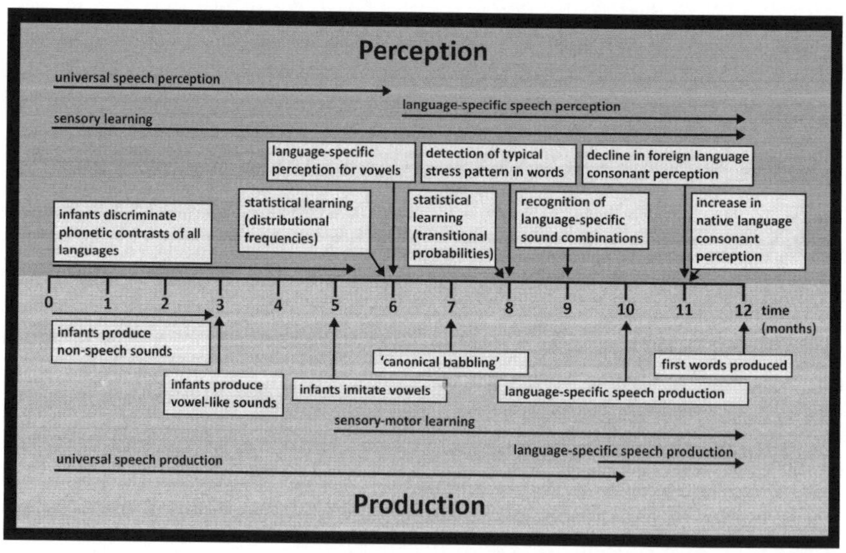

Three to Four Years and Characteristics at Ages Four to Five Years

Whereas children typically utter two-word sentences around two to three years old, by three to four years of age, they combine four words or more into longer sentences. Their conversational content includes describing experiences, friends, and events that have occurred at preschool or

Copyright © Mometrix Media. You have been licensed one copy of this document for personal use only. Any other reproduction or redistribution is strictly prohibited. All rights reserved.
This content is provided for test preparation purposes only and does not imply an endorsement by Mometrix of any particular political, scientific, or religious point of view.

other places outside of their home. By the preschool years, children typically speak clearly and fluently so non-family members can understand what they say most of the time. By the time they reach the ages of four to five years, children speak in voices that adults find easy to listen to, and can form long, detailed sentences with compound or complex structures (e.g., "We went to the beach today, but we had to come home early because my sister didn't feel well" and "I want to have a pony of my own like my friend Barry does, and my daddy said he'll buy me one when he wins the lottery."). Children of these ages can tell long, involved stories using their imaginations that stay on topic and use standard grammar. Other than incorrect/imperfect articulation of some of the more difficult consonants, their pronunciation is mostly accurate. They easily communicate with familiar adults and peers, and they may engage strangers in conversations.

Phonemes Produced Correctly by Ages from 3 to 8.5 Years

According to some researchers, 75% of typically developing children correctly produce the following speech sounds by 3 years. Devocalized/unvoiced phonemes: Stops – p as in up, k as in car, t as in to; fricative – h as in he. Vocalized/voiced phonemes: Stops – b as in be, g as in go, d as in do; fricative – zh as in measure; glides – y as in yes, w as in we; nasals – ng as in sing, m as in me, n as in no. By 3.5 years, they pronounce the devocalized fricative f as in if; by 4 years, the devocalized fricative sh as in she, devocalized affricate ch as in chew, and voiced liquid l as in look; by 4.5 years, the devocalized fricative s as in so, vocalized fricative z as in is, and vocalized affricate j as in jaw; by 5 years, the voiced liquid r as in red. By 6 years, children can usually pronounce the voiced fricative v as in voice. By 8 years, they typically acquire the voiced fricative th as in this. By 8.5 years, most children correctly pronounce the devocalized fricative th as in thing.

Phonemes Present at Various Ages			
Age (years)	Produced by 50% of children	Produced by 75% of children	Produced by 90% of children
2-2.5	/ə/ /v/ /dʒ/ /j/ /nt/	/n/ /ŋ/ /f/ /s/ /z/ /ʃ/	/p/ /b/ /t/ /d/ /k/ /g/ /m/
2.5-3	/br/ /tr/	/v/	/ə/ /n/ /f/ /r/ /w/ /h/
3-3.5	/bl/ /sp/ /st/ /sw/	/j/ /nt/	/ŋ/ /v/ /s/ /z/ /ʃ/ /tʃ/ /dʒ/ /l/
3.5-4	/ð/ /dr/ /fr/ /gl/ /gr/ /kr/ /pl/ /pr/ /sl/	/kw/ /st/ /sw/	/j/ /nt/
4-4.5	/θ/	/br/ /kr/ /pl/ /sp/	/kw/
4.5-5		/pr/ /sl/ /tr/	
5-6		/ð/ /dr/ /fr/ /gl/ /gr/	/bl/ /pl/ /sp/ /st/ /sw/
6-7		/θ/	/ð/ /br/ /dr/ /gl/ /gr/ /kr/ /tr/
7-8			/θ/ /fr/ /pr/ /sl/
*Note that the norms reported above are specifically from a sample of males. Acquisition of phonemes varies slightly between males and females.			

Speech Intelligibility

Intelligibility is how clearly listeners can understand children's speech. Significantly less intelligible speech for children's age ranges is a key characteristic of speech disorders. Young children's speech intelligibility frequently varies markedly between single-word versus conversational speech, familiar versus unfamiliar conversational topics, and familiar versus unfamiliar listeners. Within families, children may understand younger siblings' speech better than the parents do. Generally, a child's speech is typically 25% intelligible to parents by 18 months;

Copyright © Mometrix Media. You have been licensed one copy of this document for personal use only. Any other reproduction or redistribution is strictly prohibited. All rights reserved.
This content is provided for test preparation purposes only and does not imply an endorsement by Mometrix of any particular political, scientific, or religious point of view.

50% to 75% intelligible by 24 months; and 75% to 100% intelligible by 36 months. However, the broad range of individual differences among normally developing children must also be taken into account. One set of criteria (Weiss, 1982) for intelligibility is 26% to 50% by 2 years; 51% to 70% by 2½ years; and 71% to 80% by 3 years. Regarding intelligibility to strangers, i.e., unfamiliar listeners, most experts concur with Flipsen's (2006) formula: 25% intelligible to strangers by 1 year, 50% by 2 years, 75% by 3 years, and 100% by 4 years of age. According to some experts (see Gordon-Brannan and Hodson, 2000; Pascoe, 2013), children older than 4 years with less than 66% intelligibility to unfamiliar listeners should be considered for SLP intervention.

Morphological and Syntactic Expressive Language Development

Stage I

According to Brown (1973), children go through four stages in expressive language development. Stage I, typically between ages 15 to 30 months, includes MLUms (mean length of utterance measured in morphemes) around 1.75, increasing gradually; and, once they develop 50- to 60-word vocabularies, stage I sentence types. Sentences conveying operations of reference include nomination, e.g., "that truck" meaning that's a truck; recurrence, e.g., "more milk" meaning there is more milk; negation-denial, e.g., "no poopy" meaning I didn't poop; negation-rejection, e.g., "no more" meaning I don't want more; and negation-nonexistence, e.g., "kitty go" meaning the kitty has gone. Sentences indicating semantic relations include action + agent, e.g., "Mommy kiss" meaning Mommy is kissing; action + object, e.g., "pull cart" meaning pulling the cart; agent + object, e.g., "lady hat" meaning the lady wears a hat; action + locative, e.g., "in tub" meaning I am in the tub; entity + locative, e.g., "teddy bed" meaning the teddy (bear) is on the bed; possessor + object/possession, e.g., "Sarah house" meaning Sarah's house; entity + attributive, e.g., "water cold" meaning the water is cold; and demonstrative + entity, e.g., "that car" meaning not this car.

Stages II, III, and IV

Brown identified stage II as developing between 28 to 36 months old. MLUms range from 2 to 2.5. Children develop the present progressive tense, adding *-ing* to verbs, e.g., "he singing"; the prepositions *in* and *on,* e.g., "in box" and "on box"; and *–s* regular plural noun endings, e.g., "my toys." Children aged 36 to 42 months typically move to stage III, developing MLUm ranges of 2.5 to 3 and irregular verb past tenses, e.g., "me went" or "him fell"; the *–'s* possessive noun/pronoun ending, e.g., "lady's book"; and the uncontractible copula form of the verb *to be* as the only verb in a sentence, e.g., "Is it Johnny?" Children aged 40 to 46 months typically demonstrate stage IV language development, consisting of a range of 3 to 3.7 MLUms and featuring new developments including the use of the articles *a* and *the* to modify nouns, e.g., "a toy" and "the truck"; regular verb past tenses, e.g., "he played"; and also, the use of third-person regular verb present tenses, e.g., "kitty brings toy."

Stage V

In his research, Brown found that children aged 42 to 52 months and older typically progressed into the highest stage of early expressive language development, stage V. This stage involves a range of 3.7 to 4.5 MLUms. Children's spoken language use now includes, developing in the order of presentation here, third-person irregular verb forms, e.g., "she *does*" or "he *has*"; the use of the verb *to be* as an uncontractible auxiliary verb in a sentence, e.g., "*are* they coming?"; the use of the verb *to be* as a contractible copula, i.e., the only verb in a sentence in the form of a contraction of the subject and verb, e.g., "*we're* ready" or "*they're* here"; and also the use of the verb *to be* as a contractible auxiliary verb, i.e., a verb "helping" the main verb, as in the present progressive tense, and in the form of a contraction of the subject and verb, e.g., "she's coming" or "they're going."

Copyright © Mometrix Media. You have been licensed one copy of this document for personal use only. Any other reproduction or redistribution is strictly prohibited. All rights reserved.
This content is provided for test preparation purposes only and does not imply an endorsement by Mometrix of any particular political, scientific, or religious point of view.

Language Development During Adulthood and Old Age

Although the majority of language development is most obvious in children because young children gradually develop the use of longer utterances, larger and more advanced vocabularies, and increasing morphological, grammatical, syntactic, and semantic complexity; and middle childhood and adolescence include further increases in vocabulary, abstraction, sentence length and complexity; adults also display additional gains in the sophistication of their vocabularies and the complexity of their sentence structures. This is particularly true of adults who continue their formal educations, engage in occupations involving significant spoken and written language use and specialized terminology, read regularly for work and pleasure, and engage verbally in social conversations. Some adults not participating in any of these activities may maintain language use similar to the levels they reached during late adolescence. As adults age, they may have difficulty retrieving specific words from memory, even without dementia. Those developing dementias typically lose much/all their verbal expressive ability as their conditions progress. For example, Alzheimer's disease patients frequently forget people's names; have difficulty recalling specific nouns/verbs during speech; use shorter, simpler sentences; eventually have trouble formulating thoughts into sentences; speak less; and some ultimately become nonverbal in later disease stages.

Influential Factors in Children's Speech and Language Development

Children with family histories of speech/language difficulties/delays are more likely to have problems themselves. Children need adequate stimulation to develop communication skills: If parents do not play with, talk with, and read to them enough, these skills will not develop optimally. Insufficient speech opportunities, e.g., having dominant siblings or being "babied"/talked for, also inhibit speech-language development. Attention deficits/short attention spans negatively impact speech-language development. Delayed/disordered motor development can have impacts on speech production; delayed/disordered cognitive development typically affects language development; and global/general developmental delays are accompanied by delayed language development. Some children evidence specific difficulties in learning language, which may be secondary to specific learning disabilities; or they show a lack of interest in linguistic activities and preference for physical activities and other nonverbal modalities. Children whose coordination or control of speech mechanisms (e.g., tongues/lips/muscles) is poor tend to have impaired speech development and spoken communication. A variety of medical problems can impair normal speech and language development. Lack of "communicative intent," i.e., communication awareness, causes inadequate communicative development. Speech-language development can be delayed or impaired by conductive hearing losses from wax buildups, middle-ear infections, and fluid. Moving/other environmental changes and emotional/behavioral problems are additional factors.

Presbycusis

Effects on Communication for Aging Adults

As reported in *The ASHA Leader* (Humes, 2008), of the American Speech-Language-Hearing Association, depending on the definition of hearing loss, roughly one-third of adults aged 65 and older undergo sufficient hearing loss to impair their everyday communication abilities. As people age, their hearing typically loses sensitivity. The most common tendency is to lose hearing acuity for sounds at the highest frequencies first. Although human speech mainly falls into the middle-frequency ranges, high-frequency loss impairs the ability to detect or differentiate among unvoiced consonants and consonant clusters such as s, t, p, k, h, sh, and ch first. For example, as hearing acuity diminishes, people can have difficulty telling the difference between words such as *fish* versus *fist*. As hearing loss progresses, even voiced phonemes can become difficult to distinguish, especially consonants and even vowels with higher frequencies. Thus, the initial complaint of aging individuals is not that they cannot hear certain sounds or others' speech, but rather that they can

Copyright © Mometrix Media. You have been licensed one copy of this document for personal use only. Any other reproduction or redistribution is strictly prohibited. All rights reserved.
This content is provided for test preparation purposes only and does not imply an endorsement by Mometrix of any particular political, scientific, or religious point of view.

hear what people say but cannot understand it. In other words, the first communication problems experienced by aging adults are with the ability to discriminate speech sounds in conversation rather than with hearing speech overall.

Process and Impacts on Receptive Communication

As adults age, the cilia or hair cells, i.e., nerve cells in the cochlea of the inner ear, often begin to die off, reducing cochlear ability to transmit sound impulses via the acoustic/auditory nerves to the brain. This sensorineural hearing loss is permanent and irreversible; hearing aids can boost residual hearing, but they are less effective than with conductive hearing losses. Cochlear implants can provide some hearing to some people, but this is generally reserved for those who are already deaf. Sensorineural hearing loss secondary to cochlear pathology typically begins and is most prominent in the higher frequencies. At typical conversational loudness, which is around 60 to 65 dB, such high-frequency hearing loss makes it impossible for older adults to hear low-intensity, high-frequency speech sounds. Many of these phonemes are consonants carrying information. Hence an older adult who cannot detect or discriminate among unvoiced, high-frequency consonants such as s or t, cannot distinguish *sun, ton,* and *fun*, either hearing these all as *"un"* or being unable to determine whether the initial sound is s, t, or f.

Common age-related cochlear deterioration not only renders some speech sounds inaudible to affected listeners, it also damages the ability to encode the frequency content of phonemes, known as spectral resolution. This can further affect speech understanding. In addition to actual acuity, central auditory processing functions—the ability of the central nervous system's auditory regions to process and interpret speech sounds—can also deteriorate with age. On top of this, age-related cognitive decline involves linguistic knowledge, attention, memory, and multiple brain areas in addition to audition of speech sounds. This complicates research into age-related problems with speech understanding. Most instruments testing central auditory processing deficits in older adults have involved speech stimuli. Since many older adults studied have peripheral hearing loss, this confounds attempts to measure central auditory processing based on speech understanding. Moreover, research finds up to half of older adults with central auditory processing deficits also have overlapping cognitive processing deficits. Thus, central auditory processing measures commonly requiring cognitive processes such as divided attention and memory storage and retrieval (e.g., presenting different words to each ear) can be confounded by coexisting cognitive processing deficits as well as peripheral hearing losses.

Neurological Disorders and Oral and Pharyngeal Swallowing Functions

Oral and pharyngeal dysphagia can be caused by many neurological disorders. These may be categorized clinically as degenerative or nondegenerative. Degenerative disorders are subcategorized into movement disorders, dementias, etc., based on primary clinical presentation and are typically progressive. The most common nondegenerative disorder causing dysphagia is stroke. The most clinically significant result of dysphagia is aspiration. Functional abnormalities in swallowing include preparatory phase disorders, problems initiating swallowing responses, poor bolus control, and reduced hyolaryngeal elevation. Swallowing abnormalities secondary to neurological disorders are usually not specific to the disorder type. Videofluoroscopy is best for defining specific swallowing dysfunctions, supplemented by careful clinical examination and history. In some cases, videoendoscopy can also help. Both videofluoroscopy and videoendoscopy are useful not only diagnostically, but for determining and teaching maneuvers to prevent aspiration and promote swallowing. Feeding tubes should be considered when significant aspiration is unavoidable. Teams including an SLP, a gastroenterologist, and a neurologist are recommended for the best management of oropharyngeal dysphagia secondary to neurological lesions.

Copyright © Mometrix Media. You have been licensed one copy of this document for personal use only. Any other reproduction or redistribution is strictly prohibited. All rights reserved.
This content is provided for test preparation purposes only and does not imply an endorsement by Mometrix of any particular political, scientific, or religious point of view.

Effects of Stroke

Around 700,000 Americans and 2,000 individuals per 1,000,000 globally suffer strokes every year. Whereas 20% of strokes are hemorrhagic, 80% are ischemic, caused by cardiac embolism (blood clot) or atherosclerosis of the internal carotid arteries. The specific location of the cerebrovascular accident or stroke determines variations in symptoms. For example, hemiparesis on the same side as the lesion (ipsilesional), aphasia, dysarthria, and hemispatial neglect (deficit in spatial awareness and attention on one side from the inability to process and perceive stimuli on that side, caused by damage to one hemisphere of the brain) are often symptoms of supratentorial (above the tentorium cerebelli, including the cerebrum) infarcts. Ataxia; reduced pain and temperature sensation on the lesion side; diminished trunk and limb sensation and pain on the opposite side of the lesion; and velar, pharyngeal, and laryngeal paralysis on the lesion side are frequent symptoms of lateral medullary (on one side of the medulla oblongata) infarcts. Stroke-induced dysphagia symptoms vary and can include delayed oral transfer, retention in the oral lateral sulci, pharyngeal swallowing initiation delay, lowered hyolaryngeal elevation, and aspiration.

Effects of Disorders and Injuries on Swallowing and Feeding Abilities

Cerebral palsy involves damage to the parts of the brain governing the strength, control, and coordination of various muscles. The associated chronic neurological problems depend on the location(s) and severity of damage, and can include swallowing as well as walking, talking, etc. Traumatic brain injuries affecting brain areas controlling chewing and swallowing can cause dysphagia. Traumatic injuries generally cause more diffuse damage than strokes. Malignant and benign brain tumors infiltrating the regions controlling swallowing can also cause dysphagia. Moreover, surgical and radiation treatments for tumors can themselves compromise swallowing. As tumors grow, secondary swallowing disorders can become progressive, unlike those caused by strokes or traumatic brain injuries. Iatrogenic (medically induced) dysphagia can result from medication or surgery. Older psychotropic medications can cause tardive dyskinesia, i.e., repetitive involuntary movements, including orobuccolingual (mouth, cheek, and tongue) dyskinesia. Neck surgeries, e.g., carotid endarterectomy or cervical spinal fusion, can damage cranial nerves and cause dysphagia, often co-occurring with dysphonia. Postoperative edema (swelling due to fluid accumulation) can also exacerbate post-operative dysphagia.

Dementias and Movement Disorders

Dementia patients often have swallowing difficulties, plus eating problems caused by bolus transfer deficits in the mouth; agnosia, compromising the ability to recognize and accept food; and limb/manual apraxia interfering with the ability to manipulate eating utensils. Alzheimer's disease dementia, Lewy body dementia, frontotemporal dementia (from severe frontal and temporal lobe atrophy), and vascular dementia secondary to single or multiple strokes or microvascular disease all interfere with cognitive functioning, including executive function and the ability to perform activities of daily living, including eating. Degenerative metabolic disorders of the cerebellar and extrapyramidal pathways of the central nervous system cause movement disorders. Parkinson's disease, progressive supranuclear palsy, olivopontocerebellar atrophy involving atrophy of multiple systems, and the hereditary autosomal diseases Huntington's disease and Wilson's disease all produce neurological symptoms, which can include dysphagia. Amyotrophic lateral sclerosis (ALS, aka Lou Gehrig's disease), another progressive disorder, causes dysphagia when affecting the corticobulbar tracts; it also causes limb weakness, spasticity, and impaired dexterity, interfering with self-feeding, when affecting the corticospinal tracts. Its later stages cause loss of motor functions with further impact on eating. Multiple sclerosis (MS) can cause fatigue, sensory impairment, heat sensitivity, muscular weakness, and swallowing problems.

Copyright © Mometrix Media. You have been licensed one copy of this document for personal use only. Any other reproduction or redistribution is strictly prohibited. All rights reserved.
This content is provided for test preparation purposes only and does not imply an endorsement by Mometrix of any particular political, scientific, or religious point of view.

Severe Brain Injuries

From studying trauma center patients with severe brain injuries, some researchers (Mackay, Morgan, and Bernstein, 1999) have concluded that such patients frequently demonstrate swallowing disorders, as well as cognitive and behavioral symptoms. They found that patients with severe brain injuries and swallowing abnormalities require significantly longer times to initiate eating and attain completely oral feeding than those who swallow normally; hence, they need nonoral supplementation for three or four times longer than those with normal swallowing functions. Via videofluoroscopic swallow studies, the researchers identified abnormal swallowing in more than half (61%) of patients studied. The most common symptoms were reduced tongue control and loss of bolus control. Many patients (41%) aspirated liquids/foods. Whereas patients with normal swallowing reached oral feeding within 19 days, those with abnormal swallowing took 57 days. On the Rancho Los Amigos (RLA) scale, initiating oral feeding required level IV; complete oral feeding required level VI. Risk factors for disordered swallowing included lower RLA scores and Glasgow Coma Scale (GCS) scores; having a tracheostomy; and longer than two weeks of ventilation time. Lower RLA and GCS scores upon patient admission were also risk factors for aspiration.

Stages of Swallowing

Involving multiple nerves and roughly 30 muscles in the mouth and throat, swallowing consists of four stages:

1. The oral preparatory stage entails voluntary actions. Through jaw movement, chewing with the teeth, the secretion of saliva, and a good seal between the lips, an individual prepares a food bolus.
2. In the oral stage, the tongue is raised and rolled backward, making contact first with the hard palate and then with the soft palate to move the bolus back toward the esophagus.
3. In the pharyngeal stage, the soft palate is raised and retracted; the larynx is closed; breathing is suspended; the upper esophageal sphincter is relaxed and opened; and the bolus is then propelled into the esophagus. When the pharyngeal stage is mistimed, food/liquid enters the airway instead of/in addition to the esophagus, causing coughing and choking from "swallowing the wrong way"; food/liquid progressing to the lungs is aspiration.
4. In the esophageal stage, food moves from the esophagus into the stomach through involuntary action. Factors that can affect normal swallowing include appetite, dining environment, food presentation, self-feeding ability, posture, bolus size, bolus viscosity, fatigue, cognitive influences, odors, hygiene, stomach/bowel/other physical comfort, affect, and prior experiences.

Education for Individuals at Risk for Eating and Swallowing Problems

SLPs can educate people at risk for swallowing problems and/or with suspected swallowing disorders about several simple precautions and guidelines to follow when eating and drinking. For example, they should sit upright and be aware of their posture when eating and drinking. They should turn off TVs, radios, computers, tablets, phones, or video games to establish comfortable, quiet, distraction-free environments for meals. Clients with dentures should keep these clean and ensure they fit correctly; and they should wear dentures, glasses, and/or hearing aids while eating and drinking to ensure adequate sensory perception, processing, judgment, and coordination. People should not talk and eat simultaneously. They should not rush their mealtimes, which can cause swallowing abnormalities, including aspiration, not to mention indigestion, heartburn, or hiccups (from swallowing air). Clients must not swallow too much food or liquid at a time. If their SLP recommends thickening liquids, clients must apply this uniformly to all liquids they drink;

Copyright © Mometrix Media. You have been licensed one copy of this document for personal use only. Any other reproduction or redistribution is strictly prohibited. All rights reserved.
This content is provided for test preparation purposes only and does not imply an endorsement by Mometrix of any particular political, scientific, or religious point of view.

thicken to the consistency the SLP recommended; and carry the thickening agent with them for drinking liquids outside the home. They should avoid crackers, toast, biscuits, rice, and other dry/crumbly foods.

Directionality and Amplitude of Movement of Hyoid Bone During Swallowing

Researchers have obtained imaging of the swallowing actions of individuals by first having them swallow barium, a highly chemically reactive, alkaline, soft earth metal that is clearly visible in X-rays, and then using videofluorography to measure the position of the bones and/or organs involved. During the process of swallowing liquids and chewed-up solid foods, the individual's hyoid bone is found to move both upward and forward. However, researchers (see Ishida, Palmer, and Hiiemae, 2002) have found that the amounts of upward and forward movement do not correlate. Forward movement does not appear to change significantly between the first and second swallows or between solids and liquids. In contrast, upward movement of the bone varies greatly: It is bigger with the first swallow than the second one, bigger for solid foods than liquids, and sometimes observed to be very small. Researchers have concluded from studying images of the hyoid bone's movement during swallowing that processes within the mouth mainly affect the bone's upward movement, whereas the upper esophageal sphincter's opening and other pharyngeal processes affect the bone's forward movement.

Epidemiology of Dysphagia in Neurological Disorders

Estimates are that globally, 400,000 to 800,000 people with central nervous system (CNS) disorders develop neurogenic dysphagia annually. Partly because of different methods of selecting patients, such as through case series or by selecting consecutive patients, etc., and different methods of evaluating them such as with diagnostic evaluations, clinical evaluations, or questionnaires, the prevalence of swallowing disorders with different neurological disorders is variable. Researchers have found that using clinical swallowing evaluations and/or patient complaints as bases for identifying dysphagia generally results in underestimates of its prevalence. The general consensus among clinicians and researchers is that neurogenic dysphagia is most commonly the result of stroke. Videofluoroscopic swallow studies identify dysphagia in about 65% of acute stroke patients. Among those diagnosed with dysphagia, about half experience aspiration. However, it is important to note also that among acute stroke patients who aspirate liquids or foods, an estimated 40% to 70% aspirate silently, without coughing when the matter reaches the trachea or without changes in their voice when it reaches the true vocal folds. Part of the underestimation of the incidence of aspiration is attributable to this lack of overt signs in patients.

Oral/Pharyngeal Swallowing Problems Secondary to Neurological Disorders

According to various researchers, the incidence of dysphagia in patients who have amyotrophic lateral sclerosis (ALS, aka Lou Gehrig's disease) is 100%. Due to the progressive nature of the degeneration in the central nervous system, ALS patients will eventually develop difficulties with swallowing along with other neurologically based motor control issues. Patients with Huntington's disease are reported to have an 85% incidence of swallowing disorders, and 65% of patients having suffered acute strokes are found to have dysphagia. Cervical spinal surgery has a 50% rate of causing swallowing disorders. Patients who have been diagnosed with Parkinson's disease, which causes progressive problems with neurological motor functions, have a 50% incidence of swallowing difficulties. Although 16% of individuals with progressive supranuclear palsy are diagnosed with dysphagia in the early stages of the disease, 83% of those in its later stages develop it. Approximately 44% of patients with diagnoses of olivopontocerebellar atrophy are reported to experience dysphagia. Among people with multiple sclerosis, 34% have dysphagia. Those with Alzheimer's disease include 32% with dysphagia. Frontotemporal dementia causes dysphagia in

Copyright © Mometrix Media. You have been licensed one copy of this document for personal use only. Any other reproduction or redistribution is strictly prohibited. All rights reserved.
This content is provided for test preparation purposes only and does not imply an endorsement by Mometrix of any particular political, scientific, or religious point of view.

30% of patients. Traumatic brain injuries cause dysphagia in 25% of patients. Dysphagia affects 2.5% of patients after undergoing carotid endarterectomies.

Symptoms Indicating Aspiration Risk for Patients Who Suffered Acute Strokes

Swallowing difficulties are common sequelae of acute strokes. According to research (see Daniels, 2006), the following symptoms of swallowing problems that indicate risk for aspirating liquids, foods, and/or medications taken by mouth are associated with the following findings: An abnormal voluntary cough indicates aspiration risk. This indicator is documented by the findings that upon being commanded to cough, patients give no response, a verbal response, or a weak coughing response. Another indicator of aspiration risk is an abnormal gag reflex. This is associated with findings that when the back of the tongue, back wall of the pharynx, or the faucal arches are stimulated by touch, one or both sides of the velar or pharyngeal walls display weak or no contraction in response. Dysarthria, a speech disorder diagnosed with findings of impaired phonation, resonance, prosody, articulation, or breathing, is another indicator of aspiration risk in acute stroke patients. Findings of impaired vocal pitch, intensity, or quality are associated with a diagnosis of dysphonia, an additional aspiration risk indicator in the acute stroke patient population. The finding of voice quality changing after swallowing water also indicates a risk for aspiration.

Damage to Voice, Speech, and Language Functions Caused By Head Injuries

Traumatic head injuries can cause damage to voice, speech, and language because of the high probability of injury to parts of the brain responsible for these functions. One tendency observed in research is that males between the ages of 15 and 24 years are more likely to incur head trauma because their lifestyles involve behaviors that increase the risk of injuries. Additional populations that are more vulnerable to head injuries are adults aged 75 years and older and young children. The primary causes of injury in the elderly, infants, and toddlers are falls in and around the home. Another significant source of head injury to infants and toddlers is being shaken violently (shaken baby syndrome). Among adolescents and adults, car and motorcycle accidents are the primary sources of head trauma. An additional major cause in these age groups is injury sustained during violent crimes. Traumatic head injuries cause death for an estimated 200,000 Americans annually, resulting in hospitalization for another 500,000 or more. Among individuals surviving head injuries, mild to moderate problems threatening independent living affect roughly 10%. An estimated additional 200,000 people sustaining head injuries are left with serious conditions needing close supervision or institutionalization.

Voice Disorders

Humans vocalize in speech; in laughing, crying, screaming, and singing; and in the cooing and babbling of infants. Other vertebrate animals also vocalize, e.g., barking, meowing, growling, screaming, whinnying, mooing, or bleating. When the vocal folds move close together and the diaphragm pushes air from the lungs past the vocal folds, they vibrate, producing voice. Like fingerprints, each individual voice is unique, contributing to defining health, personality, and mood. Voice difficulties are estimated to affect about 7.5 million Americans. Voice disorders affect three voice components: pitch, loudness, and quality. Pitch, i.e., how high/low sounds are, is determined by the frequency of the sound waves produced. Frequency reflects vibration speed. Faster/more vibrations per second have higher frequencies; slower/fewer vibrations per second have lower frequencies. Voice disorders can cause higher/lower pitches than normal, pitch breaks, and/or lack of control over pitch variations. Loudness is perceived sound amplitude or volume. Voice disorders can cause insufficient or excessive loudness and/or impair loudness control. Quality involves distinctive sound attributes. Voice disorders can make voice quality weak, hoarse, squeaky, guttural, etc. Many people with normal speech skills experience extreme communication difficulties

Copyright © Mometrix Media. You have been licensed one copy of this document for personal use only. Any other reproduction or redistribution is strictly prohibited. All rights reserved.
This content is provided for test preparation purposes only and does not imply an endorsement by Mometrix of any particular political, scientific, or religious point of view.

from impaired vocal mechanisms when cancers, infections, surgeries, or injuries damage the nerves controlling the larynx.

Incidence and Causes in the US

According to the National Institute on Deafness and Other Communication Disorders, a division of the National Institutes of Health under the US Department of Health and Human Services, an estimated 7.5 million Americans have voice problems. One type of voice disorder is spasmodic dysphonia, caused by involuntary muscular movements in the larynx. Although people between 30 and 50 years old are the population wherein the first signs of this disorder are found most often, it can affect anybody. Research findings suggest that more females than males seem affected by spastic dysphonia. Another voice disorder, caused by the human papillomavirus, is laryngeal papillomatosis. It involves tumors growing in the vocal cords, larynx, and/or nasal air passages leading to the lungs. 60% to 80% of patients are children, most often younger than three years old. Voice problems accompany cleft palate, the fourth most common birth defect occurring with roughly 1 in every 700 live births. Around 5% to 8% of children born with cleft palate—more than 130,000 Americans—have velocardiofacial syndrome, which can include heart defects, speech and feeding problems, facial anomalies, and minor learning difficulties. Common voice symptoms of cleft palate include hypernasality, weak voice, and hoarseness.

Speech Disorders in American Populations

About 8% to 9% of young children are identified with speech sound disorders. Approximately 5% of first graders are identified with observable speech disorders. The causes of most of these speech problems are unknown. Minimal brain dysfunction, i.e., minor neurological damage, often with no other symptoms, can cause systematic articulation disorders, e.g., substitution of glottal stops for consonants in some children, when slightly impaired neuromuscular control reduces articulatory strength or coordination. Articulation disorders include the omission, distortion, and/or substitution of speech sounds (and occasionally interjection of superfluous phonemes). Another speech disorder is stuttering, which affects the speech rate and rhythm. Stuttering includes the repetition of phonemes, syllables, or words; prolongation of phonemes; complete blocks in producing initial speech sounds; and hesitations before and during speech. Of more than 15 million people worldwide who stutter, more than 3 million Americans are estimated to stutter. Although people of all ages may stutter, young children aged 2 to 6 years whose speech and language are still developing stutter more often. Stuttering is three times more common in boys than girls. Most children outgrow stuttering; adult stutterers are estimated to be 1% of the American population.

ASDs in the US

According to the US Centers for Disease Control and Prevention (CDC, 2014), autism spectrum disorders (ASDs) affect roughly 1% of the world's population. In America, more than 3.5 million individuals have ASDs. ASDs represent the fastest growing developmental disability in America, having increased from an estimated 1 in 150 children in 2000 to an estimated 1 in 68—an increase of 119.4%, growing in increments of 6% to 15% annually between 2002 and 2010. Boys are three to four times likelier than girls to have ASDs. Roughly 75% of individuals with ASDs have coexisting intellectual disabilities; others have normal or high intelligence. ASDs frequently impair communication skills as well as social skills and behavior. About half of affected individuals are nonverbal, and half are verbal. Among the verbal, individuals with ASDs range from echolalia (parroting others' utterances) only, to normal or advanced speech and language development, and everything in between. Some ASD individuals with well-developed speech and language may be capable of extensive monologues on subjects of interest to them, but they are incapable of the give-and-take of normal social conversations. Such characteristics, combined with frequent deficits in

Copyright © Mometrix Media. You have been licensed one copy of this document for personal use only. Any other reproduction or redistribution is strictly prohibited. All rights reserved.
This content is provided for test preparation purposes only and does not imply an endorsement by Mometrix of any particular political, scientific, or religious point of view.

interpreting and using nonverbal social signals, affect communication for many members of the ASD population.

Speech Development and Speech Disorders

Speech develops in a gradual process from infancy through childhood. Muscular actions in the head, neck, chest, and abdomen are regulated by cranial nerves and must be precisely coordinated to produce intelligible speech. Children eventually learn how to control these muscles by practicing for years during interactions with parents and siblings and everyday social conversations. About 5% of children have obvious speech disorders by the time they are in the first grade. Speech disorders can involve incorrect production of speech sounds, i.e., articulation or phonological disorders, or problems with speech rate and rhythm, i.e., stuttering. The causes of the majority of articulation and stuttering disorders are unknown. Although children with developmental disabilities often exhibit some speech sound disorders, the majority of preschoolers with speech disorders are developing normally otherwise. The speech of children with specific articulation disorders may be unintelligible to unfamiliar listeners in some cases; in others, intelligibility is affected to some extent.

Speech Sound Disorders

Speech disorders include phonological or articulation disorders, which affect pronunciation and intelligibility to varying degrees, and stuttering or rate and rhythm disorders, which impair communication to varying degrees. In the research literature, differences among the diagnostic standards used cause varying estimates of the prevalence of speech sound disorders. These range from 2% of eight-year-olds to 24.6% of five-year-olds, with a median of 8% to 9%. However, the consensus of researchers is that boys have higher rates of specific articulation disorders than girls, with male-to-female ratios ranging from 1.5:1 to 2.4:1. Speech sound disorders often co-occur with specific language impairment, especially in children who have been referred for clinical services. Risk factors for developing speech sound disorders include having a family history of speech disorders and chronic otitis media. Recurrent middle-ear infections can cause conductive hearing loss. The resulting inadequate audition of speech sounds can in turn cause delayed and incorrect production of speech sounds in children.

Language Disorders

Whereas speech disorders impair the production of speech sounds, language disorders impair the ability to process linguistic content when listening to and/or speaking language. About six to eight million Americans have some type of language disorder. Based on research findings, the first six months of life are most critical for children's language development. Full competence in any language requires exposure before school age, as early as possible, and ideally from birth. One language disorder is aphasia, caused by neurological damage. Expressive/Broca's aphasia affects the ability to retrieve vocabulary words from memory, form complete spoken sentences with correct syntax and grammar, and produce logically connected spoken language. Receptive/Wernicke's aphasia affects the ability to understand spoken language one hears. An estimated one million Americans have aphasia, with some 80,000 acquiring it annually. A childhood disorder involving seizures (which most children outgrow) and impairing receptive and expressive language is Landau-Kleffner syndrome, reportedly affecting more than 160 children from 1957 through 1990. Many children without organic etiologies demonstrate delayed language development from cultural/environmental deprivation, e.g., not having parents talk with, read to, play with, and give them sufficient cognitive, linguistic, and social stimulation.

Studies have identified critical periods for language acquisition within the first few years of children's lives. Language disorders have differential impacts on children versus adults: Children

Copyright © Mometrix Media. You have been licensed one copy of this document for personal use only. Any other reproduction or redistribution is strictly prohibited. All rights reserved.
This content is provided for test preparation purposes only and does not imply an endorsement by Mometrix of any particular political, scientific, or religious point of view.

not using language normally since birth/acquiring language impairments in childhood lack complete language development. Adults with full language development can acquire language disorders from strokes, head injuries, brain tumors, or dementias. Others never developed normal language skills and have language disorders secondary to intellectual disabilities, autism spectrum disorders or other congenital/acquired neurological disorders. Deaf/hearing-impaired individuals growing up using American Sign Language (ASL) may have adequate language development; those without ASL/similar languages often have incomplete language development. Children without sensory/neurological developmental disorders but clinically significant language impairments are diagnosed with a specific language impairment (SLI). SLI prevalence estimates vary across research studies due largely to varying diagnostic standards. Also, recovery patterns during early preschool years affect prevalence variations. School-age children exhibit far more stability across age. SLI prevalence during preschool and early elementary school ranges from 2% to 8% with a median of 5.95%; more in boys than girls, with ratios from 0.98:1 to 2.30:1. SLIs correlate strongly with reading problems. SLI risk factors include parental history of speech/language/learning problems and limited parental education. Breast feeding is a protective factor, even with limited parental education.

Etiology

Genetic Influences on Speech and Language Problems

Investigations into environmental and genetic influences on speech and language problems have found evidence of genetic etiologies for children's difficulties with articulation and language development as well as environmental factors. Some researchers (see DeThorne et al., 2006) studying data reported by surveyed parents of twins around 6 years old as the bases for behavioral genetic analyses and phenotypic associations between the speech and language status of children and direct testing of their early reading development found that children's speech and language difficulties were highly heritable. For example, one study estimated a 0.54 probability of inheriting expressive language deficits and a 0.97 probability of articulation problems. Moreover, children with histories of speech-language problems received significantly lower scores on a variety of early reading-related skill measures than children without speech-language problems. From such results, researchers conclude that not only are children's speech and language disorders affected by genetic factors, but moreover that children having histories of speech or language problems are at risk for lower early reading-related performance. Children with histories of problems including receptive language, expressive language, and articulation seem to have the highest risk.

Genetic Influences on Children's Language and Related Cognitive Abilities

In looking for evidence of genetic effects on typical and below-normal cognitive performance by children, some researchers (Hart, Petrill, and Dush, 2010) examined the Children of the National Longitudinal Survey of Youth database (CNLSY; US Department of Labor, 1979–2009) to establish whether genetic factors affected achievement in language, reading, and mathematics and if so, to what extent. Their analyses of receptive vocabulary, word decoding, reading comprehension, and mathematics tests supported their estimates that among both groups and the full CNLSY sample, heritable factors were implicated. All of these estimates were statistically significant and showed effects of moderate sizes. Moreover, when comparing these estimates to the results of earlier twin studies and adoption studies of the same topics, they were all within the same confidence intervals. These studies and others provide support for the conclusion that genetic factors significantly affect children's achievement. The study cited above furthermore shows that genetic sources of normal and deficient language skills, as well as reading and math skills, can be generalized to more populations than those represented by samples using twins and adopted children.

Copyright © Mometrix Media. You have been licensed one copy of this document for personal use only. Any other reproduction or redistribution is strictly prohibited. All rights reserved.
This content is provided for test preparation purposes only and does not imply an endorsement by Mometrix of any particular political, scientific, or religious point of view.

Genetic Factors in Stuttering Etiologies

Although exact etiologies for stuttering remain elusive for researchers to define, they have discovered much evidence that genetic factors contribute to dysfluency disorders. Historically, widespread clinical observations that stuttering tends to run in families have prompted more systematic investigations. Since 1937 (Bryngelson and Rutherford), stuttering incidence has been found to be more than 2.5 times higher in people with family histories of stuttering than without—46% versus 18%. Consensus among many such studies confirms similar data patterns. Literature reviews (see Yairi, Ambrose, and Cox, 1996) found in the majority of studies that 30% to 60% of stutterers had stuttering in their families, versus 10% in the families of people who did not stutter. Other related work (Ambrose, Yairi, and Cox, 1993) found that among stuttering children, 71% had immediate or extended family histories of stuttering, 43% had immediate family histories, and 28% had at least one parent with a stuttering history. These findings prompted further research into genetic factors. Longitudinal twin studies (see Dworzynski et al., 2007) conclude that early childhood stuttering is highly heritable for both persistent and recovered stuttering, and it is higher for identical than fraternal twins, with little effect from the shared environment.

Characteristics and Genetic Factors of Language Impairment in Children

Language impairment causes children difficulty in understanding spoken language, knowing word meanings, and expressing thoughts with correct word and sentence formation. Studies also find slower processing speeds across widely varied linguistic and nonlinguistic tasks in children with language impairment. Different subtypes of language impairment have been proposed, including one involving semantic and pragmatic deficits and another involving lexical and syntactic deficits. Linkage analyses searching throughout the genome for inherited areas accompanying language disorders implicate locations on chromosomes 12, 13, 16, and 19. The FOXP2 gene has been identified as causing a complex speech and language disorder and differences in brain structures when it is disrupted and as a transcription factor regulating other genes' functions, including those of the CNTNAP2 gene, which has also been implicated as a candidate for language impairment—especially regarding the ability to imitate nonwords. Researchers believe that CNTNAP2 is more likely to affect isolated skills important to language functions, and FOXP2 is more likely to affect multiple abilities concurrently due to its regulating other genes.

Dyslexia

Dyslexia includes difficulty recognizing words with nonstandard spellings; sounding words out; perceiving phonemes, syllables, and other discrete units within connected speech; and accessing mental vocabulary for rapid-naming tasks. Neuroimaging showing different brain activation patterns during reading in individuals with dyslexia support biological origins, as well as underactivity in two of three left-hemisphere regions normally active during reading; higher right-hemisphere activation instead in some individuals; differences in left-hemisphere white and gray matter shape and density; and structural differences in cortical neuron organization. In newborns with family dyslexia risk, differences in event-related neurological responses to sounds have been identified. Observations that dyslexia seems to be hereditary and runs in families are consistent with the biological bases for many of its characteristics. Linkage analyses across the genome implicate nine potential regions, named DYX1 through DYX9, as well as another region on chromosome 6 near region DYX2. Several studies have replicated these findings. Six candidate genes have been proposed within these nine regions. Some of these genes are important to the development of the embryonic brain.

Review Video: Disorders that Impair Reading and Writing
Visit mometrix.com/academy and enter code: 306758

Copyright © Mometrix Media. You have been licensed one copy of this document for personal use only. Any other reproduction or redistribution is strictly prohibited. All rights reserved.
This content is provided for test preparation purposes only and does not imply an endorsement by Mometrix of any particular political, scientific, or religious point of view.

Genetic Etiologies for Speech Sound Disorders

Speech sound disorders encompass different types. For example, children misarticulating certain sounds, e.g., lisping on /s/ and /z/, are described as having articulation disorders; in contrast, children only misarticulating within specific contexts, e.g., at the ends of words or in consonant clusters, are described as having phonologically based disorders. Children diagnosed with childhood apraxia of speech demonstrate characteristics including incorrectly producing multiple speech sounds including vowels, markedly unintelligible speech, and prosody that sounds robotic. Based on evidence that many children having speech sound disorders in preschool subsequently struggle with reading in school, recent (e.g., 2005, 2006, 2007, 2011) molecular genetic studies of childhood speech sound disorders have sought to identify connections. Linkage analyses of genomic regions associated with dyslexia do show accompanying implications for speech sound disorders, suggesting the two conditions share genetic risk factors. One study including multigenerational familial speech sound disorders found motor deficits in adult relatives of children having childhood apraxia of speech. Genomewide linkage analysis uncovered new implicated regions, one overlapping with a newly identified chromosome region for dyslexia. This novel approach to genetics in speech sound disorders has prompted genomewide studies of next generations.

Developmental Language Disorder

Symptoms of language disorders are identified in up to 1 of every 20 children. According to the National Institutes of Health (NIH), language disorders with unknown causes are termed developmental language disorders; however, ASHA, probably more accurately, terms these idiopathic. Children typically develop difficulties with receptive language skills before the age of four years. Mixed language disorders affect both receptive and expressive language skills. Brain injuries can cause some mixed language disorders, which are sometimes misdiagnosed as developmental disorders. Although intellectual deficits seldom cause language disorders, children with other developmental conditions such as hearing loss, learning disabilities, autism spectrum disorders, etc., may have coexisting language disorders. Language disorders and language delays are different. A child with delayed language develops speech and language skills in the same manner and sequence as typically developing children but reaches milestones at later ages and develops language skills more slowly. However, a child with a language disorder does not develop speech and language skills in normal ways. The child might develop certain language skills but not others. The child's language skills may also develop in different ways than they usually do.

Apraxia of Speech

Apraxia of speech is a speech disorder characterized by difficulty with the accurate and consistent motor production of speech. It is not caused by physical paralysis or weakness of the facial, jaw, tongue, or lip muscles, but rather by deficits in the brain's ability to coordinate and control the movements of those muscles to produce speech. Speech apraxia is sometimes divided into "acquired" and "developmental" types; however, ASHA prefers the term childhood apraxia of speech over developmental speech apraxia because childhood speech apraxia, like other developmental disorders, can be either congenital or acquired during childhood as speech is developing. In apraxia of speech acquired at any age, damage to regions of the brain regulating speech causes impairment or loss of existing speech abilities. Head injuries, brain tumors, strokes, and illnesses affecting the brain can cause acquired speech apraxia, which can co-occur with dysarthria and/or aphasia when damage affects the brain regions associated with these. Unlike delayed speech development, the symptoms of childhood apraxia of speech usually continue beyond the developmental period.

Copyright © Mometrix Media. You have been licensed one copy of this document for personal use only. Any other reproduction or redistribution is strictly prohibited. All rights reserved.
This content is provided for test preparation purposes only and does not imply an endorsement by Mometrix of any particular political, scientific, or religious point of view.

Developmental Disabilities

Federal resources such as the Individuals with Disabilities Education Act (IDEA) legislation guaranteeing a free, appropriate public education within the least restrictive environment to all students with disabilities; Medicaid rules determining federal health insurance coverage of services and programs to individuals with disabilities; and clinical sources such as the *Diagnostic and Statistical Manual of Mental Disorders* (DSM) published by the American Psychiatric Association, which provides definitions, classifications, and codes for various mental disorders, commonly define developmental disabilities as disabilities that have onsets before an individual reaches the age of 18 years; are chronic and severe; can be attributed to impairments that are physical, mental, or both; are likely to continue indefinitely; significantly limit the individual's functioning in major life activity areas such as receptive and expressive language, learning, self-care, mobility, self-direction, economic self-sufficiency and independent living; and require individualized supports, special services, etc. for extended times or throughout life. Therefore, many disabilities in infants, children, and adolescents up to age 18 qualify as developmental disabilities including intellectual, cognitive, or physical disabilities; mental illnesses; genetic syndromes; behavior disorders; learning disabilities; and speech and language disorders, delayed speech, and delayed language development.

Review Video: Least Restrictive Environment
Visit mometrix.com/academy and enter code: 100354

Impacts of Disabilities on Speech and Language

Some common characteristics of intellectual disability (ID) are delayed development of speech and language skills. For example, children with moderate and severe ID often begin to speak at later than normal ages, acquire smaller vocabularies, take longer to learn to read and write or never develop functional literacy skills, read at lower levels than their chronological ages, have limited or no understanding of abstract concepts, and speak using simpler sentence structures. Some may have unclear speech. Those with profound ID are frequently nonverbal or can only utter a few words. Among children with autism spectrum disorders (ASDs), some have coexisting ID and some do not. Of those who do, some are completely nonverbal; some speak only in echolalia, i.e., parroting others' utterances but producing no original speech or language; some can communicate needs, thoughts, and feelings, but only through very limited repertoires of words and phrases; and some with less extensive cognitive and behavioral impairment communicate more normally. Those having ASDs without ID, particularly the higher functioning, often have well-developed vocabularies and sentence structures and fluent speech, but they may exhibit singsong or robotic prosody. Whereas some have difficulty initiating and maintaining conversational exchanges, others can converse normally.

CP and MD

Depending on its severity, **cerebral palsy** (CP) impairs neurological control of many muscular functions, including the movements of speech muscles as well as body movements. A common symptom of CP is spasticity, which involves muscular rigidity and lack of coordination and control. Some individuals with CP may have spastic dysphonia, meaning that the spasticity of their muscles interferes with speech sound production. This is usually a symptom of more severe cases of CP. Those with mild CP may evidence only more subtle physical effects, for example, a slight limp, weakness, or difficulty with certain movements. More severe CP can result in hemiplegia, paraplegia, or quadriplegia and greater difficulty with phonation and/or movement and coordination of the speech mechanisms. Children and adolescents who have coexisting CP and intellectual disability may vocalize but be nonverbal. **Muscular dystrophy** (MD), particularly the

Copyright © Mometrix Media. You have been licensed one copy of this document for personal use only. Any other reproduction or redistribution is strictly prohibited. All rights reserved.
This content is provided for test preparation purposes only and does not imply an endorsement by Mometrix of any particular political, scientific, or religious point of view.

oculopharyngeal and myotonic forms, can cause severe speech and swallowing disorders. Oculopharyngeal MD impairs muscular contractions of the pharyngeal wall and laryngeal elevation, causing oral weakness and swallowing problems. Myotonic MD also has pharyngeal impacts, especially in control of the cricopharyngeal and chewing muscles.

ALS

Amyotrophic lateral sclerosis (ALS), a progressive disease, causes motor neurons in the brain, brainstem, and spinal cord to degenerate and die, causing gradual muscle atrophy and impairing initiation and control of muscular movements. Bulbar ALS affects motor neurons in the brainstem, affecting speech and swallowing muscles. Early symptoms include dysarthria, which prevents normal loudness and clarity of speech; slurred speech; nasal speech; stiff/spastic, tight, or weak speech muscles causing difficulty pronouncing words; and decreased control of breathing, making longer conversations or sentences difficult or impossible. Eventually, ALS completely destroys the patient's ability to speak or even vocalize. As the respiratory muscles become progressively weaker, an individual with ALS cannot speak loudly enough for others to understand them. Bulbar ALS can also cause dysphagia as muscular weakness makes chewing and swallowing difficult. At first this interferes with managing solid or hard foods; but as weakness progresses, individuals have trouble swallowing pureed foods, liquids, and even their own saliva. ALS also causes fatigue, depleting patients of the energy to have conversations and finish eating meals even before they lose these abilities completely.

Huntington's Disease

Huntington's disease (HD) is inherited and causes progressive brain cell degeneration, which impairs cognition, behavior, and motor control. Motor symptoms include impairment of voluntary movements, chorea, i.e., involuntary, uncontrolled movements such as writhing or jerking; dystonia, muscle contractures and/or rigidity; and impairment of balance, gait, and posture. HD symptoms affecting voice and speech production include dysarthria, i.e., weakness and incoordination of the speech muscles causing slurred speech; apraxia, i.e., disrupted brain programming and sequencing of speech muscle movements; poor speech rate control, causing overly slow or rapid speech; difficulty coordinating the voice with breathing; and in some cases, impaired voice quality, e.g., breathy voice, overly loud or soft voice, hoarse voice, or harsh vocal tone. HD also commonly causes dysphagia. In fact, according to research statistics, aspiration pneumonia is the number one cause of death for HD patients. Impaired motor control causes impulsive eating, problems controlling intake rates, inability to coordinate breathing and swallowing, and involuntary oral/pharyngeal muscle movements. Patients frequently aspirate liquid or food into the lungs, leading to infection—i.e., aspiration pneumonia.

Parkinson's Disease

Cognition and language are affected in some **Parkinson's disease** (PD) patients, causing difficulty with quick thinking, multitasking, understanding complex spoken sentences, retrieving words, and formulating ideas in a timely manner. PD patients frequently report knowing a word they want to say but being unable to access it. These symptoms combined can cause conversational pauses, confusing others about when to take turns speaking and leaving PD patients behind in rapidly paced group discussions. PD often causes flat/lack of facial and vocal expression, reducing the meaning that patients can communicate. It also impairs their ability to recognize emotions expressed by words and facial expressions. Additionally, PD motor impairment limits the ability to make communicative physical gestures. Changes in voice and speech sounds affect around 90% of PD patients at some point. Lower vocal volume is most common; a hoarse or breathy voice quality can develop. This interferes with communication, particularly with partners having hearing losses. Some PD patients speak more slowly; a small proportion of others speak so rapidly they trip over

Copyright © Mometrix Media. You have been licensed one copy of this document for personal use only. Any other reproduction or redistribution is strictly prohibited. All rights reserved.
This content is provided for test preparation purposes only and does not imply an endorsement by Mometrix of any particular political, scientific, or religious point of view.

sounds, seeming to stutter. Another PD symptom is difficulty coordinating talking and walking: Patients have difficulty doing these concurrently, demonstrating impairments in both.

Congenital Heart Diseases

Deficits or delays in the development of language skills are identified in many children who have complex **congenital heart disease**. Although they may score within the broad average ranges on tests of language, children who have complex congenital heart diseases are found to perform more poorly on average in linguistic tasks when their performance is compared to that of their normally developing peers who do not have congenital heart disease. A higher probability of deficits or delays in speech development is a known characteristic of children who have hypoplastic left heart syndrome and transposition of the great arteries. For example, research has found that children with transposition of the great arteries, combined with tiny septal defects of the ventricles, can have delays in communication development. Research has also found that decreased skills in expressive and receptive language were identified in one out of four children who had transposition of the great arteries.

Multiple Sclerosis

Multiple sclerosis (MS), an inflammatory degenerative disease of the central nervous system, causes demyelination, i.e., destruction of the myelin sheaths that insulate and protect brain cells and nerve fibers and facilitate their transmission of impulses. The most common problem affecting communication in MS is dysarthria, which up to half of patients experience. Weakness and spasticity in the speech muscles cause slurred speech, unclear and/or slow articulation, monotonous pitch, and breathy or harsh voice quality. MS also causes breathing problems and ataxia (incoordination), including of the speech-breathing process. Weak respiratory muscles can also decrease the lungs' vital capacity (air volume), reducing vocal loudness. Impacts vary from mild to profound. Common misunderstandings are assuming that MS patients are drunk because of slurred speech; deaf because of unclear speech; or "stupid" because of unvarying pitch, lower intelligibility, etc. Language symptoms include problems with comprehension, naming, repetition, word fluency, and sentence construction. Research finds that most MS patients who have dysarthria also have linguistic impairments.

Central Auditory Processing Disorder

Roughly 5% of school-aged children have **central auditory processing disorder** (CAPD). Their hearing acuity is normal, as evidenced by their hearing normally in quiet environments such as soundproofed rooms when sounds are presented one at a time. However, they typically cannot recognize minimal differences between phonemes in words, even when they can hear them loudly and clearly enough. Thus, background noise poses problems for students, who are frequently in noisy settings, with CAPD. They typically have difficulty with following directions and conversations; reading, writing, and spelling; math word problems; and organizing and remembering information. They are easily distracted or excessively bothered by sudden/loud noises and/or are upset by noisy surroundings. Main CAPD problem areas are the following:

- **Auditory background**—background noise distracts attention; loosely structured, noisy classrooms are frustrating.
- **Auditory memory**—retaining lists, directions, or study material, immediately and/or for later.
- **Auditory discrimination**—between phonemes in words, e.g., cat/bat; interfering with reading, writing, spelling, and following directions.

Copyright © Mometrix Media. You have been licensed one copy of this document for personal use only. Any other reproduction or redistribution is strictly prohibited. All rights reserved.
This content is provided for test preparation purposes only and does not imply an endorsement by Mometrix of any particular political, scientific, or religious point of view.

- **Auditory attention**—trouble focusing listening and maintaining attention long enough, e.g., to school lectures or teacher instructions, to complete requirements/tasks.
- **Auditory cohesion**—with cognitively higher level listening such as understanding verbal math problems or riddles, or drawing inferences from discussions/conversations.

Deafness

Deaf individuals who have not been raised using American Sign Language (ASL) or similar languages/communication systems typically demonstrate significantly delayed and/or deficient language development. This includes not only acquisition of vocabulary words and semantic comprehension of word meanings, grammatical comprehension of parts of speech, syntactic comprehension of sentence structure and word order, pragmatic comprehension of social language use, and literacy skills for reading and writing, but also the understanding of concepts that have impacts on cognitive development. Although concepts can be learned through nonverbal (e.g., visual) modalities, the primary auditory basis of language hinders language development for deaf people without alternative language. However, those raised using ASL typically demonstrate better, though different, language development. ASL has its own grammatical and syntactic structures; for example, whereas spoken English places the subject first in sentences, e.g., "I am a student," ASL places the sentence "topic" first, e.g., "(topic:) student" followed by "I." Because of ASL's different organization, and because many aspects of language (not just speech) have auditory foundations, deaf language development differs from and lacks certain features of hearing language development. However, those using ASL or other systematic communication systems still have far superior language development to those without them.

People who have hearing impairment but still have some residual hearing have a harder time developing speech than those with normal hearing, but they have a comparatively a much easier time than those who are totally deaf. Some deaf individuals can learn to develop speech through feeling vibrations—of others' speech and of their own vocal cords, speech therapy, and a great deal of hard work and practice. However, it is extremely difficult for them to monitor the pitch and volume of their speech without hearing it. As a result, what speech they can produce is limited and characterized by abnormal vocal quality, lack of regulation of loudness and pitch, and lack of normal intonation and prosody. Those with residual hearing who can use hearing aids can usually control the loudness, pitch, and intonation of their voices to produce fairly normal-sounding speech, but often display typical articulatory distortions. For example, /r/ is a phoneme notoriously difficult for hearing-impaired individuals to hear and reproduce accurately. They often pronounce it more like a cross between /r/ and /w/. Another difficult phoneme is /s/, which hearing-impaired people may pronounce more like /t/.

Down syndrome

Because individuals with **Down Syndrome** (DS) have different head and neck structures, they are more prone to nasal, sinus, upper respiratory, ear problems, and velopharyngeal insufficiency (VPI). DS children typically have anatomical differences including hypoplastic (less mobile) nasal bones; macroglossia (enlarged tongue); smaller, narrower nasopharynxes and oropharynxes; smaller Eustachian tubes; and a decreased angle of the Eustachian tubes to the hard palate. Anatomical differences cause DS children symptoms including tongue protrusion, drooling, mouth-breathing, nasal congestion and drainage, snoring, sleep apnea, and acute and chronic otitis media. They are also frequently treated for nasal, sinus, upper respiratory, and ear disease with tonsillectomies and/or adenoidectomies, which benefit many by reducing/eliminating snoring, sleep apnea, mouth-breathing and nasal drainage, but themselves can cause VPI and related hypernasal speech. DS structural abnormalities causing hypernasality include short soft palates and short, high-arched hard palates. DS functional factors contributing to postsurgical hypernasality

Copyright © Mometrix Media. You have been licensed one copy of this document for personal use only. Any other reproduction or redistribution is strictly prohibited. All rights reserved.
This content is provided for test preparation purposes only and does not imply an endorsement by Mometrix of any particular political, scientific, or religious point of view.

include hypotonia, delayed oral-motor development, and slower motor learning. Tonsillectomies with/without adenoidectomies are often performed for sleep apnea and other obstructive symptoms. However, DS children have smaller adenoidal pads than normal, so adenoidectomy may not only fail to improve ear and nose problems, but may additionally cause chronic ear drainage, respiratory problems, VPI, and hypernasality.

Otitis Media

After the common cold, **otitis media** (OM) is the second most frequent early childhood illness. In acute OM (AOM), middle-ear fluid is infected; in OM with effusion (OME), fluid is not infected. Chronic OME lasts more than eight weeks. Almost all children have at least one AOM/OME episode; at least 80% have three or more episodes before three years of age. Frequent, persistent OME is more prevalent in children with Down syndrome, fragile X syndrome, Turner syndrome, Williams syndrome, cleft palate/other craniofacial anomalies, attending childcare, exposed to secondhand smoke, from low-income families, and with OME family histories. Around half the time, OME causes temporary mild-to-moderate conductive hearing loss, which could disrupt language processing speed, affecting phonological, vocabulary, syntactic, and conversational comprehension and expression—e.g., inaccurate and/or incomplete phonological encoding and perception of grammatical morphemes. OME-related hearing loss could disrupt auditory attention in noisy environments. Children with persistent hearing loss >20 dB from OME and special populations have increased risks for speech-language/developmental difficulties. ASHA recommends regular hearing, speech, and language screening of children with chronic OM; routine hearing and middle-ear screening of children with chronic OME receiving speech-language treatment; optimal listening environments; and early intervention for speech/language difficulties/delays/disorders.

Conductive vs. Sensorineural Hearing Loss

Conductive hearing loss originates in the outer or middle ear, preventing sound from reaching the inner ear. Causes include wax buildups, ear tumors/growths, otosclerosis (a bony middle-ear growth immobilizing the ossicles, preventing sound conduction), eardrum perforation or scarring, middle-ear fluid, and middle-ear/ear canal infections. People with conductive hearing loss typically perceive sounds and speech as uniformly faint. Because air conduction is affected but they can hear their own voices inside their heads through bone conduction, their speech is usually quieter, not louder. **Sensorineural hearing loss** originates in the inner ear when cochlear hair cells and inner-ear nerves are destroyed or eventually die. It is commonly caused by aging (presbycusis), beginning with high frequencies. Additional causes include loud noise exposure; injury; viral infection, e.g., measles or mumps; meningitis; stroke; diabetes; high fever; ototoxic medications; Meniere's disease, which also affects the vestibular system, disrupting balance as well as hearing; acoustic neuromas or similar tumors; and hereditary factors. People with sensorineural hearing loss can often hear speech but not understand it because their discrimination among speech sounds is impaired. Because the problem is with neither air nor bone conduction, their speech is usually louder.

Dysarthria

Dysarthria is caused by damage to the central or peripheral nervous system that impedes the transmission from neurons in the brain to the muscles used for speech. Dysarthria can affect all processes of speech production, including breathing, phonation, resonance, articulation, and prosody. Among the six forms of dysarthria, four result from upper motor neuron damage: spastic dysarthria, caused by pyramidal tract damage; hyperkinetic dysarthria, caused by damage to the basal ganglia in the extrapyramidal tract; hypokinetic dysarthria, caused by damage to the substantia nigra, also in the extrapyramidal tract; and ataxic dysarthria, caused by cerebellar damage. One type results from lower motor neuron damage: flaccid dysarthria, caused by cranial

Copyright © Mometrix Media. You have been licensed one copy of this document for personal use only. Any other reproduction or redistribution is strictly prohibited. All rights reserved.
This content is provided for test preparation purposes only and does not imply an endorsement by Mometrix of any particular political, scientific, or religious point of view.

nerve damage. Mixed dysarthria is caused by damage to both upper and lower motor neurons. The neurological damage leads to paralysis, weakness, and/or incoordination of speech musculature. The difference between dysarthria and apraxia, which both have neurological etiologies, is that whereas apraxia involves damage to the brain's ability for generating programs required for the coordination of speech motor movements, dysarthria involves damage to the brain's ability to transmit the correct messages to the speech muscles.

Apraxia of Speech

Apraxia of speech is caused by damage to regions of the brain controlling the coordinated movements of speech muscles. The muscles themselves are not physiologically weak; the signals the brain normally sends to the mouth have been disrupted by neurological damage. The nature of this damage determines the severity of individual cases. Strokes are among the most common causes. Additional causes include traumatic brain injuries, brain tumors, dementias, and progressive neurological diseases. People with speech apraxia know which words they want to utter, but their brains have trouble coordinating the muscular movements required to produce all word phonemes. Their speech errors are typically inconsistent. They may recognize errors, and upon retrying, they may/may not articulate correctly or produce something entirely different. Errors include distortions, omissions, and/or substitutions. Additional symptoms include slow speech rates; impaired prosody and rhythm; lip and tongue groping for specific phonemes and words; producing automatic speech such as greetings better than purposeful speech; and in the severest cases, inability to say anything. For instance, patients may be unable to control their lips and tongue to form a word's initial phoneme, let alone the rest of it.

Adult Dysphagia

The most frequent causes of dysphagia in adults are neurological disorders. These can include strokes, Parkinson's disease, and amyotrophic lateral sclerosis (ALS) among other causes. Additional etiologies for most adult swallowing disorders are changes to the oral cavity, pharynx, or larynx caused by surgery, e.g., for cancer, and esophageal structural and motility abnormalities. Swallowing consists of three phases: oral, pharyngeal, and esophageal. In the oral phase, disordered swallowing can be caused by anything affecting jaw, lip, tongue, and palate functions. This includes structural defects such as cleft palates, dental malocclusions, poor dentition, or surgical changes to the oral cavity and neurological disorders such as strokes, Parkinson's disease, ALS, and other neurological conditions can impair the brain's coordination of the oral musculature. This impairment can then disrupt swallowing. In the pharyngeal phase, neurological disorders as well as surgical changes to the epiglottis and/or vocal folds can impair airway protection, enabling laryngeal instead of esophageal bolus transfer, causing aspiration. Neurological disorders also can delay initiation of swallowing, causing bolus pooling within the pharynx. In the esophageal phase, esophageal stricture or obstruction, gastroesophageal reflux, and decreased esophageal motility cause most swallowing problems.

Aphasia

Aphasia is a communication disorder involving language processing. Broca's aphasia affects expressive language, while Wernicke's aphasia affects receptive language. Aphasia is caused by damage to the regions of the brain responsible for receptively understanding language and/or expressively formulating it. The neurological damage that leads to aphasia causes difficulty with listening, reading, speaking, and writing, but it does not impair cognitive ability, voice quality, or articulation of speech sounds. This damage is most frequently done by stroke. Additional causes include traumatic brain injuries, brain tumors, and progressive neurological disorders or diseases. Depending on the location and extent of neurological injury, aphasia can coexist with apraxia, dysarthria, or dysphagia. Historically, scientists believed Broca's aphasia was isolated to the left

Copyright © Mometrix Media. You have been licensed one copy of this document for personal use only. Any other reproduction or redistribution is strictly prohibited. All rights reserved.
This content is provided for test preparation purposes only and does not imply an endorsement by Mometrix of any particular political, scientific, or religious point of view.

hemisphere and Wernicke's aphasia to the right hemisphere; however, later neuroimaging has found language functions to be more diffuse, affecting more areas. In Broca's/**expressive aphasia**, patients have trouble with word retrieval; they may substitute related or unrelated words for intended words; transpose syllables/phonemes within words; substitute made-up words/nonwords; have trouble forming sentences; fluently string real and nonwords together that make no sense; have trouble writing and spelling and adding/subtracting, counting money, telling time, and understanding other numerical concepts.

Receptive Aphasia vs. Expressive Aphasia

Whereas expressive or Broca's aphasia primarily impairs the ability to formulate spoken and written language, receptive or Wernicke's aphasia primarily impairs the ability to understand the spoken language that one hears or reads. Scientists have previously assigned the former to the left and the latter to the right hemisphere of the brain, but technological advances have since found language processes to be less localized. Strokes are the most common causes of aphasia; brain injuries, brain tumors, progressive neurological diseases, and anything else that causes neurological damage to the brain regions that process language are less common causes. More anterior damage can cause nonfluent, choppy speech; more posterior damage often leaves speech fluent, but containing made-up or incorrect words and impairs comprehension of others' speech. Patients with Wernicke's/**receptive aphasia** typically have more trouble listening and reading than speaking and writing. They often take figurative expressions literally, misinterpret jokes, misunderstand long sentences and rapid speech, and have trouble understanding speech in groups/with background noise. Patients with severe Wernicke's aphasia can speak fluently but not understand anything others say. They may attempt to cover lack of comprehension by using generic utterances, e.g., "You look nice today" or "How's the weather?" to avoid responding directly to others' speech that they cannot decipher.

Structural and Gastrointestinal Functional Etiologies of Dysphagia

Some structural etiologies of dysphagia include cleft palate, cleft lip (the palates and upper lip fail to close at/near the midline, leaving a division/cleft), micrognathia (undersized jaw), macroglossia (oversized tongue), and other craniofacial anomalies; laryngeal cleft; laryngomalacia (congenital flaccidity/softening and collapse of the larynx), tracheomalacia (flaccidity leading to collapse of the tracheal support cartilage), and pharyngomalacia (collapse of the pharyngeal wall); choanal atresia (a congenital disorder wherein the back of the nasal airway or choana is blocked by tissue); glottic web (a continuous sheet of mucosal tissue connecting the vocal folds) or subglottic stenosis (narrowing of the airway below the glottis); vocal fold paralysis, which can result from cardiac surgery; and many others. Some functional etiologies of dysphagia in the gastrointestinal system include gastroparesis (partial paralysis of the stomach muscles causing delayed stomach emptying); esophageal dysmotility (disruption in the esophagus's normal process of coordinated muscular contractions that transport food to the stomach) disorders—e.g., spasticity caused by unbalanced nerve pathways controlling esophageal muscle contraction and relaxation, causing muscle spasms, achalasia caused by esophageal sphincter rigidity, or scleroderma, an autoimmune disease causing esophageal scar tissue buildup; ileus (intestinal obstruction); or the presence of foreign bodies in the esophagus.

Etiology of Voice Disorders

Sometimes the etiology of a voice disorder is unclear, making the diagnosis also unclear, in which cases these are deemphasized but treatment is still possible; e.g., structural findings and client stimulability levels can still support treatment goals. In investigating etiology, taking a detailed history of the disorder is important. The SLP should determine sudden/gradual onset; onset-related conditions/events; whether symptoms have been stable since onset/have progressed but

Copyright © Mometrix Media. You have been licensed one copy of this document for personal use only. Any other reproduction or redistribution is strictly prohibited. All rights reserved.
This content is provided for test preparation purposes only and does not imply an endorsement by Mometrix of any particular political, scientific, or religious point of view.

are currently stable/are still progressing; whether a single/multiple systems are involved, e.g., resonance, speech, phonation, and/or respiration; any symptom-free times since onset; and client ability to self-correct/improve symptoms. Clarifying etiology can facilitate diagnosis: It is important to differentiate initial etiology versus what is maintaining the condition. These may be different or the same. If the initial cause is also maintaining the problem, neurological factors are probable. For example, laryngeal dystonia could be a primary etiology for focal muscle spasms. However, if initial versus maintaining factors differ, structural/functional primary and secondary etiologies are included—e.g., functional factors such as muscle memory and/or muscular hyperfunction. With the same example of focal muscle spasms, if an upper respiratory infection was the primary etiology, a secondary etiology of muscle tension dysphonia could be maintaining voice problems.

Structural and functional etiologies of voice disorders can be indistinguishable or overlap. For example, when cancer affecting the voice is caused by smoking, this is functional; but a cancerous tumor is a structural abnormality. To diagnose a voice disorder, when possible, SLPs must determine the etiology of current symptoms. A multitude of causes is possible for voice disorders; hence, various other practitioners can help the SLP determine etiology. For example, some voice problems can be caused by allergy symptoms, including post-nasal drip, in which case the SLP and client should consult with an allergist; and perhaps also with an otolaryngologist when symptoms such as postnasal drip are causing irritation and hoarseness. Another factor is asthma: Being a respiratory illness, it can lead to problems with voice respiration, in which case the SLP and client should consult with a pulmonologist. Gastroesophageal reflux can cause voice issues because the backing up of stomach acid into the esophagus can cause inflammation of the larynx and throat resulting in voice hoarseness, in which case the SLP and client should consult with a gastroenterologist.

Voice Disorders Involving Muscle Tension Dysphonia

Muscle tension dysphonia is one structural/functional etiology of recalcitrant voice disorders. Muscle tension causes vocal fold hyperfunction. This laryngeal muscle tension can be nonadducted or adducted; i.e., the vocal folds do/do not adduct/draw together. One of the most common etiologies of nonadducted hyperfunction is upper respiratory infection and resulting laryngitis. Although these can precipitate voice problems, other functional factors can maintain them. For example, the upper respiratory infection causes laryngitis, which causes severe hoarseness and aphonia (loss of voice). The client first consciously whispers in response, but then s/he becomes locked into whispering. Once the infection and laryngitis are resolved, the client continues being locked into the whispering behavior. This "whisper phonation" is the most frequent pattern in nonadducted hyperfunction. In the majority of clients with this condition, no overt evidence of psychogenic factors is observed. With adducted hyperfunction, the SLP determines the role of muscle tension: If the voice improves after unloading muscle tension (when possible), then the muscle tension is impairing phonation; if unloading muscle tension worsens the voice, then the muscle tension is required for optimal phonation: The underlying problem is vocal fold paresis/bowing/other hypofunction or ataxia/spasmodic dysphonia/other dysfunction.

Requirements for Voice Disorders to Qualify as Psychogenic in Origin

Three requirements for a voice disorder to qualify as psychogenic in origin are as follows:

1. One of the aforementioned factors must exist
2. The effects on the voice must be fairly consistent
3. The voice disorder cannot be accounted for by any organic cause

Copyright © Mometrix Media. You have been licensed one copy of this document for personal use only. Any other reproduction or redistribution is strictly prohibited. All rights reserved.
This content is provided for test preparation purposes only and does not imply an endorsement by Mometrix of any particular political, scientific, or religious point of view.

Psychogenic etiologies of voice disorders include chronic states of anxiety, depression, stress, intrapersonal problems (i.e., within the individual), interpersonal problems (i.e., in interacting with others), and trauma. Types of psychogenic voice disorders include conversion aphonia, conversion dysphonia, puberphonia or mutational falsetto, and conversion muteness. In conversion aphonia, the larynx is normal, yet the client whispers involuntarily. Roughly 80% of patients are female. Onset can be sudden or gradual. While psychogenic, it can be triggered by some organic disorders. In conversion dysphonia, the voice is unreliable due to unpredictable loudness, pitch, etc., varying between normal and breathy, loud and soft, and high and low pitch. Depression and/or anxiety are common causes. In puberphonia/mutational falsetto, the voice fails to change from higher preadolescent pitch to lower adolescent/adult pitch despite laryngeal capacity. Vocal symptoms include hoarseness, monotone, breathiness, thinness, and weakness.

Psychological Factors

Psychological factors such as environmental stressors or interpersonal conflicts can lead to loss of voluntary control over the general or special senses, or over normal striated muscle movements. This loss of control is defined by psychiatrists and psychologists as a conversion reaction. Historically it was called conversion hysteria. This is a psychogenic etiology of voice disorders. In one historical (1960s) case example, a psychiatric nurse had incurred a serious back injury and was prescribed painkillers, to which she subsequently became addicted. During treatment in a psychiatric facility, she had experienced acute withdrawal symptoms including screaming and striking out at staff and had been physically restrained. Later, when she demonstrated symptoms of extreme anxiety, a staff member unfortunately and unethically threatened her, "If you scream again, I'll put you back into the straightjacket!" Terrified of a repetition of restraint, which had been traumatic the first time, the patient developed a conversion reaction: To keep from screaming again, she lost her voice completely. This is a classic example of conversion muteness (also called psychogenic mutism).

Conversion Muteness or Mute

In one study (Roy et al., 2000), researchers found that the majority of clients who received diagnoses of functional dysphonia had introverted personalities, whereas the majority of clients who had developed vocal nodules (commonly caused by chronic vocal fold abuse or misuse) had extroverted personalities. Among the conversion voice disorders (conversion dysphonia, conversion aphonia, and conversion muteness/mutism), conversion muteness is the most severe. In this disorder, the client typically does not make an attempt to articulate or phonate; or some clients may articulate without exhaling, also resulting in lack of phonation. Some common characteristics of individuals with conversion muteness include mild to moderate depression, suppressed anger, dependency, immaturity, chronic stress, and indifference to the disorder or its symptoms. Some common themes in the case histories of patients with conversion mutism include wanting to express anger, fear, remorse, or other difficult emotions verbally but not permitting oneself to do so; a communication breakdown with somebody important to the patient; and feelings of fear or shame that interfere with expressing emotions via normal speech and language.

Psychogenic Voice Disorders

When the SLP suspects psychogenic etiology for a voice disorder, the first step is to refer the client to a physician for a complete medical examination to rule out the possibility of any organic or neurological etiology. For example, if flexible endoscopy shows that the patient's vocal folds adduct (come together) when the patient laughs, clears the throat, coughs, etc., but they do not adduct during attempts at communicative speech, the voice disorder's etiology must be psychogenic because the vocal folds are otherwise functional for phonation, only not during speech. This apparent contradiction can be explained when the client is not aware that clearing the throat,

Copyright © Mometrix Media. You have been licensed one copy of this document for personal use only. Any other reproduction or redistribution is strictly prohibited. All rights reserved.
This content is provided for test preparation purposes only and does not imply an endorsement by Mometrix of any particular political, scientific, or religious point of view.

coughing, and other nonspeech actions are produced by using the same mechanisms that are used for speech. After diagnosing a psychogenic voice disorder, when taking the case history the SLP should probe more deeply than during typical case histories but should do so very carefully. In efforts to determine the disorder's specific cause, the SLP can ask the client about any current/recent life events that might be important and inform the client that life conflicts/stressors could be affecting her/his voice.

Although referral for a mental health evaluation and psychotherapy is frequently indicated with voice disorders of psychogenic etiology, SLPs must also realize that clients frequently deny psychological factors and reject immediate referrals to psychiatrists/psychologists. Because it is therefore less effective for SLPs to make mental health referrals right away, SLPs should lead discussion gradually toward the subject and educate clients about reasons/needs for professional counseling. Education includes establishing the relationship of stressors and other life factors to voice disorders and eliminating/reducing client perceptions of stigma associated with psychological symptoms, evaluation, and treatment. During speech-language therapy, SLPs should avoid telling clients with psychogenic voice disorders that they could speak normally if they wanted: This constitutes blaming and is inaccurate because psychogenic symptoms are just as involuntary as others. Instead, the SLP can explain the physiological symptoms, e.g., vocal fold separation (abduction), or inability to initiate vibration. To prevent iatrogenic (clinician-induced) symptoms, SLPs should never tell clients with voice disorders to rest their voices through protracted silence/whispering. Disuse can cause vocal fold flaccidity and additional dysphonia and/or anxiety, leading to secondary voice disorders.

Anatomy of the Airway

Respiratory System

The respiratory system is made up of the nasal cavity, pharynx, larynx, trachea, right and left bronchi, and lungs, which branch into bronchioles and alveoli. The respiratory system has two divisions. The upper respiratory tract is comprised of the nasal cavity and pharynx and their associated structures. The lower respiratory tract consists of the larynx, trachea, bronchi, and lungs.

The diaphragm and muscles of the thoracic wall are responsible for the bellows movements necessary for breathing. The process of external respiration (breathing) involves the inspiration of oxygen and the exhalation of carbon dioxide. Normally, respiration occurs through the nasal cavity.

Copyright © Mometrix Media. You have been licensed one copy of this document for personal use only. Any other reproduction or redistribution is strictly prohibited. All rights reserved.
This content is provided for test preparation purposes only and does not imply an endorsement by Mometrix of any particular political, scientific, or religious point of view.

Patients who are congested or under exertion breathe through their mouths. Those with airway blockages are neck-breathers with stomas.

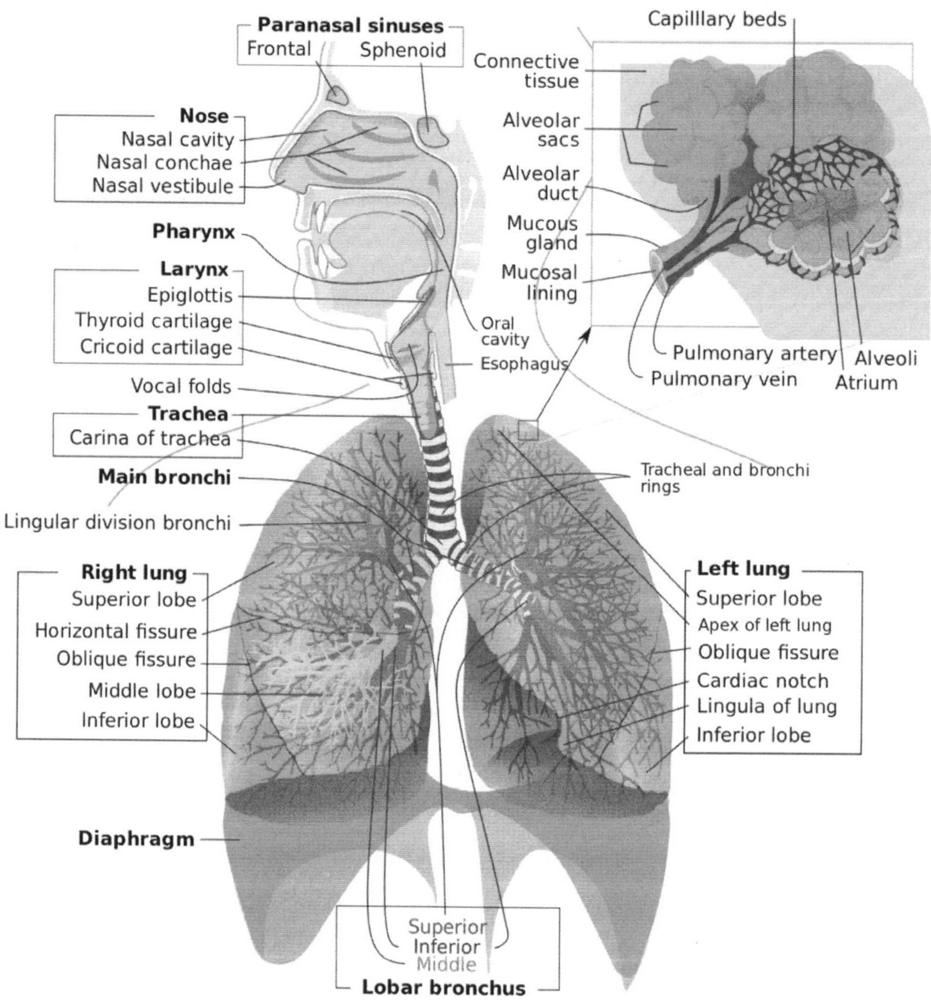

Review Video: Respiratory System
Visit mometrix.com/academy and enter code: 783075

Control of Respiration

Respiratory neurons in the medulla, pons, and brainstem control the speed and depth of respiration and are responsible for maintaining its normal rhythm. The normal respiration rate in adults is 12-20 breaths per minute. Infants breathe faster; the newborn rate is 44 breaths per minute. The respiratory neurons stimulate motor neurons in the spinal cord to cause the contraction of the muscular diaphragm and intercostal muscles. The respiratory neurons also receive information from receptors about the levels of carbon dioxide (CO_2), oxygen (O_2), and hydrogen (H) in the body, as well as the degree of stretch present in the lungs and chest. Chemoreceptors in the carotid arteries inform the respiratory neurons when the concentration of oxygen falls; chemoreceptors located in the medulla, carotid arteries, and aorta keep track of the levels of carbon dioxide and hydrogen. Breathing can be controlled consciously to a certain extent but is basically an autonomic function.

Copyright © Mometrix Media. You have been licensed one copy of this document for personal use only. Any other reproduction or redistribution is strictly prohibited. All rights reserved.
This content is provided for test preparation purposes only and does not imply an endorsement by Mometrix of any particular political, scientific, or religious point of view.

MECHANICS OF RESPIRATION

Respiration occurs when the air pressure within the alveoli differs from the air pressure external to the body. The air pressure in the lungs is altered by changes in the size of the thoracic cavity, which occur as a result of the contraction and relaxation of the muscular diaphragm and intercostal muscles. The muscular diaphragm is primarily responsible for allowing respiration. Inhalation is brought about by two actions that increase the size of the thoracic cavity. The contraction of the diaphragm causes it to flatten, lengthening the thoracic cavity, and the contraction of the intercostal muscles pulls the rib cage upward, widening it. With the enlargement of the thoracic cavity, the pressure within decreases and air enters the lungs. Air is then pushed out of the lungs as the muscular diaphragm and intercostal muscles relax and the volume of the thoracic cavity decreases.

INTERNAL AND EXTERNAL RESPIRATION

Internal respiration refers to the exchange of oxygen, carbon dioxide, and trace gases at the cellular level. **External respiration** refers to the exchange of oxygen, carbon dioxide, and other gases between the lungs and blood, commonly known as breathing. The passage of gases through the respiratory system can be traced as follows:

1. **Inspiratory neurons** in the respiratory center of the medulla oblongata (brain stem) tell the body to inhale.
2. **Nostrils** and **mouth** warm inhaled air by moving it over nasal conchae and sinuses.
3. Air passes through the **pharynx** to the **larynx** (voice box).
4. The **epiglottis** flips to cover the esophagus.
5. Air passes into the **trachea** (windpipe).
6. **Diaphragm** contracts and flattens to raise the ribs as breathing occurs.
7. **Intercostal muscles** between the ribs pull the ribs up enabling the chest to expand and air to pull inward.
8. Trachea splits into the left and right **bronchi** that connect to the **lungs**. The bronchi split into fine branches called **bronchioles**.
9. Bronchioles end in thin-walled, grape-like **alveoli** where the red blood cells absorb oxygen (O2) from the inhaled air and give off carbon dioxide (CO2).
10. **Expiratory neurons** in the brain stem tell the diaphragm and ribs to relax and exhale carbon dioxide into the atmosphere.

Review Video: Pulmonary Circuit
Visit mometrix.com/academy and enter code: 955608

NASAL CAVITY

The inside of the nose is the nasal cavity. The external nares (nostrils) are its outside openings; the internal nares (conchae) are its posterior openings; and the vestibule refers to the front (anterior) portion. Air is taken in through the external nares, warmed, humidified, and filtered by the conchae. The posterior part of the septum is made of bone, and the anterior part is cartilage. The nasal cavity is divided into left and right halves by the nasal septum (vomer). The hard palate forms the cavity floor. The nasal cavity is lined with mucous membrane. The goblet cells of the mucous membrane secrete mucus to trap particles of dust and debris. Ciliated cells wave hairs to stop large particles from advancing any further into the respiratory tract.

PHARYNX

The internal nares lead to the **pharynx**. Mucous is swept back in the nasal cavity to the pharynx, where it is swallowed and excreted through the digestive tract. Air is humidified and warmed in the nasal cavity before passing into the pharynx to prevent damage to the lining of the deeper

Copyright © Mometrix Media. You have been licensed one copy of this document for personal use only. Any other reproduction or redistribution is strictly prohibited. All rights reserved.
This content is provided for test preparation purposes only and does not imply an endorsement by Mometrix of any particular political, scientific, or religious point of view.

respiratory passages. The pharynx is the common opening from the nasal cavity to the rest of the respiratory tract, as well as the digestive tract. It is split into three regions: the **nasopharynx**, **oropharynx**, and **laryngopharynx**. The nasopharynx is the upper (superior) part of the pharynx; it extends from the internal nares down to the uvula and contains the pharyngeal tonsil. The oropharynx runs between the uvula and epiglottis. The laryngopharynx lies below the upper edge of the epiglottis and opens to the esophagus.

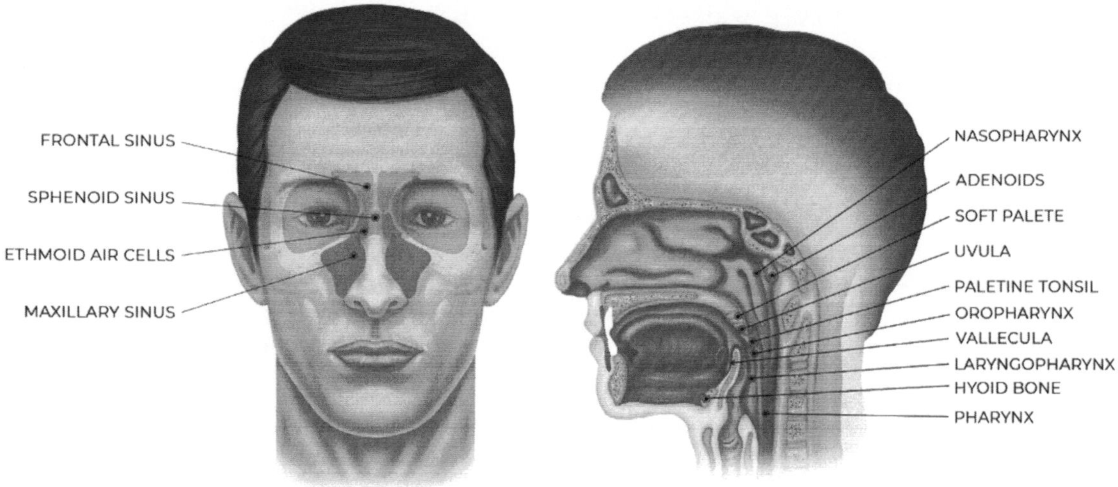

Larynx

The **larynx** is comprised of a cartilaginous skeleton, muscles, ligaments, and mucosal lining. The cartilages making up the larynx are the thyroid, cricoid, and arytenoid. The largest and most superior of these is the thyroid cartilage, or Adam's apple. The cricoid cartilage is the most inferior of the cartilages. If the patient's airway is closed by trauma, foreign body obstruction, or edema from anaphylaxis, the cricoid can be punctured to permit breathing (cricothyrotomy). The arytenoid cartilage lies between the cricoid and thyroid cartilages. The thyroid cartilage is attached to the epiglottis. It covers the opening of the larynx during swallowing to prevent food and fluid from entering the larynx. The **vallecula** is a depression that lies anterior to the epiglottis. The larynx contains the **vocal folds** (vocal cords) for speech and provides an entrance to the lower respiratory passages. The movement of the intrinsic muscles of the larynx alters the shape and tension of the vocal cords, adjusting voice pitch.

Trachea

Also called the windpipe, the **trachea** is a tube comprised of connective tissue, cartilage, and smooth muscle. Its lateral sides are made of cartilage, which protects the trachea and keeps the structure open for the passage of air. The posterior position of the trachea consists of ligamentous membrane and smooth muscle. The smooth muscle can alter the trachea's shape. The esophagus is positioned posterior to the trachea's back wall. Cilia in the trachea push mucus and particles of foreign matter toward the larynx. Their movement allows the mucus and foreign matter to enter the esophagus, where it can be swallowed. The trachea splits into the right and left mainstream bronchi at the carina.

Primary Bronchi

The **primary bronchi** (extrapulmonary bronchi) are large passageways that conduct air into the lungs; no gas exchange takes place. They form where the trachea splits at the carina and run from

Copyright © Mometrix Media. You have been licensed one copy of this document for personal use only. Any other reproduction or redistribution is strictly prohibited. All rights reserved.
This content is provided for test preparation purposes only and does not imply an endorsement by Mometrix of any particular political, scientific, or religious point of view.

the mediastinum down into the lungs. The two primary bronchi are different shapes. The right bronchus is shorter, wider, and positioned more vertically than the left bronchus. If a patient has an obstructed bronchus, it is more likely the right one. The primary bronchi are supported by C-shaped cartilage rings and split into the secondary bronchi as they enter the lungs. This site, where the bronchi, vessels, and nerves enter the lungs, is called the hilus.

Bronchial Tree

The primary bronchi split to form the **secondary bronchi**, and the secondary bronchi divide to form the **tertiary bronchi**. The tertiary bronchi reach into the lobules of the lungs and continue to branch into the bronchioles. The bronchioles divide many times to form the terminal bronchioles, which split into respiratory bronchioles. Each individual respiratory bronchiole also divides and becomes an alveolar duct. The alveolar ducts terminate in the alveoli, clusters of air sacs that resemble clusters of grapes. A single alveolus is 0.1-0.2 mm in diameter. Each one is surrounded by capillaries. It is here in the alveoli where the exchange of respiratory gases (oxygen for carbon dioxide) occurs.

Lungs

The **lungs** (pulmones) are the main organs of respiration. They are light enough to float in water, elastic, smooth, shiny, and spongy. When touched, the tiny, grape-like alveoli crackle. The lungs are covered in a double-walled sac called the pleura. The base of each lung rests on the diaphragm, which raises and lowers the lungs. The right lung is the larger of the two lungs, comprised of three lobes, versus two lobes in the left lung. The lung's lobes are separated by fissures on the surface of the organs. Each lobe of the lung is split into lobules that are separated by connective tissue. Major blood vessels and bronchi do not pass through the connective tissue, so surgeons can remove diseased lobules fairly easily. The right lung contains 10 lobules, and the left lung holds nine. As the primary bronchi enter the lungs, they split into secondary bronchi.

Review Video: Lung Sounds
Visit mometrix.com/academy and enter code: 765616

Pleura

The **pleura** is the thin membrane that protects the lungs. The parietal pleura lines the inside of the chest cavity; the visceral pleura covers the lungs. The space between the two is called the pleural space. The visceral pleura lubricates the surfaces of the lungs by secreting small amounts of fluid. The lungs expand and contract during respiration, and pleural fluid allows the different lung surfaces to glide smoothly across each other. Pleurisy is a painful condition in which the pleura become inflamed as a result of fluid collecting in the pleural space (wet pleurisy) or the two membranes rubbing together (dry pleurisy). A pleural rub may be audible with a stethoscope (auscultation) if the patient has pleurisy, pleural effusion, pneumonia, pulmonary infarction, neoplasm, lupus, or asbestosis.

Articulation Anatomy

Types of Consonants

Consonants are formed by shaping the airflow and voice in various ways using the dental anatomy. Consonants can be voiced or unvoiced, forming different phonemes as a result. The types of consonants are often described as the **manner of articulation.**

Manner of Articulation	Description

Copyright © Mometrix Media. You have been licensed one copy of this document for personal use only. Any other reproduction or redistribution is strictly prohibited. All rights reserved.
This content is provided for test preparation purposes only and does not imply an endorsement by Mometrix of any particular political, scientific, or religious point of view.

Stop (plosive or occlusive)	Sounds produced by a block and release of airflow. These are also called plosives, as the air explodes out after the stop.
Fricative	Sounds produced by passing air through a tight space, causing sound by friction.
Affricate	A combination of a stop and an affricative, caused by a block of airflow, released into a tight space, causing a short fricative sound.
Nasal	Sounds produced by voicing through the nasal cavity. Operate similarly to stops, but are voiced nasally throughout.
Approximant (Liquids and Glides)	The larger category containing liquids and glides, which are consonants that do not strongly obstruct the airflow.

Anatomical Terminology

Anatomy	Related Adjective
Lips	Labial
Tongue	Lingual
Teeth	Dental
Alveolar Ridge	Alveolar
Palate	Palatal
Velum	Velar
Uvula	Uvular
Larynx	Laryngeal
Glottis	Glottal

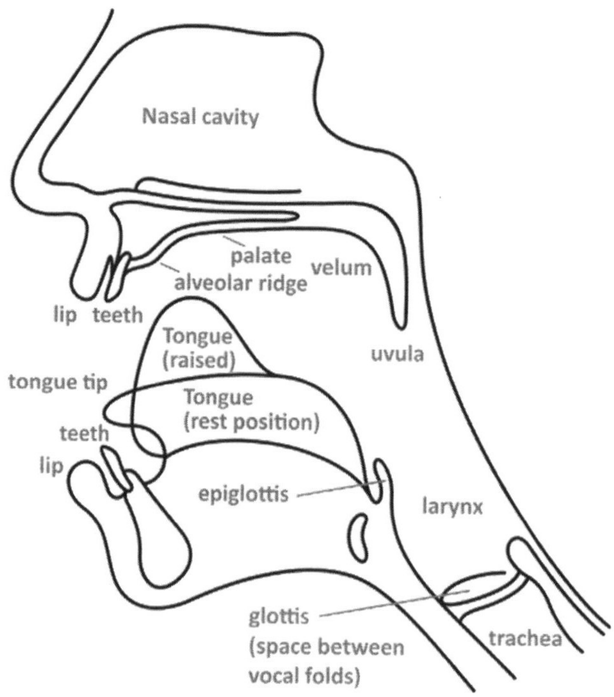

Combining Consonant Types and Anatomical Position

Many of the anatomical terms are used in describing placement in speech articulation. For instance, a voiced labiodental fricative is a sound that uses the voice, the lips and the teeth (derived from labio-dental), and passes air in a way that produces friction. The sound produced is the /v/ sound.

Copyright © Mometrix Media. You have been licensed one copy of this document for personal use only. Any other reproduction or redistribution is strictly prohibited. All rights reserved.
This content is provided for test preparation purposes only and does not imply an endorsement by Mometrix of any particular political, scientific, or religious point of view.

Identifying the manner of the consonant and the anatomical location may help in identifying articulation errors and help with communicating strategies for correction.

Manner of Articulation	Voicing	Bilabial	Labiodental	Dental	Alveolar	Palatal	Velar	Glottal
Stop	Unvoiced	/p/			/t/		/k/	
	Voiced	/b/			/d/		/g/	
Fricative	Unvoiced		/f/	/θ/	/s/			/h/
	Voiced		/v/	/ð/	/z/			
Affricate	Unvoiced					/tʃ/		
	Voiced					/dʒ/		
Nasal	Unvoiced							
	Voiced	/m/			/n/		/ŋ/	
Liquid	Unvoiced							
	Voiced				/l/ or /r/	/r/	/l/	
Glide	Unvoiced							
	Voiced	/w/				/y/		

Chapter Quiz

Ready to see how well you retained what you just read? Scan the QR code to go directly to the chapter quiz interface for this study guide. If you're using a computer, simply visit the online resources page at **mometrix.com/resources719/priispedtssli** and click the Chapter Quizzes link.

Copyright © Mometrix Media. You have been licensed one copy of this document for personal use only. Any other reproduction or redistribution is strictly prohibited. All rights reserved.
This content is provided for test preparation purposes only and does not imply an endorsement by Mometrix of any particular political, scientific, or religious point of view.

Identification and Assessment of Communication Impairments

Screening

Social Communication Disorder Screenings for Children

Whenever an adult suspects that a child has a social communication disorder, or as a part of a comprehensive speech and language evaluation of any child about whose communication adults have concerns, the SLP should conduct a screening of the child's social communication skills. Social communication skills screenings typically include the following: norm-referenced measures, as reported by parents and teachers; observations, interviews, and other tools based on competency; and a hearing screening to rule in or out a hearing loss as a factor potentially contributing to difficulties with social communication. According to experts, if the results from social communication skills screening of children diagnosed with attention-deficit/hyperactivity disorder (ADHD) is indicative of concerns regarding a child's speech and/or language, including receptive, expressive, and pragmatic language development, parents/teachers/other adults should refer the child to a pediatric SLP; and screening should include screening for comorbid conditions that are common with ADHD, e.g., family problems, psychosocial difficulties, and speech-language problems. Regarding otitis media, experts advise routine hearing screenings and referral to ear/nose/throat specialists and/or audiologists as indicated, because children's emotional and social development can be affected by chronic or multiple middle-ear infections.

Review Video: Developmental Screening Strategies
Visit mometrix.com/academy and enter code: 100353

Newborn Hearing Screenings

According to ASHA, in American hospitals, newborn hearing screenings are the current standard of care. According to the US Centers for Disease Control and Prevention, 97.9% of infants born in 2011 had hearing screenings within a few weeks of birth. The main reason for newborn hearing screenings is to identify babies likely to have hearing losses and who need more assessment. An additional reason is to identify babies having medical conditions that can cause hearing losses with later onsets and to create plans to continue monitoring their hearing. Babies not passing newborn hearing screenings are immediately referred for comprehensive audiological evaluations. The objective of these evaluations is to confirm any hearing loss by the time infants are 3 months old. Permanent childhood hearing loss, regardless of type, is the target of screening programs, but within different populations, e.g., neonatal intensive care units or well-infant nurseries, different protocols are most useful. When babies pass hearing screenings, they do not necessarily have normal hearing across all frequencies: Frequency-specific or minimal hearing losses are not identified by newborn hearing screening programs. Hence, it is important to monitor hearing, speech, and language milestones from birth through childhood.

Periodic Hearing Screenings During Early Childhood

Out of 1.6% of babies not passing newborn hearing screenings, the US Centers for Disease Control and Prevention estimates almost half may not get the follow-up diagnostic and/or intervention services recommended. Moreover, after newborn screenings, children can sustain hearing loss—with delayed onset due to genetic factors, or through injuries or illnesses. The National Institute for the Deaf estimates that roughly 6 to 7 children per 1,000 will likely have permanent hearing loss by

Copyright © Mometrix Media. You have been licensed one copy of this document for personal use only. Any other reproduction or redistribution is strictly prohibited. All rights reserved.
This content is provided for test preparation purposes only and does not imply an endorsement by Mometrix of any particular political, scientific, or religious point of view.

school age. Periodic early childhood screenings make timely diagnoses and interventions more likely. Audiologists and SLPs can help lay screeners to follow screening protocols and practices in various early childhood settings. As an example, federal Early Head Start programs for economically disadvantaged young children require hearing screenings within 6 weeks of enrollment. Consequently, the majority of states have Early Hearing Detection and Intervention coordinators and Early Childhood Hearing Outreach training teams. Screening and follow-up diagnosis data in 2008 showed that about 2 of every 1,000 children were being identified with permanent hearing loss previously undetected, and another 18 per 1,000 were receiving identification and treatment for conductive hearing loss. In another example, Parents as Teachers required in 2011 that otoacoustic emissions hearing screenings of all children within three months of enrollment.

Speech Sound Screening

Whenever a parent, teacher, or other adult suspects that a child has a speech sound disorder, or as a component of a comprehensive speech and language evaluation of a child when concerns exist about the child's communication, the child's phonology and articulation may be screened by the SLP. The purpose of such screenings is to identify children who need additional speech-language or communication assessment or for referrals for other professional services. Typical speech sound screenings include: standardized screening instruments with normative data and/or cutoff scores; informal, SLP-designed measures tailored for populations to be screened—e.g., conversational speech samples and/or reading sentences/passages aloud for older students; age-/developmentally appropriate spoken and written language comprehension and production; a hearing screening, to rule in/out the contribution of hearing loss to speech problems; an oral-motor function screening; and an orofacial examination, to assess facial symmetry and identify any structural causes of speech sound disorders, such as ankyloglossia ("tongue-tie" or abnormal palatal adhesion of the tongue), malocclusion (overbite, underbite, crossbite), or a submucous cleft palate.

After the SLP screens a child's production of speech sounds as part of a comprehensive evaluation for speech-language/communication disorders or to investigate a suspected phonological/articulation disorder, some outcomes from the screening include giving parents and teachers suggestions for preventing speech-language impairment and encouraging normal development of speech sounds. A next step the SLP may take is formulating plans for monitoring the child's speech and language development. Another next step based on screening results may be referring the child for response to intervention or similar multitiered support systems when applicable. In addition, the SLP may discover that the screening results indicate the need to refer the child for further speech and language assessment. When this is the case, the additional assessment may include comprehensive speech sound assessment, indicated if the child's phonological system is incompatible with his/her linguistic community and/or age-inappropriate; comprehensive language assessment if screening suggests delayed/disordered language development; complete audiological assessment to establish whether hearing loss is involved; and comprehensive oral-motor/oral musculature evaluation for possible physiological causes. Screening may also indicate referral for medical/other services.

Screening for Spoken Language Disorders

If a language disorder is suspected, most often in a child, the SLP will conduct a screening of the child's spoken language skills. The screening will not yield a diagnosis; instead, it will indicate whether additional, more comprehensive assessment is needed or not. Some of the typical components of a spoken language screening include: collecting information from a child's parents and/or teachers indicating their concerns about the languages spoken by the family and the child and the child's skills in each language if this is applicable; performing a hearing screening to

Copyright © Mometrix Media. You have been licensed one copy of this document for personal use only. Any other reproduction or redistribution is strictly prohibited. All rights reserved.
This content is provided for test preparation purposes only and does not imply an endorsement by Mometrix of any particular political, scientific, or religious point of view.

establish whether a hearing loss could be contributing to problems with the child's language development; administering standardized screening instruments whose sensitivity and specificity have been documented as adequate and which include normative data and/or cutoff scores; administering informal measures, which the SLP may design specifically for the relevant population (for example, preschool ages, school ages, adolescence); and screening the child's articulation if needed. Based on screening results, the SLP may recommend a complete audiological assessment, a comprehensive language assessment, and/or a comprehensive phonological/articulation assessment if the child demonstrates an age-inappropriate and/or linguistic community-inappropriate phonological system.

Screening Instruments

- The **Phonological Screening Assessment** (PSA; Stevens and Isles, Speechmark Publishing, 2001) can be administered to both children and adults. Administration takes 10 to 15 minutes. Stimulus items were selected from among the 100 most common words acquired by children. Intended as a tool for initial screening, the PSA is described as giving a comprehensive, accurate overview of phonological problems.
- **The Adolescent Language Screening Test** (ALST; Morgan and Guilford, Pro-Ed, 1984) is designed for ages 11 to 17 years. It takes 10 to 15 minutes to administer. The ALST screens the adolescent's language content, form, and use. It includes seven subscales that respectively measure phonology, morphology, sentence formulation, receptive vocabulary, expressive vocabulary, concepts, and pragmatics.
- **The Denver Articulation Screening Exam** (Frankenberg and Drumwright, Denver Developmental Materials, 1973) can be administered to children from the ages of two years and five months to seven years. It takes five minutes to administer. This screening tool assesses speech intelligibility and detects articulation disorders.

Dysphagia

Various medical conditions can indicate the possibility of dysphagia. For example, an individual may have a history of strokes; a diagnosis of Parkinson's disease, multiple sclerosis, cerebral palsy, muscular dystrophy, amyotrophic lateral sclerosis, or motor neuron disease; traumatic head injury; mouth and/or throat cancer; or Alzheimer's disease. Many medications also cause dry mouth (xerostomia, i.e., decreased saliva production), which makes it very difficult to swallow dry foods. Frequent coughing and/or choking, particularly when drinking thin liquids, are signs of dysphagia, as are pain or discomfort when swallowing; intolerance for certain and/or multiple consistencies, e.g., hard foods, lumpy foods, thick soupy foods, yogurtlike textures, or liquids in general; weight loss; sudden increases in body temperature; elevated respiratory rates; and a "wet" or gurgly sounding voice. To evaluate risk for aspiration and address it with preventive management, SLPs should ascertain whether dysphagia exists, whether the client can safely eat orally, aspiration risk, what consistencies the client can handle, which stage(s) of swallowing is/are involved, the problem's severity and prognosis, and the need for referrals to other professionals. They should also consider the client's alertness level, cognition, communication, vision and hearing, oral hygiene, positioning, and need for feeding aids/assistance.

Evaluation Process in Public School Systems

Public school systems include policies and procedures to address student dysphagia in their policy manuals. By adhering to system-supported processes, school districts aim to develop procedures that will be consistently followed districtwide. School-based services for feeding and swallowing disorders include a referral process, parent notification and involvement, screening, evaluation, and IEP and/or 504 plan development. The process of school-based evaluation starts with a referral, which may be initiated by a member of the school staff, a professional from outside of the school, or

Copyright © Mometrix Media. You have been licensed one copy of this document for personal use only. Any other reproduction or redistribution is strictly prohibited. All rights reserved.
This content is provided for test preparation purposes only and does not imply an endorsement by Mometrix of any particular political, scientific, or religious point of view.

a parent/guardian or member of the student's family. The referral is made to a multidisciplinary team of professionals employed by the school district who have training in dysphagia screening, identification, and treatment. After this initial referral, the school will contact the student's parents/guardians to obtain their informed consent for evaluation of the student's eating, drinking, and swallowing; discuss the evaluation process with them; and collect information about the student's health and medical histories and home feeding. Reviewing the referral is considered a component of the screening process. Interviews with parents and teachers are also part of screening and evaluation. The results of the screening may indicate an interdisciplinary, comprehensive feeding and swallowing evaluation.

Swallowing Screening

Although the research literature on swallowing mostly describes relatively narrow screening procedures focusing solely on identifying observable signs of aspiration, ASHA defines swallowing screening as a broader range of procedures addressing a variety of elements. A swallowing screening is generally a minimally invasive assessment procedure allowing SLPs to determine the following quickly: dysphagia probability; referral need for additional swallowing evaluation; the safety of feeding a patient orally for hydration, nutrition, and medication administration; and the need to refer the patient for hydrational and/or nutritional support. The SLP can use a screening procedure to identify whether a patient is at risk for dysphagia, and/or whether NPO (*nil per oris*, nothing by mouth) status is indicated. Individual patient factors that can represent dysphagia risk and/or need for NPO status include a medical diagnosis, such as a stroke, that often causes swallowing impairment; a known history of dysphagia; observable signs of aspiration; overt patient complaints or signs of difficulty with swallowing; and a reduced level of consciousness. SLPs can use screening procedures to determine if any of these present dysphagia risks and/or indicate NPO orders.

The following are five different models for swallowing screening procedures:

1. SLPs train nursing staff to perform swallowing screenings. Based on screening, nursing staff refer patients to SLPs for comprehensive swallowing assessment as indicated. SLPs may stay in ERs during transitional periods. Senior nursing staff may attain skill sufficient for training future nursing staff.
2. Physicians perform swallowing screenings during medical evaluations, requesting further SLP swallowing assessment when observing signs of patient swallowing problems. Swallowing screenings by nursing staff tend to be more structured than those by physicians.
3. Model (1) or (2) is applied; an automatic referral within 24 to 48 hours or another specified time frame is made for SLP swallowing assessment for all patients with specific diagnoses or admitted to acute stroke units. In this model, components can include frequent presentations/in-service trainings to medical residents and/or attending physicians, and continuing in-service training modules provided to nurses during new-hire orientations or annual education days.
4. All patients receive automatic referrals to SLPs for swallowing screening or assessment upon admission.
5. On an on-call basis, nursing staff contact SLPs to request swallowing screenings for patients presenting in the emergency room with symptoms or conditions know to pose potential dysphagia risks.

Many medical facilities have reviewed the research literature on screening procedures that have been used in the past to develop the tools they use to screen patient swallowing function. Not all specific characteristics of such swallowing screening tools necessarily have high-level evidence to

Copyright © Mometrix Media. You have been licensed one copy of this document for personal use only. Any other reproduction or redistribution is strictly prohibited. All rights reserved.
This content is provided for test preparation purposes only and does not imply an endorsement by Mometrix of any particular political, scientific, or religious point of view.

support them. Regardless, the tools and/or checklists that medical facilities generally use tend to include the following characteristics: some questions about the patient's risk factors and/or history; observation of the patient's alertness level; observation of signs that the patient has voice quality and/or motor-speech abnormalities; observation of signs indicating dysphagia, such as a weak cough, an inability to control saliva, etc., which can be identified without giving any food or liquid to the patient; and in the cases of some screening tools, presenting the patient with small amounts of water, other liquid, or food. Many of these screening tools have been designed in the forms of flowcharts or decision trees. As an example, as soon as the answer to one of the questions identifies an increased risk of dysphagia, facility personnel end the screening procedure and initiate referral to the SLP.

Screening Procedures Historically and Currently Used for Dysphagia

The research literature includes swallowing screenings via: cervical auscultation; the laryngeal cough reflex, using tartaric acid inhalation to test cough response as a laryngeal sensation integrity marker; pulse oximetry to detect decreased oxygenation of arterial blood as a potential aspiration indicator; observing coughing during/after swallowing water; observing altered voice quality after swallowing as a possible indicator of aspiration; applying decision-making algorithms considering multiple factors; observing water swallowing trials plus oral-motor and motor-speech examinations to detect specific clinical signs; observing routine oral intake or planned swallowing trials for coughing or other overt signs of difficulty; evaluating pharyngeal sensation or gag reflex; reviewing medical history for categories of etiological risk; and patient/caregiver interviews/questionnaires about historical/current swallowing problems. Many stroke center and acute care facility standards dictate dysphagia screening of all stroke patients before giving anything orally, as documented by the Joint Commission on Accreditation of Healthcare Organizations (2004). Screening methods include the 3-oz. water swallow test, the Burke water swallow test, and other water-swallow tests; the Simple Standardized Bedside Swallowing Assessment, Toronto Bedside Swallowing Screening Test, and other screening protocols incorporating brief oral-motor and sensory function plus water-swallow tests; and bedside clinical swallow examinations.

Approaches to Assessment and Evaluation

Ethnographic Interviewing

ASHA warns SLPs and other professionals against making assumptions or generalizations about clients or their families on the bases of general racial, ethnic, cultural, or social information. The cultural, social, and familial values of specific individual clients and their families are better determined via ethnographic interviewing techniques. This is important because clinical interactions and interventions frequently succeed based on the clinician's understanding of client and family perspectives, perceptions, expectations, and wishes. Whereas interviewers establish their own agendas based on what information they want for traditional interviews, clients and their families help interviewers determine which information is important in ethnographic interviews. For ethnographic interviewing, principles include using open-ended, not yes/no questions; restating verbatim the client's words without interpreting or paraphrasing; summarizing client/family statements, offering opportunities to correct any misinterpretations; avoiding asking questions with multiple parts and/or back-to-back multiple questions; avoiding leading questions that influence responses; and avoiding "why" questions, which are often perceived as judgmental and put clients on the defensive.

Copyright © Mometrix Media. You have been licensed one copy of this document for personal use only. Any other reproduction or redistribution is strictly prohibited. All rights reserved.
This content is provided for test preparation purposes only and does not imply an endorsement by Mometrix of any particular political, scientific, or religious point of view.

Bilingual Clients

With bilingual clients, ASHA advises professionals to use ethnographic interviewing rather than traditional interviewing to avoid making cultural generalizations and/or assumptions and obtain accurate information that is specific to the individual and his/her family. In ethnographic interviewing, the interviewer solicits the participation of the client and/or client's family members to decide which information they find most important to share, rather than the interviewer's deciding this alone as s/he would do for a traditional interview. When interviewing bilingual clients, the interviewer should obtain certain information to learn about the client's language history. Some of the information that the interviewer should elicit includes the client's ages when s/he acquired both his/her L1 and the L2; which language(s) the client uses at home, school and/or work; how long the client has been exposed to each language; the client's language of choice when interacting with peers; the client's progress receiving English as a second language/English language learner services, or adult education classes for learning English language; the client's academic performance; and the language(s) used within the client's family.

Case Histories

Basic Information

Because clients with various speech/language/hearing/communication disorders, as well as babies and young children, often cannot provide information themselves, SLPs must convey accurate, detailed information for physicians and other professionals to inform treatment. SLPs should include all contact information they will need for correspondence and billing, plus birth date/age; and for minors, parent names and which language(s) they speak at home. Detailed family histories are important because autism spectrum disorders and specific speech problems can have genetic factors and knowing about problems running in a family can help physicians make diagnoses. Symptoms should also be described in detail; including conditions/situations of occurrence—e.g., stress, nervousness, or anger exacerbating stuttering symptoms. Any unusual aspects of client gestation and birth, e.g., oxygen loss or prematurity, which can lead to speech problems, should be included. SLPs should write case histories with concise, clear wording. They should also include all information honestly, even those that are seem as embarrassing or sensitive, e.g., behaviors symptomatic of Tourette's syndrome or secondary behaviors associated with severe stuttering, some of which can be quite bizarre. Experienced physicians will not judge these and will need the information for correct diagnosis and appropriate treatment.

Case Histories of Hearing

Ask the client's reason for seeing the SLP; whether they have noticed hearing difficulty, what kind(s), for how long; when they believe it started; whether it involves one or both ears; and whether the difficulty occurred suddenly or developed gradually. Ask if they experience tinnitus (ringing/noise in the ears); have a history of ear infections; or if they have noticed ear pain, discharge from the ears, or dizziness. Ask if the family history includes any hearing loss; if it is more difficult to hear male, female, or children's voices; whether other people comment about how loud they set their TV volume; whether others have told them their conversational speech is too loud; if they often ask others to repeat what they say; whether they hear but cannot understand others' speech; if they have been exposed to noise at work, home, in military service, or during recreation; and whether they have more trouble following conversation in certain situations, e.g., large groups, cars, noisy restaurants, or theaters. For children, ask parents about health history, speech and language development, recognition and response for unexpected loud sounds; existing disabilities; and any previous hearing screening/assessment results.

Copyright © Mometrix Media. You have been licensed one copy of this document for personal use only. Any other reproduction or redistribution is strictly prohibited. All rights reserved.
This content is provided for test preparation purposes only and does not imply an endorsement by Mometrix of any particular political, scientific, or religious point of view.

Questions to Ask Parents

The following are things for SLPs to ask parents about their child when developing a case history:

- **Referral reason**: parental concerns with child communication, what parents have done trying to help their child learn to talk, speech-language therapy outcomes they would want, and parental willingness to incorporate SLP-suggested activities into daily routines.
- **Pregnancy, birth**: Full-term/premature, birth weight, Cesarean/vaginal birth, any pregnancy and/or delivery complications, maternal health during pregnancy, medications during pregnancy, length of hospital stay, whether mother and infant were discharged together, and any required follow-up physician visits and reason(s).
- **Medical history**: Any hospitalizations and reasons; serious injuries, and what; major illnesses; whether parents consider the child healthy currently.
- **Medications/allergies**: Known allergies, any current medications, and frequent ear infections.
- **Vision/hearing**: Whether newborn hearing screening was passed; most recent vision/hearing testing, results; any middle-ear tubes, and if so, how parents describe child hearing before and after tube insertion; one ear is better/worse; whether tubes are still present.
- **Family history**: Number of siblings/half-siblings/step-siblings, names, ages; with whom the child lives; parental visitation rights; others in the family with the same communication difficulties; any reward/consequence system for child behavior, and if so, explain; things the family enjoys doing together.
- **Milestones**: Ages of child babbling; first word; two-word combinations; crawling; walking; toilet training, and if so, at what age.
- **Oral hygiene/feeding**: Whether the child sees a dentist; can eat foods of different consistencies without choking, gagging, spitting, coughing, or other difficulties; breast-fed/bottle-fed, and how long; whether the child feeds herself/himself; continues bottle-drinking; loses liquid when drinking from bottles/cups; loses food when eating from utensils; sucks her/his thumb; continues using a pacifier, and if so, how often; breathes through the nose or mouth; and any concerns about mouth function for speaking/eating.
- **Articulation**: Speech intelligibility, intelligibility to strangers, child reactions to not being understood, and phonemes the child produces/other sounds.
- **Language**: Receptive comprehension; following simple one- and two-step directions (get examples); everyday noun use (examples); number and list current vocabulary words; jargon; whether parents understand content of child's speech; multiple word combinations (examples); communicative speech intonation; examples of how the child expresses needs/wants; whether the child uses words or gestures more (examples).
- **Day care**: Same/different behavior as at home, ability to follow routines, and amount of time spent with peers.
- **Prior therapy services**: Whether child receives/received therapy currently/in the past; if so, how beneficial it was.
- **Bilingual**: Length of US residence; primary language; preferred language; the same difficulties in both languages, and if so, explain.

Comprehensive SLP Assessment Components

Comprehensive SLP assessment should contain a case history of the client including medical status; education; occupation; and linguistic, cultural, and socioeconomic backgrounds; an interview with the client and family; a review of client hearing, vision, motor, and cognitive status; standardized and/or nonstandardized assessments of specific aspects of the client's speech, spoken language,

Copyright © Mometrix Media. You have been licensed one copy of this document for personal use only. Any other reproduction or redistribution is strictly prohibited. All rights reserved.
This content is provided for test preparation purposes only and does not imply an endorsement by Mometrix of any particular political, scientific, or religious point of view.

nonspoken language, cognitive communication, and swallowing functions; an identification of the potential for effective compensations and intervention strategies; the selection of standardized instruments for assessing speech, language, cognitive communication, and/or swallowing, taking into account whether the ecological validity of the instruments has been documented; and which follow-up services the SLP recommends for monitoring client communication and/or swallowing status, and assure that needed intervention and support are provided for clients identified with speech, language, cognitive communication, and/or swallowing disorders. Although standardized test results give SLPs important information about specific areas of communication skills; informal and/or nonstandardized assessments, including pragmatic and behavioral observations in natural settings and structured and spontaneous sampling of client language, can also yield valuable information which standardized tests alone may not reveal. Sampling in varied situations affords more accurate profiling of individual functional communication.

Phonological and Language Development in Young Children

Evidence exists that when young children have delays in the development of receptive awareness, identification, differentiation, and expressive production of speech sounds, these delays are not isolated or separate from delays in the development of grammar, sentence structure, narrative, and conversation in receptive and expressive language. According to research findings, preschool-aged children with delayed phonological development are likely to also have delayed morphological, syntactic, and discourse structure development. In addition, young children typically demonstrate better phonological performance when uttering individual words and verbal labels for pictures than connected conversational speech and organized, syntactically complex narratives. Based on these findings, experts say an integral part of children's skills for organizing language in authentic communicative situations is their speech sound development and recommend integrating phonological assessment into language assessment. Some appropriate assessment methods for this purpose include engaging preschool children in storybook subjects and play activities that reflect everyday events. To prompt a preschooler to talk about action sequences within such events, assessors use scaffolding (support) techniques for oral language. Assessment describes children's abilities for expressing semantic complexity; organizing discourse structures according to intentional, causal, and temporal connections; and applying phonological, morphological, and syntactic conventions.

Static vs. Dynamic Assessment Methods

Static assessment procedures are those that have traditionally been used. In static language assessment, the procedures are standardized. The participants are passive. The examiner observes the participants and uses the assessment to identify language deficits. In contrast, dynamic assessment aims to identify an individual child's skills and learning potential. It accounts for the nature and degree of examiner investment, and it emphasizes the learning process. Dynamic assessment is process oriented and highly interactive. The participants are active rather than passive. The examiner participates rather than only observing. Rather than just identifying deficits, the examiner describes how language characteristics/behaviors can be modified. Rather than being

Copyright © Mometrix Media. You have been licensed one copy of this document for personal use only. Any other reproduction or redistribution is strictly prohibited. All rights reserved.
This content is provided for test preparation purposes only and does not imply an endorsement by Mometrix of any particular political, scientific, or religious point of view.

standardized, dynamic assessment procedures are responsive and fluid. Major outcomes of dynamic assessments are:

- Helping SLPs to differentiate between language disorders and language differences, particularly in children with linguistically and culturally diverse backgrounds. For example, when assessment incorporates short-term teaching sessions, children who can make significant changes probably have language differences, whereas children who cannot make changes regardless of short-term intervention techniques probably have language disorders.
- Affording direct implications for intervention through providing mediated learning experiences and evaluating children's responses.

One form of dynamic assessment involves a pretest-teach-posttest method. The teaching component involves a mediated learning experience (MLE). The ultimate purpose of the mediated learning experience is to help children to become independent, self-directed learners. The responsibility of the SLP is to do whatever is needed to enable a child to learn new strategies that facilitate their continuing to learn. In dynamic assessments using MLEs, the examiner purposefully teaches the child strategies, observes the child's responses to this instruction, and then adjusts the instruction based on those responses. In the pretest phase, the SLP assesses the child's current language performance. In the teaching phase, the SLP provides an MLE; helps the child develop strategies to improve his/her language performance; and observes how able the child is to modify his/her performance, including whether s/he can change her/his linguistic behaviors; can change these quickly; and what s/he needs to be able to apply what s/he learned in the teaching session. In the posttest phase, the SLP compares performance to pretest levels and assesses whether and how well the child transfers the strategies s/he learned to the posttest task.

The four components and their rationales in MLEs used in dynamic assessment of language development in children are as follows:

- **Intentionality**: Tell the child the reason for the MLE, i.e., intent to change the child's linguistic functioning, and its target—to create awareness and teach the child.
- **Meaning**: Focus attention, helping the child attend to important task features and ignore unimportant ones—to help the child understand why the task is important.
- **Transcendence**: Introduce abstract concepts; bridge events and ideas beyond the immediate task; e.g., asking "Have you ever...?" and "What would happen if...?"—to help the child think in hypothetical terms.
- **Competence**: Help the child think through how they will apply a targeted strategy and develop a plan; discuss appropriate occasions for applying certain skills, to teach the child self-regulation and active participation in his/her own learning.

The following are three components of child modifiability in response to MLEs:

- **Responsiveness**: How well the child responds to the MLE; attends and maintains task attention; demonstrates efficient learning strategies; uses skills such as looking, comparing, verbalizing.
- **Transfer**: How well the child applies targeted skills between items/tasks/sessions/situations; and applies learned strategies soon after learning them.
- **Examiner effort**: How much support the child requires for learning and applying strategies and the nature of the support needed.

Copyright © Mometrix Media. You have been licensed one copy of this document for personal use only. Any other reproduction or redistribution is strictly prohibited. All rights reserved.
This content is provided for test preparation purposes only and does not imply an endorsement by Mometrix of any particular political, scientific, or religious point of view.

An example of testing a child's vocabulary development using dynamic assessment, including the components of intentionality, meaning, transcendence, and competence and a mediated learning experience (MLE) is explained below:

- **Intentionality**: Say you will be working on special names.
- **Meaning**: Explain that these are important to clear communication by telling people what things are. Give examples, e.g., all these pictures can be called *birds,* but without saying *duck,* it isn't clear which you mean.
- **Transcendence**: Explain that special names help us organize things by category. Use examples: e.g., if you order something at a restaurant, how would they know what to serve without a special name? If you want to go somewhere on the bus, how would you know the bus stop to get off at without a special name? Explain special names' importance to everyday communication.
- **Competence**: Ask if the child knows what to do when you present pictures. Identify thinking about and using special names and remembering to ask for things by name in class. Ask about plan development, e.g., how will we put together this puzzle/look at these books/remember to think about a new special name. During the MLE, observe the child's attention to task, single-word name understanding, and evidence of transfer. Compare posttest increases in correct words and strategy changes to pretest scores. Pre- to posttest gains indicate language differences; however, no/minimal gains indicate language disorders.

Clinical Evaluation of Feeding and Swallowing

To rule a swallowing disorder in or out, the first step is typically a clinical evaluation of swallowing and feeding. An SLP with expertise in pediatric swallowing and feeding problems may conduct this evaluation during an individual session or as a component of a swallowing and feeding team's comprehensive evaluation. Clinical evaluation covers swallowing activities during eating and drinking; secretion management; and it may also include tooth brushing and swallowing oral medications. Three categories that the SLP considers when identifying causes contributing to dysphagia are as follows:

1. **Physiological** – temporary, chronic, or progressive medical disorders involving neurological, craniofacial, pulmonary, gastroenterological, and metabolic systems.
2. **Developmental** – issues related to a child's failing to develop mature swallowing skills at the expected milestone ages. Typically, these issues are associated with the child's being deprived of appropriate, timely practice for acquiring the skills, or they are related to effects secondary to physiological and/or behavioral feeding and swallowing disorders.
3. **Behavioral** – disorders entailing:
    a. motivation to eat, drink, and/or engage in other appropriate swallowing/feeding activities
    b. interactive/social elements of feeding activities.

The behavioral category includes disruptive, aggressive, self-abusive, refusal to engage, or otherwise maladaptive behaviors. Also, some behavioral responses may be influenced by sensory issues.

The SLP's clinical swallowing and feeding evaluation typically includes, among other things: a case history based on comprehensive medical/clinical records review plus interviews with family and healthcare providers; assessment of the child's overall development physiologically, behaviorally, socially, and communicatively; observations of the child eating and drinking or being fed by

Copyright © Mometrix Media. You have been licensed one copy of this document for personal use only. Any other reproduction or redistribution is strictly prohibited. All rights reserved.
This content is provided for test preparation purposes only and does not imply an endorsement by Mometrix of any particular political, scientific, or religious point of view.

parents, family members, or caregivers, using home foods, utensils normally used, and also problematic or rejected ones; a structural assessment of the child's face, jaw, lips, tongue, hard palate, soft palate, oral pharynx, and oral mucosa; a functional assessment of the swallowing structures and muscles, including their sensation, strength, symmetry, tone, rate and range of motion, and coordination of movements; observations of the child's posture, head and neck control, developmental oral and postural reflexes, and involuntary movements in context of the child's developmental level; and a functional assessment of the child's swallowing ability, including (but not limited to) age-typical developmental skills and tasks, e.g., infant sucking and suckling, older children's chewing, oral containment, and bolus manipulation.

In addition to a case history and other observations and structural and functional assessments, the SLP conducting a clinical evaluation to rule in or out a swallowing and/or feeding disorder would include his/her clinical impressions of the adequacy of the child's airway and coordination of swallowing and breathing; an assessment of the child's skills for managing secretions and whether these skills are developmentally appropriate, which could include the adequacy and frequency of spontaneous dry swallowing and the ability for voluntary swallowing; an assessment of behavioral factors, which can include, among other things, the child's acceptance of the nipple, pacifier, cup, and spoon and the textures and range of developmentally appropriate liquids and foods that the child tolerates; an assessment of how consistent the child's skills are across the opportunity for feeding, in order to rule out any adverse effects on safety in feeding and swallowing caused by fatigue; and an assessment of any changes in the child's bolus manipulation, and/or any use by the child of compensatory, habilitative, or rehabilitative techniques for swallowing.

Medically Fragile Infants in NICUs

SLPs evaluating infant swallowing/feeding should have thorough knowledge of typical early infant development plus embryology, prenatal development, perinatal development, and common medical issues with premature and medically fragile newborns. SLPs must evaluate prefeeding skills, assess and promote oral feeding readiness, and evaluate ability for breast-feeding and bottle-feeding. Evidence-based practice in neonatal intensive care units (NICUs) is founded on underlying neurophysiological factors, infant-family bonding, family-focused environment, and specific oral sensorimotor functioning. Clinical SLP evaluations of medically fragile infants typically include: a case history including the infant's gestational history, birth history, and any relevant medical history; physical examination including respiratory status, observations regarding medical and physiological stability, and developmental assessment; evaluation of the infant's oral feeding readiness according to medical stability, ability to maintain physiological states, and nonnutritive sucking ability; developmentally appropriate clinical assessment of nutritive sucking as indicated; assessment of suckling/swallowing difficulties and associated anatomical/physiological abnormalities; additional disorders affecting feeding/swallowing; determining the optimal feeding method; assessment of feeding duration, including supplemental oxygen needs; assessment of volume limitation and fatigue issues; and assessment of parent-infant interaction effectiveness for communication and feeding.

According to ASHA, no uniform protocol exists regarding the criteria for initiating oral feeding of infants in neonatal intensive care units (NICUs). Consistency among and even within facilities concerning infant readiness for oral feeding is also limited. The medical neonatologist alone may decide infant readiness and oral feeding initiation in many NICUs; in others, the neonatologist, SLP, and nursing staff share their observations during assessment and decide about initiating oral feeding based in each individual infant's feeding and swallowing abilities. Some of the primary criteria for determining a medically fragile infant's readiness for oral feeding include the following: the infant's stability of respiration, digestion, heart rate, oxygenation, and other physiological

Copyright © Mometrix Media. You have been licensed one copy of this document for personal use only. Any other reproduction or redistribution is strictly prohibited. All rights reserved.
This content is provided for test preparation purposes only and does not imply an endorsement by Mometrix of any particular political, scientific, or religious point of view.

parameters; the infant's motor stability in terms of midline movements, muscular tone and flexion; the infant's ability to alert and stability of behavior state. SLPs and other members of the feeding and swallowing evaluation team must take into account the family's beliefs and values with respect to oral feeding and intake, together with the medical and therapeutic team's recommendations, to ascertain the most suitable time for oral feeding initiation.

Videoendoscopic/Stroboscopic Imaging and Visualization of Vocal Tract

To perform videoendoscopy/stroboscopy, the SLP must know the physiology of resonance and voice production, how to assess patient physiology, vocal tract anatomy and physiology in normal and disordered resonance and voice production, laryngeal and velopharyngeal anatomy and physiology, laryngeal pathology, impaired velopharyngeal function, and normal and disordered anatomy and physiology of voice production. Normal anatomy of the respiratory system includes the skeletal structure and the muscular parts. Normal anatomy of the phonatory system includes the skeletal framework, muscular parts, and the histology (microscopic cellular and tissue anatomical composition, structure, and function) of the vocal folds. The vocal tract anatomy includes the oral, nasal, and pharyngeal anatomy. Normal physiology includes aerodynamic principles including Bernoulli's law of the conservation of energy; the continuity law of incompressible fluids; and the aerodynamic-myoelastic theory; source-filter theory; and vocal parameters and their relationship to physiology, including frequency/pitch, intensity/loudness, and spectral energy/quality. Organic pathophysiology includes cancerous/malignant; benign; neurogenic; irritation; inflammation; trauma; and presbyphonia (aging-related). Nonorganic pathophysiology includes psychogenic; muscle tension dysphonia; maladaptive phonation habits; and phonotraumatic vocal behaviors. Congenital pathophysiology includes laryngofissure, laryngeal webbing, laryngomalacia, cleft palate, and submucosal cleft.

Coughing

The cough is a protective reflex of the airway for clearing particles, foreign matter, and mucus from the upper and lower airways. To produce a **normal cough**, one must have intact sensory innervation of airway tissues for the sensation of irritation/obstruction/presence of material and initiating coughing behavior and sufficient respiratory airflow to produce the force to shear substances away from airway walls. Coughing behavior has three phases: inspiratory, compressive, and expiratory. Effective coughing requires all three. The muscles of the inspiratory chest wall and diaphragm primarily effect the inspiratory phase, which requires coordination between inspiratory muscle contractions and activation of the posterior cricoarytenoid and cricothyroid intrinsic laryngeal muscles. Diaphragmatic and inspiratory chest wall muscle actions expand the chest cavity, increasing lung volume and enabling inspiratory airflow. Inspiratory volume ranges between 50% of tidal volume and about 50% of vital capacity during the roughly 0.65 seconds of the inspiratory phase. Inhalation determines exhalation: If the lungs cannot be inflated adequately, a suboptimal relationship between muscular length and tension during expiratory muscle contractions reduces the possible force generation during the expiratory phase, hence reducing the potential to exhale enough air forcefully enough to cough effectively.

Anatomy and Physiology Related to Speech

Anatomical and Physiological Structures Relative to Speech Pathology

- The **glossoepiglottic folds** connect the tongue's root to the front of the epiglottis.
- The **aryepiglottic folds** connect the sides of the epiglottis to the tissue covering the arytenoid and corniculate cartilage.
- The **ventricular folds**/"false vocal folds" attach to the ventricular ligaments.

Copyright © Mometrix Media. You have been licensed one copy of this document for personal use only. Any other reproduction or redistribution is strictly prohibited. All rights reserved.
This content is provided for test preparation purposes only and does not imply an endorsement by Mometrix of any particular political, scientific, or religious point of view.

- The **lateral cricoarytenoid** and **thyroarytenoid muscles** control adduction (movement inward/toward).
- The **posterior cricoarytenoid muscle** controls abduction (movement outward/away).
- The **larynx** rests atop the trachea (airway).
- The **cartilages** included in the larynx are the thyroid, cricoid, epiglottis, arytenoid, cuneiform, and corniculate.
    - The **cricoid**, **thyroid**, and **arytenoid** are important cartilages to the phonation process.
- The **intrinsic laryngeal muscles** are the cricothyroid, lateral cricoarytenoid, oblique arytenoid, transverse arytenoid, posterior cricoarytenoid, superior thyroarytenoid, thyroarytenoid-muscularis, and thyroarytenoid-vocalis.
    - The **transverse arytenoid** is the only unpaired muscle in the larynx.
    - The **internal thyroarytenoid** is called the vocalis muscle.
    - The **cricothyroid** controls vocal fold tension, contraction, and vocal pitch.
    - The **posterior cricothyroid muscle**, which is the only abductor, must contract more to enable inhaling more air. During phonation, inhalation (inspiration) is 10% and exhalation (expiration) is 90%.

Voice Production

As one exhales air from the lungs, the vocal folds are adducted or drawn together. The exhaled airflow causes the vocal folds to vibrate against one another. This vibration is the source of the voice's sound. According to the **myoelastic aerodynamic theory of phonation**, the adducted vocal folds create resistance against the exhaled air. Air pressure below the glottis then builds up, opening the vocal folds. The **subglottic pressure** is then immediately released as airflow. This increased air velocity causes air pressure to drop relative to the vocal folds' medial (inner) borders, which brings the vocal folds back together again. This air pressure decrease corresponding to the increased air speed that causes the vocal folds' approximation is known as the **Bernoulli effect**. The elasticity of the tissues produces **recoil pressure**, which also helps to draw the vocal folds back together. The length and corresponding longitudinal tension of the vocal folds, subglottic pressure, and medial compression of the vocal folds control the pitch (frequency or relative high/low sound) of the voice. Subglottic pressure and medial compression of the vocal folds also control the loudness or intensity of the voice.

Muscles and Nerves Involved

- The **lateral cricoarytenoid muscle** adducts (moves inward) the vocal folds.
- The **posterior cricoarytenoid** abducts (moves outward) the vocal folds.
- The **superior thyroarytenoid** relaxes the vocal folds and assists medial vocal fold compression.
- The **oblique** and **transverse arytenoids** move the arytenoids closer for medial compression.
- The **thyroarytenoid-muscularis** adducts (moves inward) the vocal foldsn
- The **thyroarytenoid-vocalis** regulates the vocal folds' longitudinal tension.
- **Longitudinal tension** increases when the vocal folds are lengthened and it decreases when they are shortened.
- The space between the vocal folds is called the **rima glottidis**.
- The **extrinsic laryngeal muscles** include the suprahyoid and infrahyoid muscles.
    - The **suprahyoid muscles** attach above the hyoid bone and elevate the hyoid bone and larynx.

Copyright © Mometrix Media. You have been licensed one copy of this document for personal use only. Any other reproduction or redistribution is strictly prohibited. All rights reserved.
This content is provided for test preparation purposes only and does not imply an endorsement by Mometrix of any particular political, scientific, or religious point of view.

  - The **infrahyoid muscles** attach below the hyoid bone and depress the hyoid bone and larynx.
  - The **suprahyoids** and **infrahyoids** are innervated by the facial, hypoglossal, and trigeminal cranial nerves.
- The **cricothyroid muscle** is innervated by the superior laryngeal nerve.
- All other **intrinsic laryngeal muscles** are innervated by the recurrent laryngeal nerve.
- These **laryngeal nerves** emerge to the vagus nerve, the tenth cranial nerve (X).

Assessment Procedures and Assessment

Speech Sound Production

Oral Mechanism Examination and Hearing Screening

The SLP assesses whether the client's physiological speech mechanism structures and function are adequate for producing speech sounds by conducting an examination of the client's oral mechanisms. Typically, this examination includes assessing the occlusion (bite) and any specific deviations of individual teeth; assessment of the hard and soft palates to identify the presence of any malformations such as clefts, fistulas, or a bifid uvula; assessment of the functional range of motion and strength of the jaw, tongue, velum, and lips; and assessment of tongue placement during speech and at rest to identify or rule out tongue thrust. Tongue thrust is an oral myofunctional phenomenon that can cause distortion in the production of certain phonemes (e.g., /s/, /z/, /ʃ/, /ʒ/, /ʧ/, and /dʒ/). If the SLP did not screen hearing at the time of the speech sound screening, s/he would conduct one during the comprehensive speech sound assessment, because hearing loss can cause deficits in speech sound production by interfering with auditory perception of speech sounds. Typically, the hearing screening includes examining the ear canal and eardrum with an otoscope; a pure-tone audiometric test; and assessing middle-ear function through immittance testing.

Assessing Children

Assessing children's speech sound production takes developmentally normal/appropriate errors and patterns into account, differentiating unusual/age-inappropriate/developmentally inappropriate errors. Speech sound assessment usually includes various sampling procedures as well as standardized assessment measures. Single-word testing affords identifiable production units and eliciting all speech sounds in multiple contexts, but specific phoneme production in single words may/may not match their production in connected speech. Thus, connected speech sampling yields data about phoneme production during normal conversation, storytelling/retelling, picture description, and other varied speech tasks with the clinician, peers, teachers, parents, siblings, and other varied communication partners. Evaluating the child's phonological system includes accurate production in various phonetic contexts and initial, medial, and final word positions; consonant clusters, vowel combinations, blends and other sequences; syllable shapes from simple consonant-vowel (CV) to complex, e.g., CCVCC; errors of substitution, distortion, omission, deletion, or addition; error distribution by word position; consistent distortion of different phonemes; and systematic phonological error patterns, e.g., phoneme classes such as fricatives or stops, consonant clusters/other phoneme sequences, and/or multisyllabic words or complex syllable structures.

Judging Severity of Child's Speech Sound Disorder

According to ASHA, no clear consensus exists about the best way of determining speech sound disorder severity. The SLP must make a qualitative judgment about the impact of a speech sound disorder upon a child's everyday communicative functioning. Some SLP researchers and clinicians use a descriptive continuum of disability; e.g., few substitutions and rare omissions represent mild

Copyright © Mometrix Media. You have been licensed one copy of this document for personal use only. Any other reproduction or redistribution is strictly prohibited. All rights reserved.
This content is provided for test preparation purposes only and does not imply an endorsement by Mometrix of any particular political, scientific, or religious point of view.

severity, whereas many substitutions, extensive omissions, and very limited phonemic and phonotactic repertoires represent profound severity. Others use numerical scales; for example, a quantitative approach calculating percentage of consonants correct (PCC; Shriberg and Kwiatkowski, 1982) determines severity on a mild to severe continuum. Mild severity would equate to 85% to 100% PCC; severe would equal less than 50% PCC. Percent vowels correct (PVC) and eight additional indicators have been added to this approach (Shriberg et al., 1997), which is most consistent with listener perceptions of severity. The descriptive continuum of mild, moderate, severe, and profound and the percentage calculation of correctly produced phonemes are commonly employed for their time efficiency and for the absence of more definitive methods of determining the severity of articulation disorders.

Intelligibility of child's speech: The intelligibility of a child's spontaneous speech is judged perceptually and subjectively by the listener. Intelligibility is often used to judge speech disorder severity, determine the need for intervention, and evaluate progress in speech therapy. Generally, clinicians find completely/mostly unintelligible speech in a child aged three years or older to be an indication for treatment. Researchers (Coplan and Gleason, 1988; Flipsen, 2006) provide a formula of dividing a child's age by four and converting the quotient to a percentage as a guideline for developmentally expected intelligibility: one-year-olds = 25% intelligible, two-year-olds = 50%, three-year-olds = 75%, and four-year-olds = 100%. Others (Bauman-Waengler, 2012; McLeod, Harrison, and McCormack, 2012) propose calculating the percentage of words understood in a speech sample. Intelligibility can vary by setting. Some factors affecting it include: single-word versus conversational communication levels; listener familiarity with a child's speech pattern; the speaker's voice loudness, quality; speech fluency, rate, inflection, pauses, and stress patterns; social environment, including one-on-one versus group conversation and familiar versus unfamiliar conversation partners; known versus unknown context/other communication cues; signal-to-noise ratio/background noise; and the skills of the listener.

Stimulability Testing and Speech Perception Testing

When a child makes articulation errors beyond what is developmentally normal, stimulability testing assesses the child's ability to imitate or correctly produce a phoneme that s/he has misarticulated following clinician modeling. This informs the SLP how well the child can imitate the speech sound in isolation, syllables, words, phrases, sentences, or other contexts; and helps the SLP determine cuing levels required for optimal production, for example, auditory, auditory and visual, auditory, visual, and verbal, and tactile cues. Although some test batteries incorporate stimulability subscales, not many standardized instruments or procedures exist to test stimulability. By conducting stimulability testing, the SLP can ascertain whether a child is likely to acquire the sounds s/he is misarticulating without intervention, to select appropriate targets for speech therapy, and to predict improvement through therapy. To assess whether a child can perceive the difference between a phoneme's standard production and his/her own inaccurate production, speech perception testing can be used with children who do not employ phonemic contrasts. It can determine whether misarticulations are related to generalized perceptual deficits for distinguishing minimal sound contrasts.

Assessing Child's Discrimination of Speech Sounds

Hearing/perception of speech sounds determines their production. Speech perception testing can identify perceptual deficits. One testing method is auditory discrimination: The SLP presents paired syllables, identical or with a single phoneme contrast; the child identifies "same"/"different." In picture identification, the SLP says a word; the child points at a picture illustrating that word among

Copyright © Mometrix Media. You have been licensed one copy of this document for personal use only. Any other reproduction or redistribution is strictly prohibited. All rights reserved.
This content is provided for test preparation purposes only and does not imply an endorsement by Mometrix of any particular political, scientific, or religious point of view.

two to four pictures illustrating similar-sounding words with minimal phonetic differences. Testing accurate/inaccurate pronunciation includes three task types:

- **Speech production-perception task**: Pictures are presented, a speaker says a word naming the picture, and the child identifies whether the speaker pronounced it correctly/incorrectly.
- **Mispronunciation detection task**: A computer program presents a visual picture and an audio recording of a word, either pronounced correctly or containing a single-phoneme error. The SLP asks the child to point to a visual symbol indicating correct or incorrect.
- **Lexical decision/judgment task**: Targeting a contrasting phoneme, the SLP assesses the child's ability to identify words pronounced correctly versus incorrectly by multiple speakers. The child points to a picture of the word targeted if it was articulated correctly or to an X if it was articulated incorrectly.

Speech Fluency

To assess fluency, it is best to take a sample of spontaneous conversational speech because many people who stutter can read aloud, recite poetry or memorized prose, and produce other nonpropositional speech without any dysfluencies. Stuttering dysfluencies include repetitions of phonemes, syllables, or words; prolongations of speech sounds; blocks; and secondary interjections and circumlocutions. Examples: Phoneme repetition: "You would have t-t-t-t-to...." Syllable repetition: "Lo-lo-lo-location." Word repetition: "You would have to—to—to—to...." Prolongations (vowel): "Woooould you...."; ."..see whaaaaaaat's in it"; (consonant): "Sssssssssave me a seat." Blocks: The speaker's mouth is shaped to articulate a sound, but no sound issues. The more tension that builds up, the more blocked the speaker becomes. Interjections: "We can meet---um, um, um, you know, like, around three o'clock." Circumlocutions: Using other words/phrases without problematic initial phonemes/transpositions, e.g., "the arch of marble" for "Marble Arch," avoiding initial /m/. Each involves difficulty transitioning between sounds. Some "fluent stutterers" continue speaking despite occasional/even frequent dysfluencies. More severe stutterers can develop secondary behaviors, some quite bizarre, e.g., foot stomping, fist pounding, squeezing the eyes shut, inflating the cheeks, or protruding the tongue. These are largely ineffective, but they become habits through intermittent reinforcement via occasional, coincidental relief.

Because dysfluencies are frequently obvious to listeners and disrupt communication when severe enough, it would appear simple to identify stuttering. However, it can affect things beyond observable speech, which untrained listeners cannot detect so easily. Hence, a certified SLP must diagnose stuttering. During evaluation, the SLP records the number and types of dysfluencies the speaker produces in different situations. The SLP also assesses the speaker's ways of reacting to and coping with his/her dysfluencies. Additional information includes factors exacerbating dysfluency, e.g., teasing or pressure. Depending on the client's history and age, the SLP may also assess speech rate, language skills, etc. The SLP analyzes assessment data and information about the individual to determine the presence or absence of a fluency disorder. When determining the existence of a stuttering disorder, the SLP also evaluates how much the disorder affects the individual's ability to participate in and perform daily activities. Since some dysfluencies are normal in young children's developing speech, it is important for the SLP to predict the likelihood that a young child's stuttering will continue.

Although stuttering dysfluencies can occur in individuals of any age, fewer adults than children evidence stuttering because many children who stutter grow out of it with or without speech therapy. It is also developmentally normal for young children to exhibit some dysfluencies because their speech and language skills are still in the process of developing. It is therefore necessary for

Copyright © Mometrix Media. You have been licensed one copy of this document for personal use only. Any other reproduction or redistribution is strictly prohibited. All rights reserved.
This content is provided for test preparation purposes only and does not imply an endorsement by Mometrix of any particular political, scientific, or religious point of view.

the SLP to predict whether a young child's stuttering is likely to continue into later childhood or not. The SLP can administer a series of tests, perform interviews, and make targeted observations, all of which have been designed for estimating the risk that a young child will continue to stutter. SLP experts disagree somewhat about which of the risk factors are most significant; however, the consensus among many of them is that the following factors are noteworthy: a history of stuttering in the child's family, stuttering that has lasted for six months or more, the presence of other speech and/or language disorders, and the child's and/or family's having strong concerns or fears about stuttering.

Predicting whether stuttering will continue is less critical for older children and adults than younger children because it has already continued long enough to be a problem. Evaluation is designed to assess the stuttering's overall severity, impact on communication, and daily activity participation and develop individual treatment programs. Though exact causes are undiscovered, recent research implicates genetic contributions. However, not all individuals inheriting predispositions will develop stuttering: Life events are believed to be triggers. One possible trigger is preschooler grammar development enabling longer, complete sentences. Children having no problem with one- to two-word sentences first encounter difficulty with full, more complex utterances and develop dysfluencies. Additional factors can exacerbate stuttering after it begins. Easily frustrated children, for instance, may tend to tense their speech muscles more in reaction to dysfluencies, prolonging dysfluency duration. Others' teasing or similarly aversive responses can also make stuttering worse. Emotional reactions to their stuttering and/or others' unfavorable treatment, such as embarrassment, shame, and anxiety, can cause additional interference with fluent speech.

Prevalence, Typical Onset, and Development

More males than females stutter. An estimated three to four times more elementary school boys than girls stutter. Although some children begin stuttering in elementary grades, the onset of developmental stuttering symptoms more commonly occurs between 2.5 and 4 years of age. Preschoolers, especially in the early stages of stuttering disorders, often demonstrate little or no awareness of their dysfluencies. However, school-age and older individuals develop increasing awareness of their speech problems and others' reactions to them. Individual differences in the development of stuttering are substantial. Some children's dysfluencies increase gradually over months or years; others develop significant difficulties weeks or days after onset. Children's stuttering can vary significantly in severity from day to day and week to week. Some children's dysfluencies seem to vanish for several weeks and then return for no known reason. Adolescent and adult stutterers usually have more stable symptoms than young children, yet they may still report noticeably better/worse fluency than usual during certain activities. Around 75% of preschooler stuttering ends, often within months of onset. Some individuals also improve after stuttering for years. Some children recover from stuttering with speech therapy, others without.

Common Sources of Voice Disorders

Voice disorders can result from chronic vocal strain/abuse, which can create polyps or nodules on the vocal folds, causing hoarseness and discomfort. Many vocal/resonance disorders originate from velopharyngeal dysfunction (VPD), i.e., inadequate closure of the port between the velum and pharynx, allowing air leakage into the nasal passages during speech. VPD can be caused by structural defects, e.g., cleft palate, a shortened soft palate, a deep pharynx, anomalies of the cervical spine, etc.; physiological/neurological disorders, e.g., apraxia, a motor speech disorder wherein neurological damage/deficit interferes with brain control and coordination of speech muscles; dysarthria, a motor speech disorder wherein neurological damage can affect speech rate, loudness, clarity, quality, articulation, rhythm, and breathing (as well as eating/swallowing and

Copyright © Mometrix Media. You have been licensed one copy of this document for personal use only. Any other reproduction or redistribution is strictly prohibited. All rights reserved.
This content is provided for test preparation purposes only and does not imply an endorsement by Mometrix of any particular political, scientific, or religious point of view.

secretion management); or the development of articulatory error patterns and abnormal placements, e.g., velopharyngeal mislearning. One of the best-known VPD causes is cleft palate. The palate alone may be cleft, or also the lip. Submucosal cleft palate is a cleft in the hard palate bone covered by a mucous membrane in the roof of the mouth. Clefts may be complete/incomplete and bilateral/unilateral. Coexisting abnormal muscle insertion with midline separation, or separation of the levator veli palatini muscle bundle, is common.

SPEECH EVALUATION OF CHILDREN WITH SUSPECTED VPD AND/OR CLEFT PALATE

Speech evaluation of children with suspected velopharyngeal dysfunction (VPD) and/or cleft palate aims to determine a child's current performance/activity and competence/capability. Knowing these factors informs whether the child would benefit from speech therapy: if so, when, and whether additional physical management is indicated. In addition to a thorough medical and surgical history, evaluation includes perceptual speech evaluation, articulation evaluation, dysphonia assessment, oral mechanism evaluation, standardized speech and language assessments, and instrumental evaluation. The oral mechanism evaluation examines teeth, bite, and tonsils and assesses oral cavity structures. In clients lacking cleft palate history but demonstrating hypernasal speech, three typical signs of submucous cleft palate are a notch in the hard palate's rear edge; bifid uvula; and a white/pale/bluish zone at the palate's midline. Standardized speech and language assessments provide valuable comparisons of client performance to population norms. Instrumental evaluation examines further and refutes or explains conclusions arrived at through previous perceptual analysis. Instrumental evaluation methods include nasometry, nasopharyngoscopy, videofluoroscopy/stroboscopy, and pressure-flow or aerodynamic studies.

RESONANCE AND AIRFLOW/PRESSURE EVALUATION

Children who have cleft palates and/or suspected velopharyngeal dysfunction (VPD) can have nasal air emission due to VPD, resonance disorders due to either or both cleft palate and VPD or both of these coexisting. SLPs assess resonance by having the client utter voiced sounds including vowels, vocalic consonants (e.g., /b/, /d/, /g/, /dʒ/, /l/, /m/, /n/, /r/, /v/, /w/, /j/ [the initial letter y], and /z/) and nasal consonants (e.g., /m/, /n/, and /ŋ/). They assess airflow and air pressure by having the client produce high-pressure consonants including stops (e.g., unvoiced: /k/, /p/, /t/; and voiced: /g/, /b/, /d/), fricatives (e.g., unvoiced: /f/, /h/, /s/, /ʃ/; and voiced: /v/, /z/, and /ʒ/), and affricates (e.g., unvoiced: /ʧ/; and voiced: /dʒ/). Although many people may consider resonance to be a characteristic or element of voice, in SLP, voice and resonance are actually two distinct factors of speech, each with different components of anatomy and physiology. Therefore, because the existence and/or extent of hypernasality the listener perceives in the client's voice can be hidden by dysphonia—particularly deviations in voice quality—SLPs should identify the presence of dysphonia separately.

ARTICULATION ASSESSMENT

When the SLP is evaluating articulation as part of an assessment of a client with identified or suspected cleft palate and/or suspected velopharyngeal dysfunction (VPD), the evaluation should include both a speech sample of conversation and informal, structured speech tasks such as having the client repeat consonant-vowel (CV) utterances, words, and sentences, and activities involving elicited naming. With craniofacial anomalies and resonance disorders, the articulation assessment is used for determining whether the client's speech errors are obligatory or compensatory. Obligatory errors are primary, and they are due to neurogenic or structural causes, such as velopharyngeal insufficiency or fistulas, which must be corrected through physical management. Compensatory errors are secondary, and they are learned by some children during their early speech development to make up for the inability to create enough intraoral air pressure to produce

Copyright © Mometrix Media. You have been licensed one copy of this document for personal use only. Any other reproduction or redistribution is strictly prohibited. All rights reserved.
This content is provided for test preparation purposes only and does not imply an endorsement by Mometrix of any particular political, scientific, or religious point of view.

pressure consonants normally. This inability is typically caused by cleft palate or VPD. These errors require speech therapy.

Children who have cleft palates and/or velopharyngeal dysfunction typically demonstrate speech articulation errors. These errors can be obligatory or compensatory, and children with these conditions can have both types of articulatory errors. Obligatory speech errors are directly caused by neurogenic or structural deficits or disorders, e.g., velopharyngeal insufficiency or fistulas. These must be physically managed for correction (e.g., through surgical procedures). In contrast, compensatory speech errors are developed by children as their speech develops as a way of making up for, getting around, or compensating for a lack of sufficient air pressure in the mouth for producing consonants that require more air pressure. These cannot be corrected by physical management and will respond only to speech therapy because they are learned errors (physiologically influenced) rather than physiologically dictated like obligatory errors. Errors compensating for clefts are sometimes called "cleft-type" errors. These can be difficult to identify perceptually with accuracy, requiring practice. Compensatory errors and learned, phoneme-specific nasal air emission—particularly on /s/, the other sibilant fricatives, and also affricates at times—are both types of velopharyngeal mislearning.

Standardized Instrument for Assessing Receptive Language

The **Peabody Picture Vocabulary Test** (PPVT) is a very popular norm-referenced assessment instrument. Its validity and reliability are documented; it has been used in research studies, and much research supports its use. It can be administered to children as young as 2.5 years, through 90-year-old adults. The examiner reads aloud verbal prompts on the backs of pictures presented; the test-taker points to one of four pictures corresponding to the prompt. Aside from some phrases (e.g., "It goes up," "Lying down," etc.), items are words: nouns, verbs, and adjectives with progressive difficulty. For certain ages (2.6 through 7.11), training items are provided to teach before proceeding. Although the PPVT tests vocabulary acquisition, it also assesses cognitive development: Vocabulary and intelligence correlate highly. It screens for intellectual disability and giftedness; it measures English language proficiency in English language learner students; and it can detect not only language problems, but also some visual disabilities. Being untimed, it affords equal responding opportunities. Additional benefits include response flexibility—pointing, nodding yes/no, naming, saying item numbers, saying yes/no. Nonverbal individuals/those with articulation disorders, stuttering, ASDs, Broca's aphasia, and others understanding spoken language but having expressive language/speech difficulties benefit by not having to speak, but by simply indicating word knowledge.

Standardized Instrument for Assessing Expressive Language

The **Expressive Vocabulary Test** (EVT, Williams, Pearson, 2007) is a norm-referenced instrument that can be administered to individuals aged from 2 years, 6 months to 90 years and takes 10 to 20 minutes. It includes a computerized scoring option using ASSIST scoring software, which can produce a range of scoring formats and reports. The EVT measures expressive vocabulary and ability to retrieve words from memory. It was conormed with the Peabody Picture Vocabulary Test (PPVT), its companion measure of receptive vocabulary, standardized using the same population. This enables comparing an examinee's receptive and expressive vocabulary and cognitive skills by administering both tests; ASSIST software generates comparisons. The EVT's national examinee sample was stratified to correspond to the most recent US Census data regarding race/ethnicity, gender, geographic region, and parent education/self-education level as a socioeconomic status measure. Like the PPVT, the EVT is untimed, eliminating time pressure on the test taker and the examiner. The EVT provides diagnostic analyses on five levels. It includes 38 labeling items and 152

Copyright © Mometrix Media. You have been licensed one copy of this document for personal use only. Any other reproduction or redistribution is strictly prohibited. All rights reserved.
This content is provided for test preparation purposes only and does not imply an endorsement by Mometrix of any particular political, scientific, or religious point of view.

synonym items, each requiring single-word responses. The EVT's strong scientific support and high internal consistency reliability enable meeting Reading First/other programs' assessment criteria.

Relationship Between Receptive and Expressive Language

A pediatrician and SLP (Michael and Cowan, 2010) have observed that many children referred to them for expressive speech delays are found through assessment to have age-level receptive language skills, but testing reveals deficits in understanding the social-skills-related receptive communication essential to conversation and social interactions. These experts define two main types of receptive language responses: action and conversational/social. Pointing at a picture, object, or body part, retrieving an object when asked, and following unfamiliar directions are examples of action responses. Nodding, gesturing, and facial expressions in response to questions are examples of conversational/social responses. The latter require understanding prelingual (nonverbal) communication and joint attention. These experts thus speculate that in the children found to have normal receptive language skills but delayed expressive skills, the expressive delays may be attributable to their identified deficits in conversational/social receptive language skills. Hence, they propose assessing receptive action skills and receptive communication/social skills separately and differentially to evaluate receptive communication skills more clearly and determine treatment focus.

Receptive language responses can be related to action or conversational/social. In action/active responses, for example, a child might select familiar objects, identify familiar pictures in books, follow new directions, or demonstrate receptive understanding of action verb meanings by completing requested actions. In conversational/social responses, a child might respond to questions such as "Is this where I should put this?" or "More?" by head nodding/shaking, physical gestures, and/or facial expressions, without needing to respond with any other action or activity. Receptive action skills are more related to the child's knowledge level than communication abilities; conversely, receptive communication/social skills are more related to the child's communication abilities than knowledge level. Children with age-level receptive action skills but low receptive communication/social skills typically have age-level cognitive ability but difficulties with speech and nonverbal communication skills. Children rarely test with age-level receptive communication/social but low receptive action skills. Those scoring low on both may have cognitive deficits or lack environmental exposure, and they may have speech and nonverbal communication difficulties. Children testing at age level in both receptive action and receptive communication/social skills likely has good cognitive and nonverbal communication skills, with verbal expressive speech delay being the only deficit.

Social and Action Aspects of Receptive Communication and Language Skills

One distinction in receptive language and communication skills is between receptive action responses and receptive communication/social responses. Pointing to one's facial/body parts, pictures, or objects or retrieving an object when requested and following novel directions are action responses. Responding to questions such as "Want more?" or "Do we put this there?" with gestures, nodding, and/or facial expressions are communication/social responses. Receptive language and communication skills can be assessed and defined more specifically by assessing these skill types separately. For example, if a child can point to all his/her body parts accurately when asked and identify different shapes and animals when directed, but not comprehend when asked whether s/he wants a favorite snack, this indicates sufficient receptive action skills but insufficient receptive communication/social skills. Experts believe that the latter are more important than the former to speech and communication development. Therapists can teach caregivers how to stimulate these skills during everyday routines and life experiences. Speech-language therapy should concentrate on communication/social skills in early childhood, and after

Copyright © Mometrix Media. You have been licensed one copy of this document for personal use only. Any other reproduction or redistribution is strictly prohibited. All rights reserved.
This content is provided for test preparation purposes only and does not imply an endorsement by Mometrix of any particular political, scientific, or religious point of view.

these are established, add action skills. Although expert SLPs acknowledge the importance of exposure to books and labeling environmental objects, they emphasize the critical importance of reciprocal parent-child understanding during early childhood.

Pre-School Language Scale

The **Pre-school Language Scale** (PLS, Domanski and Vieira) is administered individually to children from infant ages to 6 years, 11 months who present with symptoms or signs of language delays/disorders. Based on developmental research and milestones, the test contains two subscales for assessing auditory receptive comprehension skills and expressive skills and three additional supplements: an articulation screener, a language sample checklist, and a caregiver questionnaire. It is detailed and socioeconomically nonbiased. Depending on the child, administration takes 20 to 45 minutes. The auditory receptive subscale includes measures of attention to speakers; basic vocabulary comprehension; object play; grammatical markers; identifying rhyming words; and comparing things, etc. The expressive subscale includes naming objects; using concepts describing objects; expressing quantity; and using grammatical markers, etc. For older children, the expressive subscale includes word segmentation, analogy completion, and sequential short storytelling, etc. It has a Spanish version. Recent (2010) updates include larger normative samples incorporating children with disabilities, various ethnic and socioeconomic groups, and other diversities; research into application with ASDs; addressing IDEA regulations; an edition addressing other languages; and US Census and dialect sensitivity. It can be used with children having severe language delays. Its results can be used in portfolios.

Pragmatics

Pragmatics is the understanding of how to use language in social contexts and interactions, i.e., knowing what to say, when and how to say it, and how to communicate socially with others. Pragmatic skills include knowing one must answer questions; taking turns with others in conversations; observing and responding to nonverbal communication aspects, e.g., other people's affects (moods/emotional status), tones of voice, body language, gestures, and facial expressions; realizing one must introduce conversational topics for listeners to comprehend fully; knowing which sentence types and vocabulary words to use for initiating conversations or responding to others; maintaining/continuing topics; appropriately changing topics; knowing how to interrupt/interject politely; maintaining appropriate eye contact; and knowing how to converse formally versus informally with different people. Individuals with pragmatic deficits frequently are prone to failing to take turns, talking over others, interrupting excessively, responding inappropriately with silence, or speaking too quietly; speaking irrelevantly or about topics in which others are uninterested; including excessive detail; talking too long; assuming listeners have impossible prior knowledge and inadequately informing their stories; or, conversely, failing to assume that listeners have commonplace prior knowledge and unnecessarily overexplaining background and details.

Three major categories of communication skills included in pragmatics are explained as follows:

1. Using language for various purposes; e.g., greeting: "Hello/goodbye"; requesting: "Please get me a cookie"; demanding: "Give me a cookie!"; informing: "I'm going to take a cookie"; or promising: "I'm going to get a cookie for you."
2. Changing language corresponding to a situation's or listener's needs, e.g., giving unfamiliar listeners background information, addressing babies differently than adults, and speaking differently on playgrounds than in classrooms.

Copyright © Mometrix Media. You have been licensed one copy of this document for personal use only. Any other reproduction or redistribution is strictly prohibited. All rights reserved.
This content is provided for test preparation purposes only and does not imply an endorsement by Mometrix of any particular political, scientific, or religious point of view.

3. Following rules for conversing and storytelling, e.g., introducing conversational topics; staying on topic; taking turns during conversations; rephrasing to correct misunderstandings; using verbal and nonverbal signals appropriately; observing proxemics, i.e., personal and social space, standing appropriate distances from others when conversing; and using eye contact and facial expressions appropriately.

Pragmatic rules can vary among and within cultures: Understanding the rules accepted by conversation/communication partners is important. People with pragmatic deficits/difficulties may tell stories in disorganized ways, demonstrate minimal variety in language use, and/or say irrelevant or inappropriate things in conversation. Pragmatic difficulties in just a few situations are common for children and do not necessarily indicate disorders, but frequent, age-inappropriate problems with social language can indicate pragmatic disorders. These frequently coexist with vocabulary/grammar/other language problems.

Pragmatic Communication Deficits in Individuals with ASDs

Individuals with autism spectrum disorders (ASDs) frequently have deficits in the ability to observe and interpret the meaning of nonverbal communicative signals. For example, some people with ASDs fail to notice others' facial expressions and/or to connect them to others' emotional states. Consequently, they cannot tell whether someone is happy, sad, angry, impatient, frightened, etc. SLPs can help them gain this skill through explicit training. Someone with an ASD who has benefited from such training might demonstrate by saying, "Your mouth is turned down; that means you are unhappy" or "Your mouth turns up; you must be happy." ASD individuals also often cannot understand nonliteral meanings, such as sarcasm contradicted/not indicated by literal word meanings but expressed by accompanying vocal tone and facial expression. Though they do not come by this normal ability naturally, SLPs can teach them to attend to and analyze the nonverbal information and conclude, "S/he is being sarcastic/making a joke." The same applies to figurative language. ASD individuals tend to understand only literal word meanings. SLPs can explain metaphors, analogies, and other figurative expressions to them; with enough exposure, experience, and practice, they can learn to recognize and/or decipher figurative meanings

People with autism spectrum disorders (ASDs) often avoid direct eye contact with others. This may be attributable to sensory hypersensitivity: Individuals may avoid eye contact to prevent sensory discomfort or overload. Others can misinterpret lack of eye contact in ASDs as lack of awareness, attention, interest, or respect. Through behavioral techniques such as shaping through successive approximations, SLPs can help them learn to increase eye contact gradually to facilitate communicative and social interactions. Individuals with Asperger's syndrome and other high-functioning forms of ASDs may have good vocabularies and speak fluently, yet they may lack skills for initiating conversations and participating in normal conversational give-and-take. For example, they may be able to deliver long monologues on topics that interest them, using sophisticated terminology and concepts, but they may be unable to take turns speaking or respond to what others say. SLPs can train them to learn and consciously apply conversational techniques. Neuroimaging reveals the brain's plasticity, showing that when people with ASDs learn skills they did not develop naturally, their brain circuitry is actually rewired by the intervention. This accounts for their ability to remediate some deficits of the disorder through therapy.

Cognitive-Communication Disorders

Cognitive-communication disorders include all problems with any aspect of communication affected by impaired cognition. Cognition includes attention, perception, memory, organization, executive function, and other cognitive systems and processes. Cognitive impairments can affect areas of functioning including activities of daily living, behavioral self-regulation, social interaction,

Copyright © Mometrix Media. You have been licensed one copy of this document for personal use only. Any other reproduction or redistribution is strictly prohibited. All rights reserved.
This content is provided for test preparation purposes only and does not imply an endorsement by Mometrix of any particular political, scientific, or religious point of view.

learning, academic performance, and work performance. Communication is verbal and nonverbal. It includes the phonological, morphological, semantic, syntactic, and pragmatic domains and the activities of listening, speaking, reading, writing, and gesturing. Cognitive-communication disorders can be acquired or congenital. Some examples of acquired etiologies include anoxic, hypoxic, or toxic encephalopathy; traumatic brain injuries; stroke; brain tumors; dementias, and other degenerative and nondegenerative neurological diseases. Some examples of congenital etiologies include genetic disorders and prenatal, perinatal, and postnatal neurological diseases and injuries. Cognitive-communication disorders have high incidence and high prevalence, and they have the potential for serious consequences such as adverse impacts on quality of life; social, school and job success; personal finances; and caregivers. These characteristics make their prevention, assessment, diagnosis, and management crucial.

Background Knowledge, Experience, and Roles of SLPs

Relative to the cognitive aspects of communication, SLPs are knowledgeable regarding normal development, abnormal development, neuropsychological processes, physiological pathology, and relationships between brain functions and behaviors. Through their educational background and clinical experience, SLPs are prepared to take on various roles regarding cognitive-communication disorders. In addition to prevention, intervention, advocacy, research, education, case management, collaboration, and counseling, SLP roles include identification—identifying individuals who present with cognitive-communication disorders or are at risk for them—and assessment—selecting and using both static and dynamic procedures in assessment and diagnostic approaches that are clinically, linguistically, and culturally appropriate and identifying contextual variables contributing to or useful in remediating cognitive-communication disorders. The World Health Organization International Classification of Functioning, Disability and Health categories apply to cognitive-communication disorders:

- **Body structure and function**—neuroanatomical structures and neurophysiological and neuropsychological functions that support cognitive-communication processes.
- **Activity and participation**—capacity (executing tasks in uniform/standardized environments) and performance (executing tasks in natural environments) for everyday activities and social, academic, and work situations affected by cognitive-communication deficits.
- **Contextual factors**—personal and environmental variables facilitating/impeding function and participation; e.g., age, gender, race/ethnicity, education, cultural beliefs, lifestyle; academic curriculum, job demands, everyday communication partners' interactive and support competencies; awareness of and adjustment to disability; motivation; and accepting responsibility for change.

Characteristics of Cognitive Aspects of Communication

Research consistently shows strong correlations between intelligence and vocabulary; people with intellectual disabilities typically have smaller and simpler vocabularies than those of average or above-average intelligence. This relates not only to the acquisition of word knowledge, but moreover to concept understanding. Individuals with intellectual disabilities often think on more concrete levels as children do and may have difficulty understanding abstract ideas and the words describing them. Language and speech development are typically slower and below age level in people with intellectual disabilities. Typically, they begin to speak at later ages in childhood, acquire fewer new vocabulary words and at slower rates, and reach developmental speech and language milestones at older ages than in typical development. Not only can their language development be limited by their cognitive limitations, but also, delayed or atypical motor development in some individuals may affect their speech development. Additionally, physiological characteristics such as

Copyright © Mometrix Media. You have been licensed one copy of this document for personal use only. Any other reproduction or redistribution is strictly prohibited. All rights reserved.
This content is provided for test preparation purposes only and does not imply an endorsement by Mometrix of any particular political, scientific, or religious point of view.

those of the tongue in Down syndrome can cause some misarticulations. The general principle that receptive language understanding precedes expressive production can be magnified in some ID individuals, who may not speak much or clearly but understand far more.

Individuals with ASDs

Although individuals with ASDs can have IQ levels ranging from profound intellectual disability to gifted and many of their deficits or symptoms are social, behavioral, and/or linguistic, certain ASD characteristics have cognitive natures irrespective of intelligence. For example, they frequently have very limited/narrow interests. Those with higher intelligence will apply it to learning everything they can about only topics of interest to them, in keeping with the often obsessive character of their thinking and compulsive nature of their activities. Although this knowledge is limited in scope and breadth overall, it can also be extremely focused, in-depth, and thorough for specific subjects they find fascinating. Another cognitive aspect is that ASD individuals often learn better in some domains/subjects than others. For example, although many ASD individuals have difficulties with social interactions and some also have speech and language deficits, they may excel at learning and performance in mathematical, scientific, and analytical subjects. A salient cognitive deficit in communication for many with ASDs is in observing, understanding, and responding appropriately to nonverbal communication signals. For example, they may not recognize emotions conveyed by facial expressions, vocal tones, or gestures; figurative and nonliteral language; verbal humor; verbal irony; or verbal sarcasm.

Effects of Dementias

Because dementias typically cause progressive loss of cognitive abilities including memory, reasoning, and orientation; executive function including decision making, problem solving, and judgment; and language, dementias inevitably have adverse impacts on communication. As one example, Alzheimer's disease dementia destroys immediate, then recent, and ultimately long-term memory, including the memory for vocabulary words and familiar people's names as well as the memory for facts, information, their own past life experiences, and eventually the faces and identities of loved ones. Dementia from Alzheimer's disease not only impairs memory, which is one of its most obvious symptoms, it also impairs verbal skills and activities in addition to and beyond impairment in memory for language. Many Alzheimer's disease patients converse and speak less as their symptoms progress. This seems due not only to the loss of memory for language, but also to loss of complex skills for organizing thoughts, formulating utterances, and constructing sentences and of motivation for speech and conversation.

Assessing Need and Suitability of AAC

Although no standardized test battery exists for augmentative/alternative communication (AAC) assessment, currently recommended practices related to AAC evaluation involve several principles. For example, ASHA and AAC researchers encourage SLPs to choose assessment procedures that elicit examinee behaviors that are representative, valid, generalizable, and as applicable as possible to daily living. Obtaining evaluation results from therapy settings that are isolated and artificial can make findings less able to be generalized, reducing their applicability to informing effective interventions. An ecological inventory is one example of a valid evaluation procedure. Typical components include briefly describing the setting, persons present, and how many reasons and opportunities the examinee was given to participate and/or communicate. This is important because many people who already use AAC or are candidates to use it have fewer chances to communicate than others who speak. Hence, the assessment should include existing communication opportunities and ways for improving their quantity and quality that will optimize client participation in meaningful daily activities.

Copyright © Mometrix Media. You have been licensed one copy of this document for personal use only. Any other reproduction or redistribution is strictly prohibited. All rights reserved.
This content is provided for test preparation purposes only and does not imply an endorsement by Mometrix of any particular political, scientific, or religious point of view.

Ecological Inventory and Discrepancy Analysis

To conduct an ecological analysis for AAC evaluation, first the SLP should observe a typical, nondisabled peer of the client participating in the applicable activity in the specific setting identified. Then the SLP should list which communication behaviors this activity requires by performing a task analysis of the activity. Next the SLP would measure the client's abilities and compare them to the abilities demonstrated by the peer during the observation. The differences between the two inform a discrepancy analysis. After this, the SLP will provide the client with the technological support and/or teach the client the skills that are needed for participating in the specific activity that was used for the observation, measurement, comparison, and analysis. The SLP can use the discrepancy analysis and ecological inventory for identifying contexts in which to cultivate and improve communication skills as parts of a wider program. These assessment procedures should be carried out with different communication partners and in different settings wherein the client communicates. In addition to evaluating the client's interactions with partners familiar with the client and his/her communication methods, it is equally important to assess the client's needs for communicating with unfamiliar listeners.

Capability Assessment

When assessing an individual for potential augmentative/alternative communication (AAC) device use, the SLP needs to obtain input from multiple multidisciplinary service providers. To support this need, the SLP must gather data about the client's sensory, perceptual, motor, cognitive, literacy, reading, writing, and language competencies and then integrate this information. Then the SLP can match the individual client's skills with different AAC options whose operational requirements are most compatible. In addition to client communication needs, purposes, and opportunities, the client's capabilities will have an influence on modifications to AAC systems that may be required. The SLP must be able to adjust the assessment procedures as necessary—including departure from standardization when applicable—to achieve valid evaluations of communication and associated areas, especially literacy skills. When assessing the client's language comprehension and production skills, this SLP skill is particularly crucial. The SLP should include measures of phonological, morphological, and syntactic form; semantic content; and pragmatic language use in the assessment.

Feature Matching

Feature matching is basing AAC device/system selection on a client's communication capabilities, strengths, and needs relative to the device/system's assorted features. SLPs determine desired AAC system features according to client skills. Because client abilities change with time, SLPs must reconsider system features accordingly. Experts identify these features in the ideal AAC system: compatibility with client life aspects; affordability; ease of maintenance and repair; operability in all physical positions and environments; acceptability and motivational qualities for the client and significant others; enhancement of the client's communicative effectiveness; ability and enhancement of ongoing client growth in linguistic skills and related skills; nonrestriction of communication scopes and topics; consideration of the communication patterns and needs of the client's conversation partners; and, most importantly, the system enables the client's expression of a complete range of communication functions. To match an AAC device with client skills and requirements, SLPs must be knowledgeable about currently available equipment. If not, the SLP must refer the client to another professional with the required expertise. Also, knowing about effective use of various AAC systems for different client needs and abilities requires clinical experience and intuition because no published comparisons of device effectiveness exist.

Copyright © Mometrix Media. You have been licensed one copy of this document for personal use only. Any other reproduction or redistribution is strictly prohibited. All rights reserved.
This content is provided for test preparation purposes only and does not imply an endorsement by Mometrix of any particular political, scientific, or religious point of view.

Potential Obstacles to Using AAC Devices/Systems

Researchers have identified factors associated with knowledge, skills, attitudes, policies, practices, and other factors as potential communication barriers relative to using augmentative/alternative communication (AAC) devices/systems. The literature implies that for people using AAC and those who eventually use it, language learning environments are frequently different from those experienced by peers with typical communication abilities. For example, children with deficits in functional manipulation skills and independent mobility are limited in accessing their physical environments hence in the experiences available for language mapping. In addition, children with these disabilities spend disproportionately more time than their typically developing peers in daily care routines rather than social and play activities, further limiting their experiences. Another consideration is that according to research findings, young children using AAC devices/systems seldom receive exposure to AAC models and even less often do they receive opportunities for observing others with proficiency in AAC use. They most often receive spoken input from others instead. It is important for SLPs conducting AAC assessment not only to identify obstacles to participation, but also to design subsequent interventions addressing those obstacles.

Hearing Assessment

Observations That Indicate Need for Hearing Assessment

If a child responds to sound inconsistently, demonstrates delayed speech and language development; speaks unclearly, turns the volume up high on audio electronics, fails to follow directions, frequently says "Huh?" or "What?" or does not respond when called, the parents should have the child's hearing professionally evaluated. Adults should review the following items, and if they experience two or more, have their own hearing tested: Difficulty hearing on the phone; hearing better/worse in one ear on the phone; difficulty following conversations when two or more people are talking simultaneously; complaints from others that they turn TV volume up too high; needing to strain to understand conversations; difficulty hearing in restaurants or other settings with noisy backgrounds; ear pain, ringing in the ears, or dizziness; frequently having to ask people to repeat what they say; having members of the family and/or coworkers comment often about their missing things that were said; feeling that many people with whom they converse seem to speak unclearly or mumble; responding inappropriately to what others say due to misunderstanding it; difficulty understanding children and women's speech or higher pitched voices; noticing others' annoyance at one's misunderstanding what they say.

SLPs vs. Audiologists

Although certified audiologists test hearing, SLPs also must test hearing as part of comprehensive speech-language and hearing evaluation and when audiologists are not available, particularly in school settings. Pure-tone, air conduction audiometry is the standard. Faced away from the examiner and any mirrors/reflective surfaces to prevent visual cuing, the examinee wears earphones and raises a hand/finger on the same side/points to the ear/presses a button/says "yes" when detecting sound in each ear. The SLP presents frequencies of 125, 250, 500, 1000, 2000, 4000, and 8000 Hz, beginning at –10 dB, increasing loudness in 10-dB increments until the examinee responds. The SLP graphs hearing thresholds—the dB level at which the individual hears the sound half the time—on an audiogram, with frequencies in Hz, low to high left to right along the horizontal axis and hearing levels from –10 to 120 dB, top to bottom along the vertical axis, using a red O for the right ear and a blue X for the left. Normal hearing ranges from –10 to 15 dB at all frequencies. Slight hearing loss is 16–25 dB; mild, 26–40 dB; moderate, 41-55 dB; moderately severe, 56–70 dB; severe, 71–90 dB; and profound, 91–120 dB.

Copyright © Mometrix Media. You have been licensed one copy of this document for personal use only. Any other reproduction or redistribution is strictly prohibited. All rights reserved.
This content is provided for test preparation purposes only and does not imply an endorsement by Mometrix of any particular political, scientific, or religious point of view.

Bone Conduction Audiometry, VRA, and CPA

In cases of conductive hearing loss, e.g., an individual has middle-ear fluid, outer-ear wax, or other obstructions blocking air conduction, the SLP can use pure-tone bone conduction audiometry instead of pure-tone air conduction audiometry. This bypasses the blockage by placing a vibrator behind the ear/on the forehead through which tones are sent. Skull vibrations conduct the sound straight to the cochlea/inner ear to rule out/identify sensorineural hearing loss. For younger children aged 6–24 months, visual reinforcement audiometry (VRA) is used to screen hearing. The SLP trains the child to look at the sound source by reinforcing correct responses with visual rewards such as toys with flashing lights or movements. For toddlers and preschoolers aged 2–5 years, conditioned play audiometry (CPA) can be used. The SLP trains the child to do some activity, such as putting a stacking ring on a rod or cone, putting a block into a box, or placing a peg into a hole, every time the child hears a tone.

AEP/ABR and OAE Testing

Auditory evoked potential (AEP)/auditory brainstem response (ABR) testing provides information about inner-ear/cochlear and hearing-related brain pathway functioning. Because this test measures brainwave activity in reaction to sound stimuli, the examinee need not respond, making it a good choice for infants; individuals with physical and mental disabilities; those having difficulties with conventional, behavioral audiological testing; and those with suspected neurologically/brain pathway-based hearing loss. Electrodes are applied to the head to record brainwaves while sounds are presented. The examinee can sleep or rest during testing. Newborn hearing screening programs may use ABR: Only one loudness/intensity is presented for screening, with a pass/fail result. Otoacoustic emissions (OAEs) are minute, virtually inaudible sounds emitted from the inner ear by vibrations of the outer hair cells of the cochlea when sound stimulates it. A small probe placed in the outer ear canal can measure these emission sounds, which are produced by people with normal hearing; however, individuals with hearing losses above 25–30 dB do not produce otoacoustic emissions. OAE testing can identify outer-ear canal blockage, middle-ear fluid, and damage to cochlear outer hair cells. It is also often included in newborn hearing screening programs.

Speech Testing and Middle-Ear Testing

SLPs can confirm pure-tone audiometry results through speech testing of older children and adults by presenting speech to assess the speech reception threshold, the quietest speech someone hears half the time, and presenting words at comfortable loudness that clients repeat for word recognition, recording results on the same audiogram as pure-tone audiometry results. Speech testing can be in quiet settings to assess maximum hearing acuity and/or in noisy environments to assess difficulty understanding speech in the presence of background noise, a common symptom of individuals with hearing loss. Middle-ear testing—especially important regarding preschoolers' higher infection rates—includes tympanometry, which helps detect wax buildup, eardrum perforation, and middle-ear fluid by introducing air pressure to the ear canal, measuring eardrum mobility. Tympanograms graphing the results can identify stiff/overly mobile eardrums and holes, and they are often used with middle-ear infections. Acoustic reflex measurement helps localize hearing loss by identifying an absent reflex or the loudness needed to stimulate it. The acoustic reflex involves the middle ear's stapedius muscle pulling the eardrum slightly away from the oval window to protect hearing from loud sounds. Static acoustic impedance measures ear canal air volume, to check ventilation tube openness or identify eardrum perforation.

NNS in Infants

Nonnutritive sucking (NNS), e.g., on pacifiers, thumbs/fingers, or empty breasts/bottles, does not signify an infant's oral feeding readiness, but it is nonetheless useful for informing the subsequent clinical assessment of nutritive sucking and whether it is appropriate for feeding. Typically, skilled

Copyright © Mometrix Media. You have been licensed one copy of this document for personal use only. Any other reproduction or redistribution is strictly prohibited. All rights reserved.
This content is provided for test preparation purposes only and does not imply an endorsement by Mometrix of any particular political, scientific, or religious point of view.

SLP observation can be used to evaluate NNS patterns without requiring instrumental assessment. This noninstrumental evaluation includes the infant's oral structures and functions, e.g., integrity of the palates, jaw movement, and tongue movements for cupping and compressing; rooting ability, i.e., turning and opening the mouth, upon oral stimulation; the ability to accept a pacifier into the mouth; the ability to use positive jaw and tongue pressure to exert compression on a pacifier; the ability to use negative pressure, i.e., suction, by cupping the tongue and moving the jaw on a pacifier; the relative strength of the compression and suction; any other oral-motor dysfunctions that could be associated with motor and/or neurological disorders; and the ability of the infant to maintain the physiological state during NNS activity.

Assessment of Infants in NICUs for Feeding or Swallowing Disorder

The SLP should first assess the infant's ability for nonnutritive sucking (NNS) to evaluate the oral structures and functions, rooting; compression, suction and their strength; any other oral-motor dysfunction; and the ability for physiological state maintenance. Then the SLP should assess nutritive sucking to determine its appropriateness. If both breast- and bottle-feeding will be used, clinicians should assess the infant's sucking during both to ascertain whether the modality affects the infant's feeding performance quality, and if so, how. SLPs should show sensitivity to family beliefs and values about breast- and bottle-feeding and collaborate with mothers, lactation consultants, and nurses to identify parental feeding mode preferences. The infant's sucking-swallowing-breathing pattern, endurance, efficiency, and response to feeding should be assessed. The sucking-swallowing-breathing pattern is crucial to address safety issues, e.g., aspiration, apnea, bradycardia, and/or oxygen desaturation, which have priority in infant populations. SLPs should consider any physiological, motor, or behavioral destabilization from baseline during assessment.

Efficiency equals volume per minute and relates directly to how suction and compression are integrated. Fluid loss compromises efficiency and more frequently reflects the infant's effort at large bolus management than does poor oral-motor tone. SLPs should determine the causes for fluid loss by observing the infant's oral-motor strength and tone during nonnutritive sucking (NNS), which will show similar deficits during NS for an infant with poor oral-motor tone. Maturation typically determines feeding endurance. Endurance represents the ability to continue feeding long enough to consume the volume of milk or formula needed. SLPs can inform how they guide dynamic intervention by observing the infant's communicative behaviors during the feeding process. The baby will communicate various needs to the mother or caregiver, such as her/his ability to tolerate the size of a bolus; whether s/he needs more postural support; and whether her/his breathing and swallowing have lost synchronization. The mother or caregiver can respond dynamically to the baby's cues as they occur to optimize the feeding process.

Assessment of Breast-Feeding in NICUs to Evaluate for Feeding/Swallowing Disorder

According to the Management of Acute Malnutrition in Infants (MAMI) Project, assessment of breast-feeding should include evaluating the infant's behavior; heart and respiratory rates and other indicators of the infant's status; the behavior of the mother during feeding; the positioning of the infant; the attachment of the infant's mouth to the nipple; the efficiency and effectiveness of the infant's pattern of sucking, swallowing, and breathing; the health of the mother's breasts; and the health of the infant. Before the SLP assesses the baby's and mother's skills in breast-feeding, s/he should work together with the mother, a nurse, and a lactation consultant. In order to facilitate the safety and efficiency of breast-feeding in the neonatal intensive care unit (NICU), the SLP as a clinician should have a good working knowledge base about breast-feeding strategies. Because there are not many standardized assessment instruments to evaluate the potential of medically fragile infants in the NICU and other clinical settings for breast-feeding, ASHA advises SLPs to evaluate the variables recommended above by the MAMI Project.

Copyright © Mometrix Media. You have been licensed one copy of this document for personal use only. Any other reproduction or redistribution is strictly prohibited. All rights reserved.
This content is provided for test preparation purposes only and does not imply an endorsement by Mometrix of any particular political, scientific, or religious point of view.

Assessment of Bottle-Feeding Abilities in NICUs for Feeding/Swallowing Disorder

If the mother and hospital staff plan to feed an infant in NICU using both breast-feeding and bottle-feeding, the SLP should evaluate the infant's capabilities during both. This enables the SLP to observe whether the feeding mode makes any difference in feeding performance quality, and if so, in what way(s). Assessment of nutritive sucking (NS) should include evaluations of the baby's pattern of sucking, swallowing, and breathing; the baby's endurance (i.e., the ability to feed for durations sufficient to take in enough milk/formula for nutrition); the efficiency of nutritive sucking; and the baby's responses to feeding. When the SLP assesses bottle-feeding, s/he should evaluate heart and respiratory rates and other indicators of the baby's physical state, whether the sucking-swallowing-breathing pattern is coordinated normally or disorganized, the type of nipple used, the formula/other form of nutrition fed, the baby's positioning, the amount of formula/milk/other nutrition the baby ingests, the duration for completing one feeding, and the baby's response to intervention attempts.

Chapter Quiz

Ready to see how well you retained what you just read? Scan the QR code to go directly to the chapter quiz interface for this study guide. If you're using a computer, simply visit the online resources page at **mometrix.com/resources719/priispedtssli** and click the Chapter Quizzes link.

Copyright © Mometrix Media. You have been licensed one copy of this document for personal use only. Any other reproduction or redistribution is strictly prohibited. All rights reserved.
This content is provided for test preparation purposes only and does not imply an endorsement by Mometrix of any particular political, scientific, or religious point of view.

Planning and Managing the Learning Environment

Treatment Planning

Eligibility for SLP Treatment Services

According to ASHA, an individual is eligible for SLP treatment (as well as for assessment or further evaluation) if one or more of the following factors exist: The individual was self-referred or referred by another SLP, an audiologist, physician, teacher, family member, or interdisciplinary team suspecting a communication, speech, language, or feeding and swallowing disorder. The individual failed a communication and/or swallowing screening. The individual cannot communicate optimally or functionally across communication partners and environments. The individual cannot swallow well enough to maintain adequate hydrational, nutritional, and pulmonary status. The individual cannot swallow well enough to manage oral and pharyngeal saliva secretions. An ASHA-certified SLP has conducted an evaluation that confirms a communication and/or swallowing disorder. The individual's communication skills are not comparable to those of peers in chronological age, gender, ethnicity, linguistic background, or cultural background. The individual's communication abilities have adverse safety, health, emotional, social, educational, or occupational effects. The individual's swallowing abilities have adverse safety, health, or nutritional effects. The individual, family members, and/or guardians want to attain/maintain optimal communication and/or swallowing skills through SLP services. The individual, family and/or guardian want to improve communication skills through SLP services.

Treatment Outcomes for Communication Disorders

One area of current research into SLP topics is the effectiveness of treatment for various communication disorders. For example, collaborating researchers (van Lieshout and Namasivayam) from Canada and Santa Fe, New Mexico, respectively, and their team recently completed a large-scale study of the effectiveness of treatment for children who have speech sound disorders that are characterized by motor speech involvement (SSD-MSI). Their study, which is the first one of its kind, has supplied the largest available data set to date related to the factors that affect SLP treatment outcomes for children who have articulation disorders that involve motor speech deficits. These include children who have diagnoses of childhood apraxia of speech. The Canadian provincial government has applied the data that this study obtained to develop new guidelines and to formulate and implement a motor speech treatment protocol for preschool-aged children identified with SSD-MSI. SLP experts believe that the results of this study can also be applied for establishing appropriate clinician and parent expectation levels before intervention. Moreover, they believe these results could provide guidance for clinical practice, such as the types and amounts of treatment that this population requires.

PROMPT Therapy

The **prompts for restructuring oral muscular phonetic targets** (PROMPT) approach uses tactile-kinesthetic techniques involving touch cues to guide clients manually through the articulation of target words, phrases, and sentences. This approach develops motor control and correct oral muscle movements and eliminates superfluous movements such as inadequate lip rounding, or jaw sliding. SLPs start with individual phonemes, stimulating all involved muscles through touch to train the muscles to produce a phoneme accurately. PROMPT therapy is applicable to a broad range of communication disorders, the most common being articulation disorders, motor speech

Copyright © Mometrix Media. You have been licensed one copy of this document for personal use only. Any other reproduction or redistribution is strictly prohibited. All rights reserved.
This content is provided for test preparation purposes only and does not imply an endorsement by Mometrix of any particular political, scientific, or religious point of view.

disorders, and nonverbal status in children. Additional clients benefiting include those with autism spectrum disorders, pervasive developmental disorders, cerebral palsy, brain injuries, dysarthria, dyspraxia, apraxia, and aphasia. Two researchers (Namasivayam and van Lieshout) are currently collaborating, with funding from the PROMPT Institute in Santa Fe, New Mexico, to conduct a randomized, controlled trial to evaluate the treatment effectiveness of the PROMPT approach for use with children who have speech sound disorders characterized by motor speech involvement. They want to test whether the PROMPT approach will produce significant treatment effects that can be generalized to all this population's members.

Orofacial Myology and OMD

Orofacial myology is the science of working with the orofacial muscles, i.e., the muscles of the mouth and face and typical and atypical variations in their functions, and the associated clinical knowledge. **Orofacial myofunctional disorder** (OMD) refers to any pattern interfering with the normal growth, development, and/or function of orofacial and/or oral musculature or calling attention to its presence. A few examples of orofacial myofunctional problems include tongue thrust, including transitional tongue thrust, associated with developmental/other temporary conditions; obligatory tongue thrust, i.e., caused by physiological or structural limitations; lip incompetence, i.e., inability to achieve a resting, lips-together position without muscular strain, or a resting, lips-apart posture; and deficits in airway competency, i.e., nasal passage patency. Factors affecting treatment of OMD include effective communication and collaboration of SLPs with dental and medical specialists; understanding of relevant applied physiology and dentofacial patterns; understanding causal and contributing factors associated with OMD; understanding basic orthodontic concepts; understanding how OMD and speech are interrelated; competence in identifying factors affecting prognosis; competency to select suitable criterion-based, individualized treatment plans; professional conduct; and applicable documentation.

Factors Affecting Treatment of OMDs

To treat OMDs, SLPs must understand the roles of dental and medical specialties and procedures in interdisciplinary OMD management; know treatment modalities for skeletal and dental malocclusions, informed by etiology; know how developmental anatomy, physiology, and cognitive factors affect treatment strategies; recognize orofacial muscular adaptations compensating for dental or skeletal differences; know dental development and terminology relating to orofacial myology; and have skills for interpreting/analyzing client orofacial myology data. They must interact with dental specialists in forming realistic treatment expectations and forming suitable treatment plans; recognize orthodontic appliances and procedures; integrate knowledge about current and future orthodontic treatment procedures into treatment planning decisions for individual clients; and communicate relevant clinical findings to colleagues in other fields. They must explain to medical and dental specialists how OMDs interact with speech; identify improper lingua-dental contacts in speech and whether they produce acoustically normal/abnormal speech; recognize how nasal airway patency, dental malocclusions, and abnormal articulatory patterns interact; and understand the potential impacts of orthodontic appliances on speech functions.

When treating orofacial myofunctional disorders (OMDs), SLPs must first ascertain the probability that improper myofunctional patterns will resolve or modify spontaneously without intervention. Regarding the client's prognosis for treatment, SLPs must be able to identify associated positive and negative factors. They must apply assessment results to total dental or medical treatment plans; understand the need for interdisciplinary management of OMDs owing to factors such as oronasal airflow patterns and their complexity; and identify and understand physiological and behavioral factors that affect treatment outcomes and/or client selection. SLPs must know how to eliminate related parafunctional habits and behaviors (such as sucking, chewing) affecting oral structures and

Copyright © Mometrix Media. You have been licensed one copy of this document for personal use only. Any other reproduction or redistribution is strictly prohibited. All rights reserved.
This content is provided for test preparation purposes only and does not imply an endorsement by Mometrix of any particular political, scientific, or religious point of view.

functions. SLPs must also be able to coordinate OMD treatment programs with other dental and medical procedures; when indicated, establish home-based programs as integral treatment components; educate clients and families regarding therapy goals and procedures; understand how family linguistic, cultural, ethnic, and educational backgrounds can influence treatment planning; and, as a part of the treatment process, establish criteria for discharge and recommendations for follow-up care.

SLPs treating orofacial myofunctional disorders (OMDs) must have knowledge about infection control procedures and other elements of clinical environments appropriate for providing professional services. They must recognize oral and manual habits, labial and lingual variations in posturing, nonorganic swallowing variations, and other orofacial myofunctional conditions they should include in an orofacial myofunctional practice. SLPs need to establish that creating, reestablishing, stabilizing, and maintaining an oral environment that promotes normal orofacial growth and development processes is the most important goal of orofacial myofunctional intervention. They also need to educate the referral sources with whom they interact about the nature and goals of orofacial myofunctional treatment. With the exception of SLPs who have credentials in the applicable dental and/or medical specialty areas, other SLPs practicing orofacial myology should NOT: provide nutritional management or counseling; perform craniosacral practices or manipulations; engage in practices associated with reducing symptoms of sleep apnea or other medical conditions; or treat parafunctional problems associated with myofascial pain dysfunction and temporomandibular joint (TMJ) disorders.

Treatment Goals

Internal Consistency

Just as internal consistency reliability in test instruments means that all the items within an instrument are consistent with one another, internal consistency in designing SLP treatment plans and therapy goals means that all parts of a treatment plan must match one another. This also applies to individualized education programs (IEPs), which school-based SLPs collaborate in developing (or primarily develop themselves and help teachers/others incorporate into daily classroom/school/home activities, when SLP is the only special education need). For example, data documented must match across goals, objectives, IEPs, and progress reports. Treatment goals, objectives, and progress reports should use the same specific wording as the evaluation reports and needs identified in IEPs. School-based SLPs should not introduce target speech-language behaviors into IEP goals/objectives that are not described in IEP present levels of educational performance. SLPs can obtain data to inform language behaviors to target in treatment from sources including the following: results of criterion-referenced tests and authentic assessments in initial evaluation reports, progress reports filed before annual IEP review dates in schools, three-year reevaluation reports if the timing coincides, data collected during therapy, classroom observations in schools, and parent/family/teacher interviews focusing on communication area priorities.

Criteria for Producing Measurable SLP Treatment Goals and Objectives

In keeping with all disciplines using behavioral standards, SLP treatment goals and objectives must involve behaviors that can be observed and quantified, i.e., counted or measured. Two ways of determining whether a goal or objective can be measured are the stranger test and the dead-man test. Goals and objectives pass the stranger test if someone who does not know the client can read them and arrive at the same interpretation of the target behaviors as the SLP who wrote them. For example, "misarticulation" would not include certain phonemes for children younger than the norms for articulating them correctly. Goals/objectives pass the "dead-man" test if they are not things that a dead person could do. For example, a target behavior of "not stuttering" could be done by a dead person. However, "speaking without stuttering" passes the test because dead people

Copyright © Mometrix Media. You have been licensed one copy of this document for personal use only. Any other reproduction or redistribution is strictly prohibited. All rights reserved.
This content is provided for test preparation purposes only and does not imply an endorsement by Mometrix of any particular political, scientific, or religious point of view.

cannot speak. If the SLP has a clear idea of which specific measurement task(s) can be administered to measure both baseline skill levels and progress in therapy, then the goals or objectives that the SLP writes will be more likely to be measurable.

Description of Current Levels of Performance and Progress

When writing the therapy goals or IEP goals and objectives for SLP treatment, the descriptions of current levels of client/student performance must include objective data as baselines to use for comparison in progress reports. When updating treatment plans for ongoing therapy or for clients returning to therapy or writing IEPs for new school years, progress attained relative to previous therapy goals/toward last year's IEP goals and objectives must also include objective data. At a minimum, components to report include the effects of the communication/swallowing disorder upon the client/student's progress in daily life and employment/general education curriculum; client/student strengths, and for students, parental input about student strengths; client/student progress toward each previous goal and objective, and the client/student progress toward each new goal and objective. Another optional yet preferable component is additional information that creates an overall portrait of client/student communication skills. Using specific given conditions when reporting current levels of performance, tasks selected to measure progress, and progress as measured by identified tasks facilitates more precise measurement of skill performance, for example, "Given A level of cuing in B activity, out of 10 trials, the client/student performed at C%."

Sources of Therapy Goals for School-Based SLPs

When school-based SLPs are developing goals for speech-language therapy that they will work toward with students and include in their IEPs, the following are examples of some of the sources they can use as the bases for goals: the SLPs' own judgments, informed by their training, experience, and language model; prereferral information, e.g., exactly why the student was referred for speech-language evaluation and the presence or absence of specific language behaviors about which the IEP team was concerned; parent/teacher interviews about the areas of student communication that concerned them the most; evaluation data collected for initial or three-year evaluations, including criterion-referenced tests and language samples, SLP probes and other authentic assessments; additional data that the SLP has collected during therapy sessions; observations of the student's communication behaviors in the classroom; and referring to school curriculum and grade-level expectations, particularly for literacy language skills required for successful classroom participation. Speech-language IEP goals should not exceed two to three specific speech-language skills for one school year; these should be the two to three that all team members agree are most important for the student to achieve that year.

More General vs. More Specific SLP Therapy Goals

More specific SLP therapy goals usually will be more useful than more general goals because they describe speech-language behaviors to establish, increase, or improve and speech-language disorders to eliminate, decrease, or ameliorate more precisely; and they have more internal consistency with evaluation data, data used in progress reports, and school IEPs. The definition of specific goals includes the following criteria: The targeted communication/speech-language behavior is defined clearly. This behavior should pass the stranger and dead-man tests. In other words, if a goal does not represent a communication/speech-language behavior that a stranger can observe and recognize what the SLP intended in describing it, it is overly general; if it represents the absence/elimination of a disorder or behavior that could apply to dead people, it must be further specified in the context of the presence of behaviors that dead people could not perform. Specificity also includes measurability: The SLP should identify a specific measurement task whereby the behavior can be counted as occurring/not occurring. As one caveat, school systems report SLP concerns that using specific curricula or tests for measurement make goals/objectives

Copyright © Mometrix Media. You have been licensed one copy of this document for personal use only. Any other reproduction or redistribution is strictly prohibited. All rights reserved.
This content is provided for test preparation purposes only and does not imply an endorsement by Mometrix of any particular political, scientific, or religious point of view.

overly specific. However, planning with specific measurement tasks in mind makes goals measurable whether SLPs name them or not.

Combining Areas of Communication and Goals Based on Standardized Test Errors

When writing goals for therapy, SLPs should not combine speech articulation behaviors with language development behaviors within the same goal. For example, the SLP should not use a criterion of speech intelligibility within a language goal. Intelligibility, which is affected by speech rate, pronunciation, and other issues related to speech sound production, is a functional articulation outcome measure rather than a language goal. Hence, SLPs should avoid using the term "intelligibility" in reference to any circumstance not involving articulation or speech. Language goals and articulation/intelligibility goals should be separate. When writing language goals for treatment plans and inclusion in school IEPs, SLPs should not use errors or error patterns identified in norm-referenced test results. Experts (see McCauley and Swisher, 1984) have remarked that norm-referenced test results can likely never be used "profitably" for planning therapy goals. Although identifying specific errors/error patterns on standardized tests can provide useful information for therapy, writing language goals based on them does not enable determining the priority of those goals; hence, targeting standardized test errors frequently fails the "so what?" test (Minneapolis Public Schools, 2009).

Receptive and Expressive Language Skills Should Not Be in the Same SLP Therapy Goal

Receptive and expressive language skills are frequently at disparate levels, particularly in individuals with communication disorders. For example, in school populations, a student's general cognitive abilities and lack of experience and background knowledge frequently influence their language comprehension. Also, teachers typically provide modeling, scaffolding, visual supports, etc. that address comprehension, such as understanding vocabulary words and following directions, in all classroom activities. Another consideration is that therapy goals should be observable, measurable, and specific in order to design therapy and measure progress; but terminology related to receptive language, e.g., "comprehend" or "understand," are not measurable and are ambiguous. (They are also not observable unless the goal is written to "*demonstrate* understanding/comprehension" and specifies the task, behavior, or instrument whereby it is demonstrated.) Instead of receptive language goals, school-based SLPs can consider alternatives, e.g., writing functional goals identifying verbal and nonverbal responses students must give for successful academic and school functioning. Another alternative is to document receptive language goals under "breadth of curriculum" sections.

Planning Treatment for ELLs

When planning therapy for English language learners (ELLs) who have speech-language disorders, particularly students and younger children even more so, SLPs need to take into account the client or student's skills in the native language. SLPs and ELLs should only be working together on speech-language behaviors that are related to their specific speech-language disorders, and not on speech-language behaviors that are related to their emergent skills for speaking in the English language. A general principle when including more specific objectives under SLP therapy goals is to limit the number of objectives to three under any one goal. Criteria for determining success in SLP therapy must be specific enough to measure and compare progress against them. For example, "The client will have conversations without significant interference from stuttering most of the time" is not specific enough to determine success. But "The client will exhibit dysfluencies in 10% or fewer of utterances during 10- to 15-minute conversations" or "The client will repeat word-initial phonemes in 10% or fewer of the words s/he utters during each 15-minute conversation" are examples of more measurable criteria for successful therapy outcomes.

Copyright © Mometrix Media. You have been licensed one copy of this document for personal use only. Any other reproduction or redistribution is strictly prohibited. All rights reserved.
This content is provided for test preparation purposes only and does not imply an endorsement by Mometrix of any particular political, scientific, or religious point of view.

Direction of Change, Expected Ending Performance Level, and Sequencing

The SLP should specify the direction of change for the client, e.g., s/he will increase, maintain, or decrease an identified speech-language behavior; a specific speech/language behavior or skill that the client is to change or learn through therapy; and the condition(s) under which the client is to perform the identified speech/language behavior or skill, e.g., given a certain environment, setting, materials, and/or level of assistance, the client will perform the behavior or skill. The SLP should specify the expected ending performance level by indicating "from – to," where the "from" component is the baseline level, score, or other measurement and the "to" component is a final level, score, or measurement that is the target of treatment. Criteria for successful performance and instruments or procedures for measuring it should also be included. SLPs can sequence short-term objectives by behavior, i.e., the only part that changes is the specific speech-language behavior to be changed or learned; by condition, e.g., the specific place or setting, or the specific level of support, is the only part that changes; or by criteria, i.e., the specific ending performance target indicates when the client has mastered the objective.

Treatment for Voice Disorders in Singers

Similarly, to the knowledge that physical therapists need to treat sports injuries to specific body parts in athletes, SLPs need detailed understanding of musculoskeletal anatomy and physiology to treat voice disorders in singers. Vocally, singers are also athletes who must sustain higher levels than average of phonatory strength, agility, and stamina for executing complex laryngeal maneuvers repeatedly. SLPs often collaborate with laryngologists, particularly in hospitals, to coordinate the management of vocal problems in singers. Treatment strategies, combining surgical and medical management with voice therapy, are individualized to the client. Therefore, it is essential for a laryngologist to evaluate the problem accurately first. The majority of singers ask whether structural changes in their vocal folds are causing their voice symptoms, and they frequently are surprised to discover that behavioral habits, medication side-effects, dehydration, environmental exposures, etc. are contributing factors. When pathology requiring voice therapy from the SLP is diagnosed, medical personnel must supply the SLP with relevant information about ongoing treatments, e.g., medical and dietary management of gastroesophageal reflux; use of inhalers for asthma; and use of nasal sprays for allergies so the SLP can evaluate progress in therapy within the client's individual context.

Among discrete vocal fold lesions experienced by singing performers, the most common are fibrovascular nodules, polyps, ectasias/varices, and cysts. Following thorough laryngology assessment, the laryngologist and SLP design the treatment. When structural lesions exist, treatment is determined in the context of the individual singer's vocal needs. Initial management of structural lesions nearly always includes voice therapy from the SLP. When the lesions are vocal nodules, surgical management includes voice therapy as an integral component. Ideally, the singer will have worked with the SLP preoperatively. After surgery, following voice rest—typically for a two-week period—patients are told only to resume actively singing after optimal healing is confirmed by postoperative examination and then to do so only under the SLP's direct supervision. When voice disorders do not include structural lesions needing surgery, patients are directly referred to the SLP for voice therapy. SLPs review stroboscopy examination results, receive other relevant examination findings from team members, and discuss with them any related medical conditions affecting the voice.

Vocal Emergencies

When professional singers encounter vocal emergencies, these can have significant impacts on their training and careers, e.g., if they develop problems during or right before an important exam, a major performance, or an important recording session. Emergencies include such things as severe,

Copyright © Mometrix Media. You have been licensed one copy of this document for personal use only. Any other reproduction or redistribution is strictly prohibited. All rights reserved.
This content is provided for test preparation purposes only and does not imply an endorsement by Mometrix of any particular political, scientific, or religious point of view.

acute upper respiratory infections and loss of control over the singing voice. Like sports athletes and ballet dancers, singers usually must resume maximum performance levels immediately. This indicates the need for SLPs and laryngologists to collaborate: The physician must determine medically whether pathology is present that would make continued singing dangerous, which in turn determines whether the patient must cancel or postpone a performance and practice complete voice rest. If the singer makes an informed decision to continue performing, the SLP and laryngologist help the patient optimize general management, laryngeal biomechanics, and vocal hygiene. Multiple voice therapy sessions and repeated examinations within short time periods, and hence scheduling flexibility and availability, are often required for management. Patient investment in treatment and adequate follow-up must determine treatment efficacy to enable timely adjustments in therapy when indicated.

Specialized Skills Needed to Address Details of Treatment

Because singing performers constitute a population with unique vocal needs, the SLP treating them must have specialized skills for identifying patient concerns and appropriately customizing the details of voice therapy. This is true regardless of whether the problem is observable more readily in singing or speaking. To treat the speaking voice, SLPs who specialize in treating voice disorders need not necessarily be singers. However, for managing difficulties with the singing voice, having formal training in singing is beneficial for the treating SLP. Music knowledge, listening skills, and other additional skill sets and insights that inform and expedite all phases of therapeutic management, especially during voice treatment, are afforded by having this kind of background. Moreover, for improving the process of transferring skills and/or knowledge, having the ability to teach the concepts underlying singing techniques and rehabilitation is equally as important as being able to sing. When an individual SLP's caseload is composed of several or many singers, this is likely to increase the level of singing skill needed.

Considerations for Choices of Appropriate Treatment

SLPs may apply varied treatment approaches, e.g., holistic or symptomatic, to improve the physical efficiency of a singer's voice use. Nonetheless, understanding which physical change must occur for treatment to be effective gives SLPs an advantage. For example, the SLP may hear patient throat tension but cannot determine its source by ear. Through palpation, the SLP may discover a posterior/asymmetrical presentation of the hyoid bone relative to the hyoid lamina. This can supply clues about specific muscles that might affect vocal function. Prior medical management determines the SLP's treatment choice; e.g., a singer who has had phonomicrosurgery versus one diagnosed with unbalanced/excessive muscular tension typically have different treatments. With surgical laryngeal alterations, SLP conducting postoperative voice therapy must be sensitive to both the need to adjust vocal function and potential psychological factors. For instance, voice disorders requiring only behavioral therapy are less likely to distress singers than those requiring surgery, voice rest prohibiting spoken communication, vocal conditioning, and uncertain professional futures. And within behavioral treatments alone, different etiologies—e.g., lesions affecting glottic closure versus breathiness due to functional muscle patterns—can dictate different methods.

Research Findings About Toddlers with Developmental Disabilities

In one study (Yoder, Warren, and McCathren, 1998), investigators wanted to generate prognoses of whether prelinguistic children averaging 22 months old with developmental disabilities (but no profound/severe motor disabilities) would talk within a year. Research staff obtained structured and unstructured communication samples during initial assessment, had mothers complete a vocabulary checklist, and measured maternal responses to children's communication behaviors during mother-child interactions. Communication samples were replicated after a year. The investigators defined children who could speak five or more different nonimitative words in either

Copyright © Mometrix Media. You have been licensed one copy of this document for personal use only. Any other reproduction or redistribution is strictly prohibited. All rights reserved.
This content is provided for test preparation purposes only and does not imply an endorsement by Mometrix of any particular political, scientific, or religious point of view.

language sample as "functional speakers" and those speaking fewer than five as "prefunctional speakers." Five variables measured during initial and subsequent assessments were as follows:

1. Number of canonical vocal communication acts (vocalizations including a vowel and at least one true consonant)
2. Number of intentional communication acts
3. Rate of protodeclaratives (using gestures instrumentally)
4. Communicative Development Inventory (CDI) discrepancy ratio, i.e., ratio of words uttered to words understood on this test
5. Number of maternal responses to child communication acts

After controlling statistically for the other significant predictors, only variables (1), (3), and (4) continued predicting functional speech within a year. Hence, intentional communication acts and maternal responses did not inform prognoses for speech.

Determination of Prognosis for Clients with Aphasia

Although with aphasia patients, a prognosis may represent only the SLP's best guess, experts (Knauff et al., 2008) have identified a number of related factors from research evidence by reviewing the current literature. Integrating these findings can guide clinicians in evidence-based assessment and prognosis for recovery. The factors they identified include age; beliefs; attitudes; access to care; motivation; depression; family support; handedness; gender; education; intelligence; the size and site of the lesion, if applicable; the initial severity of the stroke causing the aphasia and the volume of the lesion, if applicable; and patterns of recovery associated with different types of aphasia. Regarding age, it is a primary risk factor for having a stroke. Therefore, older patients are more likely than younger ones to have aphasia. Individuals with nonfluent aphasia tend to be younger, and those with fluent aphasia tend to be older. The recovery rate for younger patients is higher than that for older patients. However, the studies reviewed found an individual's age at the time of the initial onset of aphasia to be an inadequate recovery predictor.

In reviewing current research literature, some investigators (Knauff et al., 2008) have identified the relationships of various factors to determining prognoses for stroke patients with aphasia. Although handedness has not been found to influence aphasia recovery independently, left-handed individuals have been reported to recover better from aphasia than right-handed ones. A suggested reason is that left-handed and ambidextrous persons seem to process language bilaterally more than the right-handed, enabling better compensation for unilateral stroke damage. The reviewers report that gender does not seem related to aphasia recovery. At younger ages, more men than women have strokes, but at older ages, this does not apply. Two studies reviewed found slightly higher aphasia incidence among women than men; another found the reverse. Regarding education as a variable, studies do not show it has a significant relationship with recovery from aphasia. However, the reviewers also note that many other variables confound the effects of educational level, e.g., general intelligence, literacy level, amount of formal education, learning disabilities, socioeconomic status, cultural characteristics, access to health care, and psychiatric disorders.

Researchers at the Medical University of South Carolina at Charleston reviewed recent studies of aphasia secondary to strokes to identify factors for clinicians to consider in determining patient prognoses for recovery. In reviewing studies, they found that premorbid intelligence was not found to have an apparent influence on aphasia recovery, despite a general belief that higher intelligence before a stroke was a prognostic indicator relative to aphasia. However, the size and location of the lesion caused by a stroke were investigated in multiple studies and found to influence recovery. Less extensive lesions confined to the cerebral cortex are correlated with better recovery from aphasia. When lesions extend into the underlying white matter, studies have reported persistent

Copyright © Mometrix Media. You have been licensed one copy of this document for personal use only. Any other reproduction or redistribution is strictly prohibited. All rights reserved.
This content is provided for test preparation purposes only and does not imply an endorsement by Mometrix of any particular political, scientific, or religious point of view.

speech fluency deficits. Also, neuroimaging studies imply that better long-term prognosis for receptive language functions is associated with left superior temporal cortical functional recovery. Recovery of language comprehension skills seems to depend critically upon the strategic placement of lesions in the left temporal lobe.

Reviewing research into relationships of different factors to recovery from aphasia of stroke patients, investigators from the Medical University of South Carolina at Charleston (Knauff et al., 2008) identified variables that did not appear to influence aphasia recovery despite prevalent beliefs that they did, and others multiple studies identified as strongly affecting recovery prognoses, some in general and some for more specific symptoms. For example, handedness as an independent factor was not found to influence aphasia recovery despite reports that it does, which is attributed to more bilateral language processing in left-handed/ambidextrous than right-handed patients. Though studies did not show significant correlations between educational levels and aphasia recovery, the reviewers noted interference by multiple confounding variables. Studies did not find gender or premorbid intelligence related to recovery. However, younger age predicts better recovery than older age. Also, initial aphasia severity is associated with initial stroke severity and lesion volume in several studies. During both acute and chronic recovery phases, aphasia severity apparently predicts language outcomes strongly: Severe aphasia during early recovery stages has a poorer prognosis during any/all later stages.

According to a review of the literature (Knauff et al., 2008), a great many interrelated factors must be considered to form a prognosis for recovery from aphasia in a stroke patient. However, the reviewers identified factors that did not appear to influence aphasia recovery in any studies reviewed and others which studies identified as having definite relationships to aphasia prognoses. Among the latter, the type of aphasia was found to be related to different recovery patterns and prognoses in several studies. For example, patients with global aphasia and Wernicke's (receptive) aphasia who have severe communication deficits during the early stages of recovery have higher probabilities of improving more overall, but lower probabilities of regaining their premorbid functioning levels than those with milder initial aphasia symptoms. Patients whose speech/language functions are the most impaired have the most potential to recover through rehabilitative treatment. Although patients with nonfluent aphasia can progress to fluent status, it is not typical for fluent patients to become nonfluent subsequently. Studies also show that with any type of aphasia, the majority of patients have milder symptoms one year after stroke.

Making Contributions to Curriculum in Schools

Making unique contributions to curriculum is identified by ASHA as being among the roles and responsibilities of SLPs working in schools. In one example, a guidance counselor gives instruction in social skills to a group of students who have been identified as demonstrating difficulties with peer interactions. For some of these students, pragmatic language deficits contribute to their social interaction problems. The SLP works with the guidance counselor in developing lesson plans the counselor will use to teach social skills. The SLP also recommends specific activities that incorporate goals for pragmatic language development. Additionally, the SLP works with some of the students directly to intensify intervention with pragmatic language. The collaboration and recommendations of the SLP are valuable because both the SLP and the guidance counselor are professionals having expertise in social skills. Yet they are not duplicating the same services because the SLP has unique expertise in the pragmatic language underlying social skills; SLP consultation and recommendations enhance the guidance counselor's services. The SLP's direct work with some students who need more intensive intervention for taking others' perspectives, metalinguistic processes, and other aspects of pragmatic language accesses the SLP's therapeutic expertise.

Copyright © Mometrix Media. You have been licensed one copy of this document for personal use only. Any other reproduction or redistribution is strictly prohibited. All rights reserved.
This content is provided for test preparation purposes only and does not imply an endorsement by Mometrix of any particular political, scientific, or religious point of view.

Current research findings affirm that the language processes of listening, speaking, reading, and writing are interrelated, and SLPs have unique abilities to make significant contributions to literacy performance in students who have communication disorders and others who struggle in school. As an example, when a school district requests that personnel volunteer to work on a summer project focusing on aligning district curriculum with the National Education Association's Common Core State Standards (CCSS), an SLP makes an application to participate because s/he believes s/he can contribute significantly to the project. This is correct, because the CCSS contain a great many language expectations across all curriculum content areas and grade levels pertaining to vocabulary, morphology, and syntax. Because of the SLP's background in language, s/he can offer valuable knowledge, insights, and recommendations for aligning curriculum with the CCSS in the areas of language arts, literacy, etc. Moreover, participating as a member of an important school district committee can promote the expertise of the SLP profession in language and literacy, and it can also help inform other educators about SLP roles in the school system.

Providing Culturally Competent Services in School Systems

With American school populations reflecting increasing demographic diversity, SLPs contribute importantly to assuring all students culturally competent services. SLPs have expertise in differentiating language disorders from English language acquisition status, cultural differences, socioeconomic factors, inadequate previous instruction, and challenges of learning regional English-language dialects. Such SLP expertise enables greater accuracy and appropriateness in identifying student needs. Also, SLPs contribute knowledge about how linguistic differences and ESL acquisition affect learning, and they can help teachers promote students' educational development. For example, a student whose parents speak Spanish has tested out of ESL services and speaks English with his friends, but she does not answer questions in class, even very simple ones whose answers the teacher has given several times. The teacher suspects auditory processing and possibly emotional/social problems. In obtaining a language acquisition history, the SLP discovers native cultural expectations for children to obey and respect authority figures. The SLP's recommendation for school professionals to meet to discuss ways of working with the family and assuring the student's comfort with classroom speaking and understanding classroom expectations. Communicating these recommendations demonstrates cultural sensitivity and allows for cultural factors before evaluation for disorders is indicated.

Distinguishing Between Developmental Disabilities and ESL Characteristics

Consider a student whose first language is Korean but who understands and speaks English, and is performing successfully in academic school subjects. This student's teacher requests an evaluation because he does not participate in class discussions; does not initiate social conversations with peers; does not ask to participate in games/play activities; does not acknowledge peer questions or comments; demonstrates pragmatic inappropriateness in the few interactions he does have; and flaps his hands and engages in other self-stimulating behaviors. The school team wants to defer evaluation because of the student's ESL status. However, the SLP recommends an evaluation of the student. This recommendation is valuable because she recognizes the reported behaviors are typical of an autism spectrum disorder (ASD), and this possibility should be further investigated before school personnel conclude the behaviors originate from linguistic and cultural differences. It is true that students from Asian cultures are typically not as demonstrative in their social interactions as students in American culture; however, the behaviors observed in this student depart significantly from what cultural influences are expected to produce, and/or they are idiosyncratic enough to suggest ASD symptoms more than cultural and language differences.

Copyright © Mometrix Media. You have been licensed one copy of this document for personal use only. Any other reproduction or redistribution is strictly prohibited. All rights reserved.
This content is provided for test preparation purposes only and does not imply an endorsement by Mometrix of any particular political, scientific, or religious point of view.

Recommendations Between Different Settings

An SLP in private practice sends a report to a school SLP, recommending that a student that the private SLP evaluated off site receive two individual 45-minute therapy sessions. The report is based on standardized and informal test results, but not on classroom observations. The diagnosis appears correct, and the report is written professionally. However, the school SLP secures informed consent to evaluate the student and schedules a series of observations of the student in the classroom. After completing observations, the school SLP contacts the private SLP to discuss overall considerations for the student, educational implications of the student's communication disorder, how long and how often to provide services, and models for service delivery to meet the student's needs best. This example illustrates the importance for SLPs in different settings to discuss their findings about shared clients and differences in their recommendations. Recommendations from SLPs in different settings can differ because private practitioners frequently view service durations and amounts differently: they may not realize the unique service delivery opportunities afforded in schools and/or the school criteria for providing services. Communication enables participants' understanding of setting differences, producing recommendations in the student's best interests.

Communication of Therapy Recommendations to Parents

A school-based SLP recommends speech-language services for a high school student. The student's parent is concerned that therapy will interfere with time for classwork and questions how SLP services are relevant to meeting Common Core State Standards (CCSS). The SLP gives a careful explanation of how therapy goals are related to learning curriculum content. The SLP points out that the foundations of curriculum depend on underlying language skills, the CCSS include many language-specific requirements, and working on language development will strengthen the student's achievement in both high school subjects and the state standardized test. By communicating not only her recommendations but also their rationales, the SLP avoided trivializing and/or dismissing the parent's concern; explained the SLP's role of speech-language support helping students meet curriculum goals, giving a reason for services that made sense to a parent of a high school student; showed how speech-language therapy goals align with CCSS, helping the parent appreciate connections between speech-language therapy and curriculum; and, by recommending therapy, addressed the fact that students with language disorders have more trouble accessing and using curriculum's academic language.

Complying with Different Ethical Treatment Principles from Multiple Sources

SLPs and audiologists must have the motivation, discipline, and knowledge to recognize and avoid potential violations of ethical principles in providing treatment services. Typically, credentialing associations and professional organizations require practitioner commitment to adhere to professional codes or standards for maintaining credentials or membership. Although many SLPs and audiologists are familiar with the ASHA Code of Ethics, and some know about the ethical codes or codes of conduct of their state board of examiners, they need to be knowledgeable about both. Because ethics is such an important element of health care, most hospitals and other healthcare organizations have established their own ethical codes and published them for their staffs, to which practitioners must also attend. Hence, most SLP and audiology practitioners are responsible for multiple professional conduct standards at the same time, and these can both overlap and conflict. Also, professional standards of ethical conduct often change with time; for example, the ASHA Code of Ethics has been amended several times since its initial publication in 1930.

Codes of Conduct and Ethics

Although SLPs and audiologists would find compliance with professional obligations easier if codes of conduct issued by state board of examiners and the ASHA Code of Ethics were made more

Copyright © Mometrix Media. You have been licensed one copy of this document for personal use only. Any other reproduction or redistribution is strictly prohibited. All rights reserved.
This content is provided for test preparation purposes only and does not imply an endorsement by Mometrix of any particular political, scientific, or religious point of view.

uniform, this ideal is not a reality. Even though most states with licensure laws base their professional conduct standards on the ASHA Code of Ethics, the codes are still significantly disparate among states. Some states originally adopted the ASHA Code of Ethics completely or largely, but over time many of these states deviated from this basis. Such deviation is attributed to states' not updating their codes pursuant to ASHA Code updates or to practical or political exigencies. As a result, most clinicians are challenged with learning and applying multiple standards, codes, and rules of ethics that can be inconsistent at times. Four areas of ethical discourse commonly shared among different rules of conduct and codes of ethics pertaining to SLP and audiological practice are the priority of client/patient welfare; independent professional judgment or prescription; guarantees of outcomes; and the use of every available resource, including referrals.

Motor Programming Approach to Treating Childhood Apraxia of Speech

Childhood apraxia of speech is a disorder of the speech motor system. The SLP who understands this can find guidance in treating it through understanding principles of motor programming and planning. Although each child with a diagnosis of childhood apraxia of speech will have an individual profile, and hence will have different needs at different times while developing communicative and speech competence, SLPs must still ascertain what contributions to a child's overall speech difficulties are made by motor speech deficits, and they also must address other possible communication and language deficits. Generally, treatment methods following a motor programming approach include these main principles:

- Treatment should provide children with intensive and frequent practice of targeted speech production.
- Treatment should focus on the correct speech movements that represent the actual skills the SLP needs to train in the child.
- Treatment should include enhanced external sensory input. This means providing not only auditory cues, but also providing visual, tactile, and cognitive cues for speech production.
- SLPs should carefully consider types of speech practice, e.g., blocked versus random and massed versus distributed.
- SLPs should give suitable feedback about performance/results.

Treatment Principles for Intervention with Phonological Disorders

Three main principles for the treatment of phonological disorders are the following:

- The systematic nature of phonology is the basis for SLP treatment.
- Conceptual activities rather than motor activities are characteristic of treatment for phonological disorders.
- The ultimate goal of treatment for phonological disorders is generalization, which promotes intelligibility.

SLPs should consider these intervention principles:

- Work at word level for meaning.
- Aim for functional generalization.
- Treat error patterns, not isolated errors.
- If using a three-position substitutions, omissions, distortions, and additions (SODA) phonological analysis, transcribe complete words to detect error patterns.
- Teach phonemic contrasts applicable to the child's error patterns.

Copyright © Mometrix Media. You have been licensed one copy of this document for personal use only. Any other reproduction or redistribution is strictly prohibited. All rights reserved.
This content is provided for test preparation purposes only and does not imply an endorsement by Mometrix of any particular political, scientific, or religious point of view.

- Show the child how different sounds convey different meanings. Also, give parents examples of their children's homonymic errors.
- Show the child that creating meaning is the function of phonology by using natural/authentic contexts that are interesting and meaningful to the child.
- "Stack" the therapy environment with multiple examples of each individual target word so children can choose activities (e.g., for *keys* and *car*, have several different keys and toy cars).
- Choose targets with potential impact on the child. (10) Select examples of phonological rules/error patterns judiciously (see Bowen, 2012).

Principles That Inform SLP Treatment of Motor Speech Disorders

Prerequisites for motor learning are motivation, focused attention, and training in phonetic placement as prepractice. Conditions of practice include motivation, goal setting and target setting (what and the number of times), instructions, modeling, setting and people involved, and numerous other factors.

- **Practice schedules** and repetitive drills (motor drills) require many repetitions of target behaviors within each practice session to enable motor learning and then habituation.
- **Habituation** is a step toward automaticity in processing speech production. Reinforcing praise should not interrupt, distract, be too noisy, or be time-consuming.
- **Model reinforcement** for parents is select and develop appealing activities, repeatedly inviting children to produce target utterances.
- **Massed practice** entails fewer, longer sessions, promoting rapid skill development but less generalization; distributed practice spreads the same practice duration over more sessions, taking longer but improving motor learning.
- **Blocked practice** includes all repeats (trials) of each target (stimulus) in one time block, enhancing performance; random practice randomizes stimulus presentation throughout each session, enhancing retention and motor learning.
- **Providing frequent feedback** individualizes feedback, frequency, and specificity.
- **Production rate and accuracy** are inversely related to some extent.
- **Incorporating varied production rates** into repetitive motor drill practice promotes habituated accuracy plus, eventually, natural rates, prosody, and automaticity.

Treatment Principles for CAS and Intervention Procedures

Childhood apraxia of speech (CAS) treatment:

- Is founded on motor learning principles
- Involves motor, not conceptual activities
- Promotes intelligibility by aiming first for habituation and then for automaticity

During intensive practice trials, pair auditory and visual stimuli. Train phoneme combinations (consonant-vowel, vowel-consonant, consonant-vowel-consonant), not isolated phonemes. Focus therapy on movement performance drills. Use systematic drills/repetitive production trials as intensively as feasible. Use small steps to construct stimulus hierarchies judiciously. Use *simple* cloze procedures and carrier phrases. Combine slower production rates with proprioceptive self-monitoring. Constantly consider the prosodic contours of utterances; pair movement sequences with rhythm, intonation, stress, and other suprasegmental facilitators. Use whispering, loudness, and singing with appropriate judgment. Early in treatment, establish a few "power words" or core vocabulary, particularly with nonverbal/minimally verbal children. To decrease frustration and facilitate communication, language development, and intelligibility, use alternative/augmentative

Copyright © Mometrix Media. You have been licensed one copy of this document for personal use only. Any other reproduction or redistribution is strictly prohibited. All rights reserved.
This content is provided for test preparation purposes only and does not imply an endorsement by Mometrix of any particular political, scientific, or religious point of view.

communication (AAC) devices or signing; reassure children's parents. Because treatment changes with time, be flexible. Assign effective, consistent, regular homework as a given (within reason). Expect children to have good and bad performance days.

Treatment Evaluation

Reliability and Population Validity

Before implementing any treatment procedure, program, or product, the SLP should consider its reliability, about which it should make information available. The SLP needs to determine whether he or she can rely on the procedure to function in a consistent manner across repeated applications. The procedure should also clearly specify its applicable uses. The SLP should consider which population the procedure applies to, and whether its evidence of it validity for use with a specific population has been documented. SLPs should use procedures mainly with populations included in existing validity data. Standardization procedures should include the linguistic, racial, and ethnic diversity of populations with whom a program will be used when this is applicable. If validity data are not available for a population, the SLP must be able to justify the use of a procedure or program and document the limitations that generalization to nonvalidated populations is not supported. The SLP should look at a product, program, or procedure for clear statements of its expected outcomes, including supporting data that show its benefits to the targeted population.

Criteria in Evaluation Related to Supporting Research Evidence

The SLP should consider whether an assessment, treatment program, product, or procedure has been reviewed, discussed, and validated in any publications, particularly peer-reviewed professional research journals, which are the most credible sources. If training manuals, brochures, newsletters, articles in the popular press, or other promotional materials are the only published information sources about the product, procedure, or program, then the SLP should look for valid research data to substantiate any claims made in promotional publications. The SLP should also look for other peer-reviewed research that refutes or supports the claimed benefits or outcomes of a procedure. Consulting such research sources will help the SLP ascertain whether an assessment or treatment procedure has been found to be statistically reliable and valid. SLPs should consider the quality of research designs used, for example, whether participant characteristics before and after administration are clearly specified, whether control groups were used, whether participant selection was randomized, and whether the study was replicated with similar results. They should also consider the level of evidence, with the result being peer-reviewed research based on a series of studies that were well designed, have been replicated, and demonstrate client benefits.

PACE

Background

A trend in education has been to design and implement **value-added assessment** (VAA) to ensure intervention effectiveness. The focus of research into VAA, however, has been mainly on teachers. Hence, concerns arose that VAA as applied to SLPs had not been addressed. Assessment specifically to evaluate school SLP performance must correctly show the active, integral, and unique role played by SLPs, who collaborate with other educators to inform curriculum decisions, provide assessments and treatments of communication disorders and problems at all grade levels in all educational settings that are culturally competent and of high quality, and thereby enhance overall student school community success and achievement. Aside from relying solely on students' standardized test scores, ASHA reviewed a variety of measures such as teacher self-reports, portfolio assessments, classroom observations, student progress logs and other instructional artifacts, and principal evaluations. Of these, it found the most comprehensive, flexible choices to evaluate SLP

Copyright © Mometrix Media. You have been licensed one copy of this document for personal use only. Any other reproduction or redistribution is strictly prohibited. All rights reserved.
This content is provided for test preparation purposes only and does not imply an endorsement by Mometrix of any particular political, scientific, or religious point of view.

performance seemed to be portfolio assessments, observations, and self-reports. ASHA then developed an accountability measure for school SLPs, the Performance Assessment of Contributions and Effectiveness.

PACE System for Evaluating School SLP Effectiveness

ASHA's **Performance Assessment of Contributions and Effectiveness** (PACE) performance objectives and indicators are as follows: showing SLP and related (such as literacy) skills and knowledge; ethical service implementation; evidence-based practices; giving students engaging, effective, educationally and culturally appropriate services; partnering with school teams to determine special education eligibility and recommend services complying with federal and state regulations for IEPs; showing competence for making suitable, comprehensive evaluation of students potentially having varied communication disorders; delivering services using dynamic, applicable methods matching widely varied individual student needs; collaborating with teachers and other professionals in serving both special and general education needs of students; collaborating with families and offering them opportunities for involvement in their children's SLP services; earning professional development/continuing education units meeting ASHA and state certification and licensing maintenance requirements; and contributing to assorted initiatives at district/building levels.

Review Video: Collaborating with Families
Visit mometrix.com/academy and enter code: 679996

Review Video: Collaborating with Other Professionals
Visit mometrix.com/academy and enter code: 100351

Recommendations for Use and Implementation Guide Components

ASHA recommends that instead of value-added assessment (VAA) systems using students' state standardized test scores as a basis, schools should use its Performance Assessment of Contributions and Effectiveness (PACE) system to evaluate specific SLP contributions to student achievement. It encourages all ASHA and state association member SLPs' active involvement in advocacy for state/local PACE adoption and for state/district accountability system developers to utilize PACE. ASHA members can propose using parts of or the entire model for developing state/local SLP accountability systems; states can do so. ASHA also suggests that groups of related service providers may want to adapt PACE as an instructional accountability independent measure or integrated component for their school-based practitioners. Implementation is designed for SLP-supervisor collaboration. In the PACE implementation guide, the PACE matrix provides performance objectives and related examples of observational evidence collected during SLP therapy and portfolio contents. Performance levels for each objective can be recorded. The step-by-step guide suggests points in time throughout the school year for implementing components. The SLP toolkit contains the self-reflection tool, which helps SLPs develop annual professional development plans by providing professional skills corresponding to performance objectives; checklist copies for classroom teachers, students, and parents to indicate their satisfaction with SLP services; and a portfolio development guide.

Components

ASHA's Performance Assessment of Contributions and Effectiveness (PACE) system contains the PACE matrix, based on ASHA's policy document entitled Roles and Responsibilities of Speech-Language Pathologists in Schools and the PACE observation form and self-reflection tool. Findings recorded on the observation form and other portfolio components are evaluated using the matrix. In addition to the Performance Assessment of Contributions and Effectiveness (PACE) matrix with

Copyright © Mometrix Media. You have been licensed one copy of this document for personal use only. Any other reproduction or redistribution is strictly prohibited. All rights reserved.
This content is provided for test preparation purposes only and does not imply an endorsement by Mometrix of any particular political, scientific, or religious point of view.

performance objectives and related portfolio and observational examples; the step-by-step guide to help schedule PACE component implementation; the self-reflection Tool to help SLPs develop yearly professional development (PD) plans; and checklists for student, teacher, and parent SLP service satisfaction, the PACE implementation guide includes the evaluator toolkit, which contains the evaluator guide and observation form. The evaluator guide provides the rationale for using PACE to evaluate SLP effectiveness, including a chart aligning the administrative support recommended with each performance objective and indicator. The observation form is for recording observational findings related to performance objectives. The matrix should be used to evaluate this observational evidence. The PACE matrix is the evaluation system's foundation. SLPs and evaluators review data recorded in the observation form, checklists, self-reflection tool, and other artifacts included in the portfolio to decide performance objective ratings. SLPs can use matrix results to develop their annual PD plans. Additionally, the PACE web page offers a glossary of terms and the PACE framework, giving an overview of performance indicators, examples of observational and portfolio evidence, and describing administrative support associated with each performance objective.

Performance Objectives

One PACE performance objective is to show knowledge and skills in SLP, literacy, and other related subjects and to implement services in ethical ways. PACE portfolios contain data recorded on the PACE observation form; student, teacher, and parent checklists; and the PACE SLP self-reflection tool. Examples of portfolio evidence that the SLP meets this performance objective include documentation that the SLP passed a national SLP examination approved by ASHA; evidence that the SLP participates in high-quality, consistent professional development (PD) programs devoted to topics concerning speech and language; and additional information provided by the SLP. Examples of observational evidence to look for that the SLP meets this performance objective includes the following: The SLP provides services across a range of communication and swallowing disorders, appropriate to the setting and encompassing all student skill levels. The SLP fulfills PD requirements, including providing in-service trainings. The SLP shows oral and written communication competencies. The SLP adheres to all risk management procedures. And the SLP organizes work space equipment and materials.

In the PACE matrix (the foundation of the PACE evaluation system), the second performance objective is to provide students services that engage them, reflect evidence-based practice, are effective, and are appropriate educationally and culturally. Data collected in the PACE portfolio from students, teachers, parents, and the SLP that indicate SLP fulfillment of this objective include the following: documentation of observations by another certified SLP/other professional familiar with communication disorders and therapy of the observed SLP's therapy practices; self-assessment(s) completed by the SLP; teacher, parent, and student (when applicable) surveys; and additional SLP input. Observational evidence to seek includes the following: The SLP engages students in therapy activities; gives individual students appropriate, accurate feedback; promotes individual student IEP goals through the activities s/he implements; demonstrates good skills in behavior management; effectively and efficiently uses the time allotted for therapy; cultivates positive student-SLP interactions; gives every student enough opportunities to respond a significant number of times; develops and implements suitable therapy plans; integrates curriculum materials/objectives in therapy sessions; shows requisite knowledge and skills for delivering/facilitating treatment with children from linguistically/culturally diverse backgrounds; documents service types and progress evidence; and advocates for indicated services to students.

The PACE system's matrix provides SLP performance objectives and evidence supporting their fulfillment. As an example, the third PACE performance objective is to collaborate with school

Copyright © Mometrix Media. You have been licensed one copy of this document for personal use only. Any other reproduction or redistribution is strictly prohibited. All rights reserved.
This content is provided for test preparation purposes only and does not imply an endorsement by Mometrix of any particular political, scientific, or religious point of view.

teams to determine student eligibility for special education and related services and recommend services complying with federal and state regulations for students with IEPs. In the PACE portfolio, wherein observational, checklist, and self-evaluation data are collected, some examples of portfolio evidence that an SLP meets this objective include the following: Established through reviewing the IEPs of an agreed-on student case files sample, the IEP goals, services, and supports documented are relevant to the student's needs and the Common Core State Standards and/or other state standards. Documentation that a certified SLP (preferred) or other professional knowledgeable about communication disorders and their treatment has observed the SLP's therapy sessions. A survey checklist from teacher(s), parent(s), and the student when applicable. A review of student case files that shows the SLP completed all evaluation and IEP documents using procedures complying with federal, state, and local specifications within required time lines, used applicable forms, shared information with all team members, and offered teachers and parents opportunities to contribute to documents as indicated. The SLP's input is additional portfolio evidence.

In the PACE matrix, the third SLP performance objective listed is partnering with the school team to determine student special education eligibility and recommending services that comply with federal and state regulations concerning student individualized education programs (IEPs). Observational evidence that an SLP meets this objective includes the following: The SLP sufficiently prepares for meetings; clearly explains IEP content using language understandable to parents and other IEP team members; explains the relationship of speech-language goals to student curriculum success; develops comprehensible, measurable goals; responds suitably to other team members' comments and questions; appropriately addresses conflicts that might arise during IEP meetings; supplies evidence that parents and other team members contributed to the IEP content; explains the relationship of IEP goals to a student's present educational levels; uses appropriate forms to complete documentation within specific time lines; bills Medicaid and fulfills other compliance requirements accurately; contributes suitable information to student transition plans; uses surveys and checklists to solicit feedback from students, teachers, and parents about compliance and documentation; supplies evidence contributing to student eligibility determinations; follows the Individuals with Disabilities Education Act, Family Education Rights and Privacy Act, Section 504 of the Rehabilitation Act, and Health Insurance Portability and Accountability Act regulations concerning compliance and documentation; and maintains student records confidentiality.

The fourth performance objective in the PACE matrix is showing skill for performing applicable comprehensive evaluations for students with varied potential communication disorders. Portfolio evidence includes the following: Case files show that the SLP's comprehensive evaluations contain varied, appropriate standardized assessments and informal assessment strategies; test result interpretation designed for making suitable recommendations; family and school staff input; observational notes; student classroom performance evidence; and additional SLP input. Observational evidence includes the following: The SLP collects case history data, develops schedules that designate time blocks for conducting assessments, uses applicable formal and informal assessment instruments, observes formal and informal testing using varied assessment strategies, develops suitable evaluation reports, analyzes and interprets assessment results for making appropriate recommendations, and reports assessment results in a timely fashion. In addition, observations should show that the SLP has the knowledge and skills required to administer or facilitate the assessment of students whose backgrounds are linguistically and/or culturally diverse.

In ASHA's PACE matrix, the fifth performance objective is for SLPs to use dynamic and fitting methods of delivering services that match each individual student's needs within the broad variety of such needs. Some examples of evidence in the PACE portfolio demonstrating that an SLP meets

Copyright © Mometrix Media. You have been licensed one copy of this document for personal use only. Any other reproduction or redistribution is strictly prohibited. All rights reserved.
This content is provided for test preparation purposes only and does not imply an endorsement by Mometrix of any particular political, scientific, or religious point of view.

this objective include the following: A copy of the SLP schedule demonstrates how the SLP varies locations and frequency of SLP support services according to individual student needs. Student IEPs contain a variety of sites and frequencies for delivering SLP services. SLP self-assessment reflects fulfillment of this objective. The SLP provides any additional input. Observational evidence that the SLP fulfills this objective includes: The SLP designs a schedule that enables completing all work activities in effective and efficient ways. The SLP develops activities that promote individual students' progress toward their specific IEP goals. The SLP alters the direction, activities, and/or feedback of a therapy session whenever a student does not understand/cannot demonstrate success regarding that session's therapy goal. The SLP also records data about the student's performance during each therapy session.

ASHA's PACE matrix evaluation system identifies its sixth performance objective for SLPs as collaborating with classroom teachers and other professionals for students in both special and general education settings. Some examples of portfolio contents to demonstrate that an SLP meets this objective include the following: A schedule for therapy that includes services delivered within the classroom, samples of response to intervention activities that the SLP has performed together with classroom teachers, logs documenting sessions wherein the SLP collaborated and consulted with classroom teachers, documentation or other evidence that the SLP has shared IEP goals and goal progress with classroom teachers, classroom teachers' completed checklist evaluations of the SLP, and additional SLP input. Examples of observational evidence that the SLP meets this performance objective include the following: The SLP shows respect for teachers and other professionals. The SLP demonstrates active listening techniques with teachers/other professionals. The SLP presents his/herself with professional attitudes and behaviors. The SLP demonstrates coteaching or collaborative instruction. The SLP responds to feedback professionally. And at IEP team meetings and other meetings, the SLP demonstrates collaborative practices.

In ASHA's PACE evaluation system, its matrix includes the seventh of nine performance objectives for SLPs working in schools as offering opportunities for family involvement in school SLP services to their children and as collaborating with their students' families. Among the products collected in the PACE portfolio, evidence that the SLP satisfies this performance objective include: a copy of the completed PACE parent checklist that indicates the parents' rating of satisfaction with the SLP's services, materials the SLP has sent to students' families giving them ways to practice SLP therapy goals with their children at home, logs of the SLP's ongoing communication with students' parents, evidence that students' parents were asked to contribute input/suggestions regarding their children's IEP goals, and any additional SLP input. Observational evidence includes the following: The SLP respects students and their families, uses active listening methods, demonstrates a professional demeanor, responds to feedback in professional ways, and shows collaborative practices with families during IEP team meetings and other conferences. Parent communication logs and/or other evidence also demonstrate that the SLP communicates regularly with students' families.

The eighth performance objective in the PACE matrix is to earn enough professional development (PD) or continuing education units (CEUs) to satisfy both ASHA and state certification and licensure requirements. Portfolio evidence of this includes completed copies of ASHA's CEU Compliance form, state PD participation records, and the ASHA Continuing Education Registry. Observational evidence includes that the SLP pursues PD by completing in-service trainings; provides in-service trainings to others; and participates in state, school, or local meetings, conferences, associations, and/or professional learning communities. The ninth performance objective in the PACE matrix is for SLPs to contribute to various district- or building-level initiatives. Portfolio evidence of this includes a record of the SLP's participation in district/building committees, examples of the SLP's

Copyright © Mometrix Media. You have been licensed one copy of this document for personal use only. Any other reproduction or redistribution is strictly prohibited. All rights reserved.
This content is provided for test preparation purposes only and does not imply an endorsement by Mometrix of any particular political, scientific, or religious point of view.

response to intervention (RTI) activities, samples of presentations the SLP has made to school staff and/or parents, the completed PACE self-assessment checklist, input from teachers and school administrators, copies of materials and resources the SLP has provided staff, and SLP input. Observational evidence includes the SLP's participation in planning school assessments, on curriculum teams, in RTI initiatives, and in other initiatives for schoolwide positive behavioral support systems.

Research Findings on Dysphagia Patients

Medical Facility Follow-Up on SLPs and Other Recommendations for Dysphagia Care

From research conducted in 2003 to 2004 by the US Department of Veterans Affairs Office of Inspector General's Office of Healthcare Inspections (OHI, 2006) to evaluate how Veterans Health Administration (VHA) medical facilities were managing the feeding of patients with dysphagia, investigators reported findings on a number of issues, including continuity of care. They identified discrepancies between patient diets listed in nursing discharge instructions, which patients sign and take home, and doctors' discharge summaries. Some patient diet orders upon discharge differed from diets identified in the most recent registered dietitian's chart notes, or from diets that the SLP recommended. The researchers attributed these discrepancies to the facts that none of the VHA facilities studied used interdisciplinary discharge forms, which enable including input from SLPs, occupational therapists, etc. into nursing discharge instructions; and in all but one location, SLPs did not attend discharge planning meetings or interdisciplinary team meetings regularly. In one facility, researchers found incorrect discharge instructions about modified diets in four of six outpatient records reviewed. In each case, modified consistency diets were wrongly upgraded to regular consistency with no restrictions. In another location, a patient was discharged with a diet more restricted than what he ate in the hospital.

Follow-Up After Discharge from Hospital Facilities

Researchers for the Veterans Administration (2006) investigating dysphagia care at Veterans Health Administration hospitals found that of the facilities they studied, SLPs at several hospitals did not follow up consistently with the patients diagnosed with dysphagia whom they had evaluated for the purposes of assessing their progress in treatment and/or whether their care plans needed to be revised. They found in addition that when SLPs did follow up, they often limited their follow-up services to feeding management, and they seldom included swallowing treatment in their follow-ups. Regarding follow-up with outpatients, via medical records reviews of outpatients with dysphagia who had been evaluated by SLPs while they were hospitalized, aspiration precautions had been issued for many during their hospitalization, and most of them had feeding guidelines issued while in the hospital. Even though most of these patients received modified consistency diet orders upon discharge and a few still required crushed medications and thickened liquids when discharged, only 16% of patients for whom follow-up was indicated were scheduled for return appointments to see the SLP.

Inpatient Follow-Up

In evaluating dysphagia patient feeding management at Veterans Health Administration hospitals, researchers for the Department of Veterans Affairs (2006) looked at continuity of care. Regarding follow-up with inpatients, the investigators identified abnormal results of swallowing evaluations for 98% of the patients in their study sample. Yet of these, only 60% had documentation in their medical charts that SLPs followed up on their treatment. For 79% of these patients, SLPs had recommended feeding guidelines; for 67%, SLPs had recommended diet modifications. According to ASHA's position statement, dysphagia management by SLPs includes providing treatment for feeding and swallowing disorders, documenting patient progress, and deciding appropriate criteria for dismissal. While swallowing management, which can include feeder training, compensatory

Copyright © Mometrix Media. You have been licensed one copy of this document for personal use only. Any other reproduction or redistribution is strictly prohibited. All rights reserved.
This content is provided for test preparation purposes only and does not imply an endorsement by Mometrix of any particular political, scientific, or religious point of view.

adjustments, and dietary modification, does not remediate the dysphagia; swallowing treatment is designed to alter swallowing physiology. The researchers identified following up on evaluations wherein SLPs offered feeding guidelines and/or recommended dietary modifications as critical to improving patient results. They found mealtime patient observation a minimal indication to ascertain feeder guideline compliance and/or patient tolerance of new diets.

In research conducted by the Veterans Administration (VA) at VA hospitals, an SLP reported to researchers that because of limited facility staff, she mainly delivered diagnostic services to dysphagia patients but very few swallowing management or dysphagia therapy services. She also reported that unless the doctor reconsulted her to provide follow-up, she did not follow up with dysphagia patients. The hospital had designated one registered dietitian (RD) as the "dysphagia dietitian," whose duties included identifying patients with dysphagia for referral to the SLP, following up with patients after swallowing evaluations, and referring any problems to the SLP. The researchers found this system inadequate, illustrating with an example: Based on the videofluoroscopy swallow study (VFSS) results, the SLP recommended one patient be taken off *nil per oris*/nothing by mouth status. After the evaluation, neither the SLP nor designated "dysphagia dietitian" monitored this patient. The unit's regular RD charted concerns about the amount consumed orally being insufficient to meet the patient's nutritional needs. Additionally, even the patient communicated concerns about choking. Serious aspiration four days after the VFSS caused aspiration pneumonia in this patient.

Researchers for the Veterans Administration have found (2006) that among Veterans Healthcare Administration hospitals studied, while SLPs at some facilities documented appropriately following up with inpatients having dysphagia after their evaluation, at other facilities, the SLPs provided inadequate follow-up services. The investigators also found wide variability among dysphagia management practices in the hospitals they studied. For example, of seven hospitals, three had one full-time employee equivalent SLP for dysphagia management; one had three; one had 4.5; and two had less than one (0.63 and 0.25, respectively), i.e., the SLP provided services to those facilities less than full time. SLPs at only two facilities were allowed to post feeding guidelines. At four facilities, SLPs provided follow-up with inpatients after evaluation 100% of the time; 29% of the time at one; 25% at another; and 0% at one. Only two facilities had policies about follow-up. At one hospital, the SLP attended discharge planning and/or interdisciplinary team meetings; at another, the SLP did not; and at the rest, SLPs attended only "as needed."

Following up is crucial to dysphagia patient safety. Researchers for the Veterans Administration (VA) reported (2006) that at a VA hospital, an inpatient referred for swallowing evaluation received an instrumental videofluoroscopy swallowing study (VFSS) evaluation from an SLP a week after referral. Based on evidence of aspiration and other abnormal VFSS results, the SLP recommended thickening all liquids, a modified consistency diet, and mealtime monitoring. The researchers were told that the SLP was following the patient. A week after SLP recommendations, researchers observed a nursing assistant monitoring the patient, who reported that was only the second time he had received mealtime assistance. The investigators observed that the patient was given thin, not thickened liquids and a regular, not modified consistency diet. He coughed throughout the meal and could not chew the meat. The nursing assistant said she did not know whether this SLP was seeing the patient or of any feeding guidelines. After exiting the dining room, the researchers observed the nursing assistant leaving the patient to finish his meal unattended. This illustrates the critical importance of following up with dysphagia patients after SLP evaluation and recommendations: Staff may not follow/even be aware of/informed of feeding guidelines and dietary recommendations.

Copyright © Mometrix Media. You have been licensed one copy of this document for personal use only. Any other reproduction or redistribution is strictly prohibited. All rights reserved.
This content is provided for test preparation purposes only and does not imply an endorsement by Mometrix of any particular political, scientific, or religious point of view.

When studying the care of dysphagia patients at several Veterans Administration (VA) hospitals, VA researchers found practice issues with monitoring and follow-up. For example, they observed that one patient did not receive the recommended diet; had difficulty eating the diet provided; and was initially monitored at one meal by a nursing assistant, but subsequently left unattended during the same meal. Moreover, the nursing assistant denied knowing of patient dietary guidelines or SLP contact. The researchers found feeding guidelines posted at the patient's bedside, including detailed instructions for thermal stimulation (changing temperature to facilitate tongue movements and pharyngeal swallowing) before meals, and aggressive oral hygiene. Yet nurse charting documented oral care only once in three days. Furthermore, a past doctor's regular diet order was never updated for recommended modified consistency and thickened liquids. Upon return observation, researchers found the patient eating in the dark unattended. He denied knowledge of feeding guidelines. Researchers noted the patient's increased risk of choking/aspiration pneumonia because the doctor failed to implement the consulting SLP's recommendations, nursing staff failed to follow his plan of care, and the SLP failed to monitor him. The investigators informed the patient's treatment team of the issues.

Despite policies and procedures that hospitals have in place, errors in both recommendations and actual practices can occur. For example, Veterans Administration researchers studying follow-up and monitoring after evaluation of dysphagia patients observed a patient at one facility. Reviewing his medical chart, they found a registered dietitian (RD) note that the patient was at risk for choking. His ordered diet consisted of mostly pureed foods and some diced foods. Yet the researchers also found he had "a standing order for bologna sandwiches." (US Department of Veterans Affairs OIG OHI, 2006) They observed the patient ignoring his meal tray, eating a bologna sandwich and potato chips. They discovered further that this patient had never received a referral to the SLP for swallowing evaluation. The researchers asked why a patient who was described by an RD as at risk for choking was being permitted to eat bologna sandwiches and potato chips. They furthermore asked why, if this patient could eat these foods, he had a modified diet order. Their observations and questions resulted in immediate scheduling of a swallowing evaluation. Regular SLP follow-ups after abnormal swallowing evaluations, and interdisciplinary care coordination, are indicated.

Management, Monitoring, and Follow-Up

Investigators conducting (2006) research for the US Veterans Administration at Veterans Health Administration (VHA) hospitals found that all too often, patients with swallowing disorders are not referred to SLPs for evaluation; or after evaluation, SLPs, physicians, and nursing staff do not follow up with patients after abnormal evaluation results. They have also found that physicians do not always order the diets recommended by SLPs or that patients are eating diets other than those ordered for them. In addition, among patients who mostly were given orders for diets with modified food consistency upon their discharge from the hospital, including some who still needed their pills crushed and liquids thickened at discharge, of those for whom follow-up was indicated, only a minority of them (16%) were scheduled with appointments for return visits to the SLP. Based on these findings, the researchers recommended improvement actions by the Under Secretary for Health, the facility managers, and the Veterans Integrated Services Network. These recommendations included assuring the accuracy and consistency of discharge instructions for diet, making sure that SLPs' and others' recommendations from swallowing consultations are followed up, and seeing that long-term orders for dietary modifications are monitored for continuing appropriateness.

Healthcare investigators for the US Department of Veterans affairs conducted (2006) research in several Veterans Health Administration (VHA) hospital facilities into the swallowing management

Copyright © Mometrix Media. You have been licensed one copy of this document for personal use only. Any other reproduction or redistribution is strictly prohibited. All rights reserved.
This content is provided for test preparation purposes only and does not imply an endorsement by Mometrix of any particular political, scientific, or religious point of view.

and care of patients with dysphagia. They found that upon discharge, outpatients often received different diet orders than those given during hospitalization without medical reason, and discharge diets ordered contradicted dietary recommendations documented by SLPs soon before discharge. They also found after SLPs provided swallowing consultations and made recommendations, hospital personnel (including physicians and nurses) did not necessarily follow up on these SLP recommendations. Additionally, in some facilities, SLPs themselves did not follow up with dysphagia patients unless ordered to by physicians. The investigators recommended actions to assure correct, consistent discharge diet instructions; follow-up on swallowing consultation recommendations; and monitoring of modified diet orders, especially of long standing, to assess their appropriateness. The Under Secretary of Health agreed and supplied improvement plans. The VHA assigned a work group to develop guidelines for the documentation and verification of discharge diet orders, assigned an SLP task force to review evidence-based practices and develop practice recommendations for follow-up post-evaluation, and developed practice recommendations for monitoring diet modification suitability.

Monitoring Long-Term Diet Orders

According to dysphagia experts, after the SLP performs a videofluoroscopy swallow study or other instrumental assessment of swallowing, s/he should observe the patient at meals and conduct clinical examinations of the patient before orders are made to change the consistencies of foods in the patient's diet. This practice can prevent having patients maintained on diets, or changed to diets, that are inappropriate for them. For example, researchers found that after abnormal swallowing assessments, SLPs had recommended changes to diet orders for 67% of the patients in their study sample; yet in their evaluation reports, 58% contained notations that the patient required no further follow-up by the SLP. When a patient identified at risk for choking was discovered eating unsuitable foods that raised this risk, a hospital immediately scheduled a swallowing evaluation. They also implemented reviews of diet orders for all long-term-care patients. Additionally, they evaluated the documentation of rationales behind orders for modified consistency diets, e.g., dysphagia, poor dentition, or risk of aspiration. Researchers observing these actions recommend that other facilities conduct similar reviews to keep patients from being indefinitely maintained on unnecessary dietary modifications.

Referral Following School-Based Early Hearing Screenings and Tympanometry

Universal newborn hearing screenings are the standard today. To support this standard, many public schools organize hearing screenings for newborns, young children, and older children. For babies and children older than seven months, if observational hearing screening reveals repeated, marked lack of appropriate response on either side or orientation to the incorrect side, even with stimulus variation and a calm, alert infant/child, hearing loss should be suspected and referral for additional testing made. To decrease unnecessary referrals via false positives, screeners should rescreen and/or perform tympanometry or pneumatic otoscopy. Tympanometry is especially useful with young children for identifying otitis media, which is most common in early childhood, and the potential for resulting conductive hearing loss. Children failing tympanometry should be referred to medical professionals. Among tympanogram curves, Type A curves represent normal middle-ear function. Type As curves imply normal middle-ear pressure, but partial immobilization of the stapes ("stirrup"). Type Ad curves are related to ossicle separation or a flaccid eardrum. Type B curves show that fluid fills the middle-ear cavity. Type C curves represent lower-than-normal middle-ear pressure, which occurs with poor Eustachian tube function and retraction of the eardrum.

If tympanometry performed on an infant or young child, results in a Type A tympanogram curve, the child's middle ear is functioning normally and no referral for further audiological evaluation is

Copyright © Mometrix Media. You have been licensed one copy of this document for personal use only. Any other reproduction or redistribution is strictly prohibited. All rights reserved.
This content is provided for test preparation purposes only and does not imply an endorsement by Mometrix of any particular political, scientific, or religious point of view.

indicated. A Type B curve indicates a fluid-filled middle ear. Screeners should rescreen after one month. A repeated Type B curve on rescreening indicates referral for medical follow-up. A Type C curve indicates negative middle-ear pressure, i.e., lower than normal. If the negative pressure is more than –200, screeners should rescreen after one month—even if the child passed pure-tone audiometric hearing screening. If the same >–200 reading is obtained, the child should be referred for medical follow-up. A Type As curve suggests that the stapes are partly immobilized despite normal middle-ear pressure. A child receiving this tympanogram should not be referred for medical follow-up unless pure-tone audiometric screening indicates hearing loss. A Type Ad curve is a sign of separated ossicles or tympanic membrane flaccidity. As with Type As, referral is not indicated unless pure-tone screening shows hearing loss. Children with myringotomy ventilation tubes already inserted typically have flat tympanogram curves; because they are already being treated, referral is not indicated.

When a student/child fails a hearing screening in a school-based screening program, the school nurse and/or other personnel will refer the child for further evaluation. The referral may be to a general practice physician, specialist physician, audiologist, or SLP. If not only hearing loss, but also resulting speech/language problems are suspected/identified, referrals include to an SLP (as well as others if medical conditions requiring treatment and/or hearing aid/cochlear implant evaluation are also indicated). State education department authorities advise developing referral tracking methods. They consider it reasonable for parents to respond by scheduling evaluation appointments within two weeks of referral. If not, parents should be periodically contacted until referral disposition is known. Parents often hesitate to admit inability to afford evaluation costs. SLPs and school nurses can help by knowing about and offering community financial aid resources. Referral tracking should note referral date, parent contact date(s) and method(s), professional evaluation date, and follow-up results. This enables evaluating screening program validity, reliability, and yield. Identifying reasons for incomplete follow-up is also important to addressing causes, e.g., lack of parental knowledge/attention/financial means and/or available providers.

Students Who Fail Hearing Screenings

Referal

If a student fails a hearing screening, the school nurse typically is responsible for following up on their referrals for further evaluation. Some state education department experts advise ideally phoning or personally visiting parents before making written referrals because this enables collecting relevant information about the child's previous history and/or prior referral outcomes, assessing parental understanding of the referral, and determining whether parents have the resources and information for referral completion. The SLP should be prepared to explain screening results to parents of younger students and/or directly to older students, and explain the importance of following up with a thorough examination. They should help parents understand whether the examination requires an SLP, audiologist, otolaryngologist, and/or primary care provider physician. School nurses, or SLPs if school nurses are unavailable, should inform parents that hearing screening was not performed in a soundproofed/sound-treated setting, and they should supply written information about any school-based program screening or evaluation results.

Follow-Up Evaluations

In addition to explaining to parents what the results of a hearing screening signify and why it is important for their child to have a more thorough follow-up examination if s/he failed the hearing screening, the SLP should distinguish to what extent an examination is indicated, i.e., whether it should be conducted by the family physician, a physician specializing in otorhinolaryngology (ear-nose-throat), an audiologist, or an SLP. The SLP should explain to the parents that more comprehensive evaluation by healthcare providers may be necessary. On the referral form, the SLP

Copyright © Mometrix Media. You have been licensed one copy of this document for personal use only. Any other reproduction or redistribution is strictly prohibited. All rights reserved.
This content is provided for test preparation purposes only and does not imply an endorsement by Mometrix of any particular political, scientific, or religious point of view.

and/or school nurse should document the findings of the hearing screening, and also record any additional observations made in the school screening setting. School nurses often request written reports from professionals conducting further evaluations. The SLP's written report should include evaluation results and any SLP recommendations for school personnel regarding the student. SLPs can help parents by including information about needed services available locally, average per-visit charges, what to expect of evaluation, and advising families using managed care health insurance to contact their providers about covered services (including treatment) and how to access these.

Treatment

Speech Sound Production Disorders

SLP treatment of disorders in the production of speech sounds focuses on helping clients to produce speech sounds or phonemes correctly, in isolation and in the contexts of syllables, words, phrases, sentences, and connected speech. Disorders in speech sound production can result from problems with phonological processes and manner of using the speech mechanisms to produce sounds correctly. SLP treatment of articulation disorders can include demonstrating to the client how to produce a specific phoneme(s) accurately, helping the client to recognize whether sounds are produced correctly or incorrectly, and practicing producing specific phonemes in different word contexts. SLP treatment of phonological process disorders can entail teaching clients the rules of speech to help them utter words accurately. Intervention depends on the client's age and assessment results. It can address any of these:

- Selecting targets for intervention according to phonological and articulatory assessment results.
- Improving listening discrimination among phonemes.
- Improving phoneme production.
- Generally facilitating newly acquired phonological or articulatory skills in varied listening, speaking, and literacy-learning contexts.
- Increasing phonological awareness of phonemes and phoneme sequences in words.
- When developmentally/age-appropriate, relating sounds to printed/written orthography.

Traditional Approach to Articulation Therapy

According to experts (see Bowen, 2012), there is no one definition of traditional articulation therapy: Different people assign different meanings to it, and it can involve various philosophies and practices. Powers (1971), who described "traditional" SLP approaches to functional speech or articulation disorders, asserted that since Travis (1931) developed and described "stimulus methods," these have continued to form the essence of most SLPs' treatment methodologies. According to Powers, the first step is always auditory discrimination training: The SLP helps the client or child to identify, name, and discriminate a speech sound from other phonemes and then to discriminate it from others within increasingly complex contexts. Various versions, but always beginning with sound discrimination, have been described by many others, including Berry and Eisenson (1956), Carrell (1968), Sloane and Macaulay (1968), Garrett (1973), and Van Riper (1978). Van Riper described the "hallmark" of traditional articulation therapy as its activity sequence of:

1. Identifying a standard phoneme.
2. Discriminating between correct and incorrect forms of the phoneme via scanning and comparison.

Copyright © Mometrix Media. You have been licensed one copy of this document for personal use only. Any other reproduction or redistribution is strictly prohibited. All rights reserved.
This content is provided for test preparation purposes only and does not imply an endorsement by Mometrix of any particular political, scientific, or religious point of view.

3. Producing variations of the phoneme and correcting those variations until correct production is achieved.
4. Stabilizing and reinforcing correct production in all contexts and situations involving speech.

Whole Language Approach to Phonological and Articulation Disorders

The **Whole Language Therapy** (Hoffman, 1993) approach is designed for children with co-occurring moderate to severe phonological disorders and expressive language disorders. To give an example of the Whole Language approach, a typical therapy session would involve conversational interactions between the therapist and child, storybooks, and storytelling by both the SLP and the child, with incorporated modeling, cues, cloze sentence completion procedures, and rebuses that tell stories. The session could involve personal pronouns, question forms, and syllable-initial, word-initial (SIWI) phonemes. For instance, the SLP might read the P.D. Eastman book, *Are You My Mother?* to the child; the SLP would model pronouns, question form(s), and an SIWI phoneme such as /h/ that are frequently used in the story. Then the SLP would retell the story, beginning with brief utterances and increasing the length gradually. During retelling, the child repeats each LSP utterance and then retells the story if s/he is able, possibly to a doll, a puppet, or a toy character or an animal. Naming objects or pictures in themselves is not included.

Language-Based Intervention Approach for Phonological Disorders

According to Tyler (2002), language-based intervention for phonological disorders is based on the evidence that children with phonological disorders frequently also demonstrate problems in other language domains. Unlike traditional approaches, this approach may not focus on phonemic errors or target them for intervention because language-based approaches encompass all aspects of language. This approach includes various conversational, naturalistic techniques. For example, the SLP uses focused stimulation by recasting and expanding conversational utterances; provides scaffolding (temporary support, gradually decreased commensurately with increasing proficiency) for producing narratives; and applies elicited production techniques such as preparatory sets, forced-choice questions, and cloze sentence completion tasks. Although research does not demonstrate that such morphological/syntactic approaches to phonology are effective across all domains, Tyler states that language-based approaches do improve some individual children's phonology. Especially for children with concurrent speech and language disorders and highly inconsistent phonological systems, these approaches seem beneficial for improving both simultaneously. In collaborative and classroom settings, a language-based approach is also a workable choice. Tyler stresses close SLP progress monitoring to ensure the effectiveness of a language-based approach for children with phonological disorders.

Criteria for Selecting Phonemic Targets in Phonological Interventions

Eight traditional criteria for selecting phonemic targets in phonological interventions are as follows:

1. Phonemes in typical developmental acquisition sequence
2. Social importance is significant for the child to increase intelligibility and to avoid embarrassment.
3. Stimulable phonemes are easy to teach and produce, motivated by early success.
4. Minimal distinctive features show children their homophonic errors.
5. Unfamiliar words
6. Sounds sometimes correctly, but inconsistently produced

Copyright © Mometrix Media. You have been licensed one copy of this document for personal use only. Any other reproduction or redistribution is strictly prohibited. All rights reserved.
This content is provided for test preparation purposes only and does not imply an endorsement by Mometrix of any particular political, scientific, or religious point of view.

7. Patterns impeding intelligibility most.
8. Nondevelopmental patterns deviating from the norm most, disrupting prosody and sounding the strangest

The following are eight newer selection criteria for the same purpose:

1. Later developing phonemes or clusters for greater systemic change
2. Prioritize "marked" consonants implying accompanying features, including fricatives imply and generalize to stops, voiceless stops, voiced stops; affricates, fricatives; clusters, singletons.
3. Nonstimulable phonemes to make them stimulable, increasing the generalization likelihood
4. Maximal distinctive features to create phonemic opposition
5. Aim for generalization by working systemically with most linguistically marked, later developing, nonstimulable sounds least supported by phonological knowledge to restructure the phonological system.
6. The sonority sequencing principle, in other words, ordering phonemes by amount of sound/oral stricture.
7. "Least [phonological] knowledge" targets. (Research into this is controversial.)
8. Lexical properties, i.e., high-frequency and low-density words (having smaller "neighborhoods" of phonetically similar words).

Fluency Disorders

Fluency disorders include stuttering, which involves repetitions or prolongation of phonemes, syllables, words, or phrases and/or blocks in producing them; cluttering, which involves abnormally rapid and/or irregular rates of speech delivery; as well as the limitations in participation and activity associated with these. Some assessment results that inform SLP treatment of fluency disorders include the severity of the disorder; attitudes toward speech and the disorder; avoidance behaviors; dysfluency and secondary behavior categories; rates of speech; instrumental measures of respiratory, laryngeal, and oral behaviors when indicated; muscle tension; emotional reactions to speech or fluency disorders; and individual coping behaviors, in general and relative to the fluency disorder. Prognosis details and information for optimal treatment planning also inform treatment. To improve elements of speech fluency and concurrent dysfluency features such that optimal participation/activity are promoted, SLPs may work in therapy to decrease dysfluency severity, abnormality, and duration in multiple contexts of communication; decrease avoidance behaviors; eliminate or decrease barriers such as listener/parent reactions and client perceptions that cause, maintain, or worsen dysfluencies; and help clients communicate in social, educational, and occupational situations for optimal participation/activity.

For clients with fluency disorders, the SLP should individualize the treatment according to the individual client's specific history, characteristics, symptoms, communication goals, and the clinical milestones that the client has heretofore attained. Although some clients who have fluency disorders seek treatment by participating in residential, intensive treatment programs, it is common for more clients with stuttering or cluttering fluency disorders to participate in individual therapy sessions that private SLP practitioners, community clinics, and hospital outpatient clinics offer. SLP treatment for stuttering typically focuses on making dysfluencies less frequent, severe, lengthy, and abnormal in varied communicative situations; eliminating or decreasing related avoidance behaviors; eliminating or decreasing obstacles that cause, make worse, or sustain stuttering behaviors, such as the reactions of others and the client's own perceptions; and helping clients who stutter to communicate more normally and effectively in different speech contexts. In

Copyright © Mometrix Media. You have been licensed one copy of this document for personal use only. Any other reproduction or redistribution is strictly prohibited. All rights reserved.
This content is provided for test preparation purposes only and does not imply an endorsement by Mometrix of any particular political, scientific, or religious point of view.

treatment for cluttering, the SLP should individualize therapy to the client's unique problems. This may include goals such as slowing the client's rate of speech, increasing the client's self-monitoring of speech, articulating clearly, organizing language, using acceptable language, interacting with listeners, using natural speech, and decreasing excessive numbers and frequencies of dysfluency.

Review Video: Fluency
Visit mometrix.com/academy and enter code: 531179

Stuttering

When working with clients who stutter, the SLP's goal is more to minimize the impacts on communication of dysfluencies when they occur than to eliminate dysfluencies, which is often more difficult. SLPs can teach clients to identify their reactions to and/or coping with dysfluencies and to learn other reactions that promote fluency and make communication more effective. For example, if a client frequently exhibits physically tense, long-lasting dysfluencies, the SLP would teach him/her to modify these until they are fairly effortless and short-lived/momentary speech breaks. As fluency management in therapy improves, clients practice newly acquired skills in real-life contexts. Although behavioral strategies are typically fairly easy for clients to apply in therapeutic exercises, everyday fluency management is much harder in early treatment stages, requiring much mental effort. Because fluency monitoring and management is simpler in a therapy room's (ideally) controlled, quieter setting but more challenging in hectic, noisy classrooms or offices, SLPs frequently work with families, teachers, coworkers, employers, etc. about what to expect from therapy, including that expecting an individual who stutters to monitor and control speech fluency in all situations at all times is unreasonable.

Preschoolers

SLPs have traditionally hesitated to treat preschooler stuttering because

- Many young children eventually "outgrow" dysfluencies.
- experts believed that therapy increased young children's awareness of dysfluencies and hence the potential that these would persist.

However, the current consensus is that early intervention is helpful for stuttering. Nonetheless, when preschoolers have only stuttered for a few months, appear at low risk for persistent dysfluency, and seem unconcerned about their dysfluencies, SLPs still often recommend "wait-and-see" approaches. When they do recommend treatment, SLPs take somewhat different approaches with preschoolers than with older children and adults. For instance, the SLP may teach parents to give feedback as praise for fluent speech (e.g., "That was really smooth!") and *occasional* feedback as observations of dysfluent speech (e.g., "That sounded a bit bumpy"); to model fluent speech; and where, when, and how to implement such techniques. Research recently implies that these interventions are very effective to eliminate or decrease stuttering symptoms for preschool-aged children.

Assistive Devices

Various electronic devices have been developed to promote more fluent speech in stutterers. The majority of these tools change the way that the individual hears his or her voice when speaking. For example, a delayed auditory feedback loop is one method. The client wears a small earphone similar to a hearing aid, which records and plays back the client's speech in his or her ear a few seconds after it occurs. This is based on a hypothesis that in people who stutter, something has gone awry with the usual, natural auditory feedback of our own speech that we normally hear. The delayed feedback seems to distract the speaker; he or she may speak a bit more loudly or harshly

Copyright © Mometrix Media. You have been licensed one copy of this document for personal use only. Any other reproduction or redistribution is strictly prohibited. All rights reserved.
This content is provided for test preparation purposes only and does not imply an endorsement by Mometrix of any particular political, scientific, or religious point of view.

over the feedback, but also more fluently. Another similar technique is playing auditory feedback at a different pitch than spoken. A third method is introducing "white noise," a continuous masking sound into the speaker's ear, which blocks background noises and perhaps faulty auditory feedback. Research continues into why some clients benefit more or less from these devices, whether device efficacy can be increased, amounts of improvement to expect using devices alone or with SLP therapy, and whether device benefits can have long-term lasting power.

Orofacial Clefts

Orofacial clefts such as cleft palate and cleft lip are birth defects caused by the failure of oral cavity and/or lip tissues to form and close correctly during prenatal development. The results of these openings in the palate/lip include hearing problems, swallowing problems, resonance disorders, and phonological/articulation disorders. Infants born with cleft palates and lips are referred immediately for multidisciplinary comprehensive evaluation by a craniofacial/cleft palate team. Only a team approach can meet the needs of this population because of their multiple medical, dental, audiological, speech-language, swallowing, and feeding needs. Because ongoing changes in structural and anatomical relationships and facial growth and development—both rapid and gradual—occur during infancy and childhood, this patient population is followed from birth through late adolescence/young adulthood. Treatment often includes one or more surgeries to repair defects. The velopharyngeal mechanism separates the nasal and oral cavities during speech to normalize resonance and articulation of pressure-sensitive phonemes. Muscles in the velum and lateral and posterior pharyngeal walls perform this action. Absent/inadequate velopharyngeal closure, i.e., velopharyngeal dysfunction, reduces intraoral pressure and admits air leakage into the nose, commonly causing audible nasal air emission and hypernasal resonance.

Because cleft palate involves an opening in the palate, a common side effect is inadequacy or failure of the velopharyngeal mechanism to close completely. This closure normally separates the oral and nasal cavities during speech. This separation enables an individual to articulate pressure-sensitive phonemes and normalizes the resonance of the voice, i.e., how much speech sound resounds in the nasal cavity. When the velar and pharyngeal muscles do not close completely or at all, this is called velopharyngeal dysfunction. This condition permits air to leak into the nose, which lowers the pressure within the mouth, increases resonance in the nose, and can also cause audible air emissions through the nose when articulating consonants requiring oral air pressure. Resonance is classified as normal, hypernasal, hyponasal, or mixed hypernasality and hyponasality. Hypernasality (excessive nasal resonance), typically when articulating vowels and vocalized oral consonants, is most common with cleft palate. SLP treatment often concentrates on improving velopharyngeal function by eliminating compensatory errors, and on improving articulatory placement. SLPs may begin by using *temporary* nasal occlusion to avert snorting development and improve airflow direction. SLPs may also use auditory, tactile, and visual feedback to help patients identify nasal airflow and eliminate incorrect velopharyngeal patterns.

CAS

Unlike delayed language development, **childhood apraxia of speech** (CAS) is not caused by environmental or educational factors but by neurological and physiological dysfunction causing impairment in the consistency and precision of motor movements underlying speech. The brain's planning and/or programming of spatial-temporal factors in movement sequences is impaired, causing speech sound articulatory and prosodic errors. Recent neurogenetic research suggests that a genetic mutation in the brain's basal ganglia may be responsible for CAS. Hence, children will not outgrow CAS as they might overcome developmental delays. CAS characteristics include more speech sound errors corresponding to longer words and more syllables, i.e., more speech movements; omissions of many speech sounds; potentially limited variety in sounds produced

Copyright © Mometrix Media. You have been licensed one copy of this document for personal use only. Any other reproduction or redistribution is strictly prohibited. All rights reserved.
This content is provided for test preparation purposes only and does not imply an endorsement by Mometrix of any particular political, scientific, or religious point of view.

and/or persistently using the simplest, earliest acquired sounds (e.g., /b/, /p/, /m/); possible nasality; vowel distortion/inconsistency; and errors perceived as unusual compared to "normal" articulatory errors. SLPs vary in approaches to CAS, individualizing therapy and treating other co-occurring speech/language problems as needed. Clients vary in response to therapy. Apraxia patients typically need intensive, frequent one-on-one treatment. Typical approaches include speech imitation development, teaching speech sound pattern rules, work on oral-motor/speech sequences, increasing syllable pattern complexity and length, multimodal approaches, word-finding, language organization, and sometimes using augmentative/alternative communication systems along with therapy if necessary.

Dysarthria

Dysarthria is actually a family of motor speech disorders rather than one single disorder. Typical characteristics of dysarthria include weak, slow, or uncoordinated movements of the speech muscles as a consequence of damage to the central nervous system or the peripheral nervous system. This neurological damage to the brain regions and nerves that control the speech musculature affects the processes of speech breathing (respiration), phonation, resonance, articulation, and prosody (normal speech intonations). The strength or force, endurance, timing, direction, and range of motion of speech movements can be impaired in dysarthria. Observable symptoms of dysarthria include weak breath support; slurred speech; inexact or weak articulatory contacts (tongue, lips, teeth, alveolus, palate, velum, pharynx, etc.); low volume (reduced voice loudness), uncoordinated respiratory stream, hypernasal resonance, and lowered speech intelligibility. Treatment concentrates on specific speech production process components such as building muscular strength and control, increasing consonant precision, and making respiration more adequate for voice production. For instance, phonation and sound production to enhance intelligibility can be a therapy focus for patients with Parkinson's disease. When natural speech is unintelligible, SLPs may use augmentative/alternative communication systems to enable functional communication.

Language Disorders

The brain's use of symbols to communicate is a definition of language, as is a particular such system of symbols. Some common characteristics of language disorders include deficits in comprehending and/or producing spoken and written language. Language disorders can include impairment in language form, e.g., phonology (speech sounds); morphology (grammatical structural units of language that determine meaning), and/or syntax (sentence structure and word sequence); semantics (the content and meaning of language); and/or pragmatics (the social communication functions of language). Children can have language disorders secondary to Down syndrome, fragile X syndrome, or other congenital syndromes; meningitis, encephalitis, or other diseases; traumatic brain injuries; or hearing losses. Adults can have language disorders from brain injuries, strokes, and dementias. SLP treatment includes remediating problems with phonology, phonics (sound-to-letter correspondences), alphabet letter recognition, patterns of spelling and morphology, sentence formation, semantic content, and/or pragmatics in speech and writing. Working on print symbols, sentence construction, and meaning can remediate language knowledge and use for listening, speaking, reading, writing, and thinking. Treatment goals may include understanding and forming complex spoken and written sentences and developing self-regulation strategies to address complex demands of language and literacy.

Receptive and Expressive Language Disorders

When an individual encounters impairment in his or her ability to communicate effectively and participate in social, educational, and occupational activities because of a language disorder involving spoken or written language, SLP intervention is indicated. SLP treatment for language

Copyright © Mometrix Media. You have been licensed one copy of this document for personal use only. Any other reproduction or redistribution is strictly prohibited. All rights reserved.
This content is provided for test preparation purposes only and does not imply an endorsement by Mometrix of any particular political, scientific, or religious point of view.

disorders targets the improvement of the client's knowledge of language and use of language for listening, reading, speaking, writing, thinking, and reasoning. This includes helping the client gain or improve the ability to recognize and distinguish among speech sounds (phonology) and written or printed symbols (orthography) in order to understand and produce understandable spoken and written language. The SLP also assists the client in understanding semantic relationships that enable accurately comprehending and expressing meanings in spoken language and understanding the syntactic structures for formulating complex spoken and written sentences and conversations. The SLP works with the client on recognizing and formulating discourse structures to understand and organize spoken and written text. Verbal and nonverbal pragmatic conventions for appropriate communication in various social situations are another important therapy focus for language disorders wherein pragmatics are impaired.

Common Symptoms in Preschool Children and Potential Therapy Goals

Children with receptive language disorders can have difficulty following directions, answering questions, understanding the meanings of physical gestures, taking turns during conversations, and identifying objects and pictures. Children with expressive language disorders can have difficulty naming objects; asking questions; using physical gestures; combining words to form sentences; using correct pronouns, e.g., "they" or "she"; learning rhymes and songs; and knowing how to initiate and maintain conversations. Early literacy skills are also affected for some children. For example, they may have difficulty telling stories that have a distinct beginning, middle, and end; naming letters and numbers; learning the alphabet; holding books right side up; looking at pictures in books; and turning book pages. Although purely receptive or expressive language disorders (e.g., Wernicke's or Broca's aphasia) can occur, often secondary to localized brain injury, damage, or deficit; it is more common for young children to demonstrate problems with both receptive comprehension and expressive production of language. Some potential SLP therapy goals include increasing the child's language comprehension and use; teaching families, caregivers, and teachers ways of communicating with the child; and helping children use augmentative/alternative communication methods as needed, e.g., picture boards, speech-generating computer software, and simple gestures.

Advice to Parents for Building Young Children's Receptive and Expressive Language Skills

SLPs can advise parents to follow these ASHA-recommended language-building practices: Talking to children a lot helps them learn new words. Reading to children daily is crucial. Parents should point out environmental words on signs outdoors, in stores, at school, etc. to children. They should speak to their children in the language the parents know best. When preschoolers talk, parents should listen and respond. Parents should encourage children to ask questions and allow them enough time to answer questions. Parents are also advised to set TV watching and electronic media use limits and use the time saved for reading together and conversing. Receptive and expressive language disorders in preschoolers can include problems with learning new words; speaking words in the correct sequence; understanding directions, questions, and basic concepts; telling stories; and participating in conversations. Numerous (>200) studies find SLP intervention to be effective for the overwhelming majority of children with language disorders. Research also supplies evidence of the benefits of the earliest intervention possible. ASHA data find roughly 70% of preschoolers with language disorders gain one or more levels on functional communication measures of spoken language production and/or comprehension after SLP intervention.

Social Communication Disorders

Individuals with autism spectrum disorders, attention deficit/hyperactivity disorder (ADHD), developmental or intellectual disabilities, and fetal alcohol syndrome frequently have problems

Copyright © Mometrix Media. You have been licensed one copy of this document for personal use only. Any other reproduction or redistribution is strictly prohibited. All rights reserved.
This content is provided for test preparation purposes only and does not imply an endorsement by Mometrix of any particular political, scientific, or religious point of view.

with social aspects of communication including pragmatics, and they can benefit from SLP treatment. Treatment modalities include augmentative/alternative communication, i.e., replacing or supplementing natural speech and/or writing using unaided symbols such as gestures, manual signing, and finger spelling and/or aided symbols such as Blissymbols, picture communication symbols, concrete objects, and line drawings; computer-based instruction in social understanding and skills; and video-based instruction/video modeling for observational learning of desirable behaviors. The underlying principles of cognitive-behavioral therapy (CBT) are that cognitive events mediate an individual's behavior and that changes in cognitive patterns or thinking can promote changes in behavior. CBT combines behaviorist and cognitive learning principles for encouraging and shaping desired behaviors. When using CBT with child or adolescent groups with ADHD, SLPs should especially emphasize a variety of areas, including listening skills and social skills in peer interactions; apply active learning strategies; and provide rewards (reinforcers) for acquiring key learning elements.

Behavioral Interventions or Techniques

Applied behavioral analysis focuses on environmental influences to observable behaviors; environmental modifications shape behavior changes. Functional communication training combines functional behavior analysis of maladaptive behaviors' communication functions with teaching more appropriate communicative replacement behaviors. Incidental teaching maximizes naturally occurring learning opportunities and reinforces successive approximations toward desired behaviors. Milieu therapy integrates various methods into natural environments, including everyday activities, not just during therapy sessions. Pivotal response training, based on the idea that developing "pivotal" behavioral skills—such as behavioral self-regulation, the motivation to initiate social interactions, the motivation and ability to respond appropriately to environmental and social stimuli, and being able to respond to multiple cues—leads to corresponding improvements in behavior. Positive behavioral support uses functional behavior analysis of maladaptive behaviors to focus on the relationship between communication and challenging behaviors. By integrating person-centered/client-centered values with applied behavior analysis principles, positive supports and responses for cultivating adaptive skills and behaviors replace maladaptive behaviors.

Social communication, emotional regulation, and transactional support is a service delivery model (not a specific treatment program) that is focused on strategies for self-regulating emotions and communicating with others. Social scripts is a prompting strategy for teaching children to use variety in language during social interactions. SLPs provide scripted visual and/or verbal prompts, which they gradually remove as children achieve more spontaneous use. Social skills groups are typically composed of two to eight individuals who have social communication disorders and an adult facilitator/teacher. In these groups, the teacher/facilitator uses instruction, role-playing, and feedback to teach members ways to interact appropriately with their typically developing peers. Social Stories™ is a very structured intervention method that explains social situations to children through telling/reading them stories, and it helps them to learn socially appropriate responses and behaviors. This intervention was originally developed for therapy with children who have autism spectrum disorders (ASDs), and it is now being applied to help children with other disorders. The SCORE skills strategy, a social skills program, is conducted in small cooperative groups, focusing on five social skills: **S**hare ideas, **C**ompliment others, **O**ffer help and encouragement, **R**ecommend changes nicely, and **E**xercise self-control.

The Denver Model, a play-based treatment approach, uses intensive one-on-one therapy, social peer interactions in school settings, and home-based instruction to develop children's social communication skills. In parent-mediated/parent-implemented interventions, parents apply

Copyright © Mometrix Media. You have been licensed one copy of this document for personal use only. Any other reproduction or redistribution is strictly prohibited. All rights reserved.
This content is provided for test preparation purposes only and does not imply an endorsement by Mometrix of any particular political, scientific, or religious point of view.

individualized, direct intervention practices that SLPs may teach them with their children to augment positive learning opportunities and skills acquisition. Research finds these effective with attention deficit/hyperactivity disorder and autism spectrum disorder (ASD) populations. In peer-mediated/peer-implemented interventions, the SLP teaches strategies for facilitating social and play interactions to children with social communication disorders. These strategies have been found to be effective with ASD and intellectual/developmental disability populations. Relationship-based interventions support child-parent bonds. For example, the Interdisciplinary Council on Development and Learning's DIRFloortime model encourages children to interact through playing with parents and others, focusing on challenging children to be spontaneous and creative; engaging the child's senses, motor skills, and feelings; and following the child's lead. Research supports relationship-based treatments for increasing social communication skills in ASD populations. Treatment and Education of Autistic and Related Communication Handicapped Children, a university-based system of regional community centers, offers diagnostic evaluations, social play and recreation groups, individual counseling, parent support and training groups, supported employment, and other clinical services.

Cognitive-Communication Disorders

Communication necessarily involves complex interaction among cognition (thinking), language, and speech processes. Cognitive-communication disorders result from cognitive deficits affecting all or any of these areas involved in communication: attention, visual-spatial neglect (visual field impairment), memory, reasoning, organization, planning, and problem-solving skills. Deficits in these areas have adverse impacts on communication because they reduce an individual's ability to comprehend spoken/written language, to express needs, wants, thoughts, and feelings in spoken/written language; and to interpret and use verbal and nonverbal communication during social interactions, i.e., pragmatics. Damage to the right hemisphere of the brain, which is often sustained secondary to a cerebrovascular accident or stroke (i.e., either the blood released by a hemorrhage destroys/damages brain tissue in hemorrhagic stroke, or blood flow to a part of the brain is interrupted due to a blocked artery in ischemic stroke), can cause cognitive-communication disorders. Traumatic brain injuries often cause cognitive-communication disorders. Encephalopathy, other diseases, and other neurological injuries or insults can also cause cognitive-communication deficits.

Deficits Targeted in Treatment

SLPs providing intervention services to clients with cognitive-communication disorders work to remediate difficulties with being able to perceive, attend to, organize, and retain information; to reason; to solve problems; and to exercise self-regulating or executive control over cognitive, linguistic, and social interaction functioning. Treatment is informed by assessment, which identifies specific deficits, skills preserved, and comparative strength areas. Intervention then addresses the deficits and uses the strengths and maintained abilities identified to enable maximum safety; independent functioning; and effective, efficient communication skills. For example, the SLP may concentrate on helping the client develop memory strategies to compensate for retention deficits, formal problem-solving strategies and how to apply these in functional activities, and enhancing attentional skills at different complexity levels. SLP treatment for cognitive-communication disorders may also be focused on enhancing the client's ability to process various kinds of information, e.g., verbal, nonverbal, and social cues. Because they frequently coincide with/within cognitive-communication disorders, SLPs may also address reading comprehension, language formation, and other specific language impairments during treatment.

Copyright © Mometrix Media. You have been licensed one copy of this document for personal use only. Any other reproduction or redistribution is strictly prohibited. All rights reserved.
This content is provided for test preparation purposes only and does not imply an endorsement by Mometrix of any particular political, scientific, or religious point of view.

KNOWLEDGE NEEDED TO TREAT COGNITIVE-COMMUNICATION DISORDERS

SLPs need knowledge of: Individual service needs (e.g., admission, delivery types, discharge, and follow-up) according to environment, personal characteristics, and support systems; intervention models, including impairment-oriented approaches such as training distinct cognitive processes and activity/participation-oriented approaches such as teaching specific functional skills; specific intervention strategies; impacts of environmental and personal context factors on cognitive-communication; impacts of neuropharmacology on cognitive-communication; differential diagnosis of cognitive, language, and speech characteristics of developmental versus acquired communication disorders; implications of specific diagnostic categories for prognosis; impact of medical treatments, context, and other factors on applying intervention strategies; least restrictive environment laws; potential effects of insufficient/excessive restrictiveness; evaluation criteria regarding evidence supporting intervention methods; comprehensive treatment plan components; characteristics and applications of available intervention materials; procedures to improve communication partners' interactive competencies and support behaviors in varied settings; characteristics and applications of available technologies; behavior modification and management principles; service delivery models; group dynamics; group intervention techniques; learning and transfer/generalization principles and theories; treatment effect maintenance and generalization facilitation and measurement methods; follow-up procedures; effective transition procedures; treatment efficacy; individual and program outcome measurement methods; family systems theory; disability impacts on individuals, families, and others; counseling principles and techniques; referral criteria; and current policies and practices for reimbursement.

SKILLS NEEDED TO TREAT COGNITIVE-COMMUNICATION DISORDERS

According to ASHA, some of the skills that SLPs need for treating cognitive-communication disorders include the following: clinical decision making that applies suitable admission, discharge, and follow-up criteria; identifying and implementing applicable treatment approaches for specific clinical populations and individuals, including training separate cognitive processes and other impairment-oriented approaches and teaching specified functional skills and other activity-/participation-oriented approaches; evaluating and choosing suitable treatment materials and programs; recognizing impacts on intervention strategy application of context and accordingly modifying environments, tasks, and others' support behaviors in pertinent settings; evaluating evidence supporting treatment strategies; developing comprehensive treatment plans, including identifying and prioritizing goals, goal-attack strategies, objectives, procedures, activities, and coordination with other agencies and services; evaluating and applying available therapy materials, and developing new materials when necessary; improving communication partners' interactive competencies and support behaviors in varied environments; applying AAC systems, computer-assisted intervention, organization and memory aids, and other applicable technologies; and applying the principles of applied behavior analysis and behavior modification.

In addition to many others, SLPs must have the following skills in order to treat cognitive-communication disorders, according to ASHA: Be able to choose appropriate service delivery models, e.g., in the classroom, pull-out sessions, individual therapy, group therapy, collaborative, consultative, home-based, or workplace-based, and modify these as required; choose suitable therapy settings that are compatible with legal requirements to provide services in the least restrictive environment according to individual needs, such as inclusive classrooms and workplaces; provide effective group therapy interventions; promote and measure the maintenance and generalization of treatment effects; document the results of therapy; evaluate the effectiveness and efficacy of treatment targeting impairment-oriented and activity-/participation-oriented goals and objectives across a range of different contexts; evaluate treatment programs; deliver effective follow-up services after clients have been discharged; provide services to promote seamless

Copyright © Mometrix Media. You have been licensed one copy of this document for personal use only. Any other reproduction or redistribution is strictly prohibited. All rights reserved.
This content is provided for test preparation purposes only and does not imply an endorsement by Mometrix of any particular political, scientific, or religious point of view.

transitions among settings (e.g., school-to-work, hospital-to-community); train frequent communication partners, including teachers, employers, caregivers, and family members, in techniques to facilitate everyday functional communication; counsel clients, family, and others about cognitive-communication intervention and related domains; make indicated referrals; and apply current formats, policies, and procedures for reimbursement.

AAC and SGD as Treatment Methods for Communication Disorders

An augmentative or alternative communication (AAC) system is any combination of aids, devices, strategies, techniques, and/or symbols that provide an alternative modality of communicating by augmenting and/or representing spoken and/or written language for individuals who are unable to communicate using conventional methods of speech and writing. SLPs provide intervention services to help clients understand and use personalized AAC systems in order for them to achieve optimal activities and participation in communication. In addition, SLPs provide services for repairing or modifying AAC systems as needed. A speech-generating device (SGD) is one type of AAC device that enables an electronically generated voice and output of audible, understandable speech. Insurers typically classify SGDs and AAC devices as durable medical equipment. Before delivering an SGD or AAC, the SLP must formally evaluate the client's cognitive and communicative skills. Some of the minimally required elements include the type, severity, and anticipated course of the current communication impairment; cognitive and linguistic abilities; whether daily client communication needs could be met equally effectively using natural communication modes; expected functional communication goals to achieve; and treatment options.

Prerequisite Elements to Assess and Plan Before Beginning Treatment

In addition to the client's current communication impairment type, severity, and expected course; client cognitive and language skills; ruling in/out any other, natural communication modalities that could meet daily client communication needs equally well; functional communication goals; and treatment options, before a client receives an augmentative/alternative communication (AAC) device/system or speech-generating device (SGD), the SLP must also provide a rationale for selecting a specific device, accessories, and/or software; show the existence of a treatment plan including a training schedule for the device chosen; and state that the client has the physical and cognitive skills to use the device selected and any accessories or software for communicating. To upgrade, replace, or change previously provided AACs or SGDs, accessories, or software, the SLP must provide information about the upgrade/replacement/change's functional benefit to the client relative to the originally provided AAC/SGD. Additional prerequisites include that the client's medical condition causes a severe voice, speech, language, or other communication impairment; the client's communication needs cannot be as effectively met using natural communication modes; other treatments have been ruled out as less effective; and the recommended device/system will improve client communication.

SLP Duties

The individual client's chronological age, developmental stage, and other life circumstances will determine the specific elements of SLP intervention involving AAC devices. In accordance with these factors, the intervention that the SLP provides can include the following duties: The SLP educates the client, family, caregivers, and others involved in the client's communication and/or treatment about the operation of the selected AAC system and demonstrates how to operate it. The SLP plans for optimizing the client's use of the AAC system, which includes educating the client, family, and/or caregivers in the system's maintenance, programming updates, and modifications for use in academic, conversational, and other contexts. The SLP may include using the AAC system during therapeutic activities for achieving communication and spoken/written speech-language goals and objectives in natural voice, speech, vocabulary, sentence comprehension, sentence

Copyright © Mometrix Media. You have been licensed one copy of this document for personal use only. Any other reproduction or redistribution is strictly prohibited. All rights reserved.
This content is provided for test preparation purposes only and does not imply an endorsement by Mometrix of any particular political, scientific, or religious point of view.

production, reading, writing, conversational turn taking, judging listener needs, and others according to client age, abilities, and participation/activity needs. The SLP may also provide services for using the AAC system for social, educational, occupational, and other multiple functions and contexts.

Types and Characteristics of Devices Considered as SGDs or AAC s for Purpose of Insurance Coverage

Although some speech-generating devices (SGDs) and/or augmentative/alternative communication (AAC) devices or systems have been designed as dedicated speech devices, this design is not necessary for insurers to consider covering products related to using AAC devices in SLP therapy and to facilitate or enable communication. For example, computers, tablets, or other devices that can run word processing programs, accounting programs, and/or serve other nonmedical functions can be considered for health insurance coverage under the same criteria as dedicated SGDs or AAC devices or systems. Software that is designed to facilitate communication through enabling a computer, a personal digital assistant (PDA), or any other device to function as an SGD will also be considered for coverage under these same criteria. PDAs, desktop computers, laptop computers, iPads, other brands of tablet devices, and similar commercial products that can be programmed to perform the same functions as an SGD satisfy the insurer definition of durable medical equipment used for SGDs and AAC systems and devices. Hence, these can also be considered for insurance coverage purposes as SGDs.

AR Services

The SLP conducts aural rehabilitation (AR) assessment in order to evaluate the impacts of hearing loss upon a client's communication strengths, weaknesses, and functioning. This includes identifying any speech, language, and/or communication impairments. These often co-occur with hearing loss because of the highly auditory basis of normal spoken and written language. SLPs provide AR treatment for the purposes of improving the communication skills of a client who has a hearing loss. This treatment includes focusing on the client's receptive comprehension and expressive production of oral, written, or signed language; client voice and speech production; providing auditory training to the client, which is necessary for clients lacking experience with hearing spoken language; instructing the client in speech reading; providing the client with multimodal training that accesses visual, tactile, and auditory-visual channels; providing communication strategies for the client to use; educating the client and her/his significant others; and providing related counseling. Examples of AR services, in addition to auditory training and speech reading, include early intervention programs for infants and young children. Audiologists provide all of the above services that SLPs provide; additionally they provide hearing aid fitting and cochlear implant programming services.

Significant hearing losses commonly cause speech, language, and/or communication impairments. AR treatment addresses the client's hearing and speech-language-communication impairments; the restrictions on participation, limitations on activities, and potential personal and environmental factors that can have impacts on the communication, functioning, health, and well-being of individuals with hearing loss. Treatment entails compensating as much as possible for the hearing loss, which may include recommending that the client be fitted for a hearing aid or receive a cochlear implant. Hearing aids can help clients with either conductive or sensorineural hearing losses, provided the loss is not profound, by electronically amplifying the sounds received. Profoundly deaf individuals, who cannot hear sounds even with hearing aids, benefit from cochlear implantation. An external microphone and processor collect sound signals in place of the outer ear and convert them to electrical impulses, bypassing the middle ear' transmit these impulses electromagnetically from an external coil; through the skin to an internal coil, which connects to

Copyright © Mometrix Media. You have been licensed one copy of this document for personal use only. Any other reproduction or redistribution is strictly prohibited. All rights reserved.
This content is provided for test preparation purposes only and does not imply an endorsement by Mometrix of any particular political, scientific, or religious point of view.

electrodes implanted in the cochlea, which send electrical signals directly to the auditory nerve, thereby stimulating it.

Hearing loss is considered the most common birth defect in the U.S, affecting up to 3 of every 1,000 newborns. Because the first few months of life are critical to language development, hearing loss that is congenital or has prelingual (before speech and language development) onset significantly affects communication development during infancy and early childhood. Because being unable to hear speech sounds clearly/at all has a direct impact on speech, language, and communication skills development, early detection of hearing loss and intervention to remediate the loss decreases the adverse effects of hearing loss. Even a mild hearing loss can delay a young child's speech and language development. This makes AR treatment vital for babies and young children. AR treatment also benefits older children and adults by improving their receptive and expressive communication abilities. Although choosing, fitting, and evaluating hearing aids/cochlear implants/other amplification devices for clients of all ages is the audiologist's job, audiologists and SLPs are equally qualified to provide AR services to clients with hearing loss. Because cochlear implant recipients must learn different ways to process sounds and maximize device effectiveness, intensive AR services benefit them.

Childhood Hearing Loss, Language Development, and Aural Habilitation Therapy

Among the consequences of hearing loss with congenital/infancy/early childhood onset, the most debilitating one is disruption of speech and language acquisition. Early detection and amplification are documented to improve hearing-impaired children's language acquisition dramatically: Infants identified with and treated for hearing losses by six months old are expected to achieve normal language development. SLPs typically provide the following:

1. Auditory perception training to augment sound awareness, identification, discrimination, and associations with meaning; develop aided listening skills; and teach handling difficult and easy listening circumstances.
2. Using environment, context, body language, facial expressions, and other visual cues.
3. Developing speech sound production skills in isolation, words, and conversation and breath control, speech rate, loudness, rhythms, and voice quality.
4. Developing receptive language understanding and expressive language usage commensurate with developmental expectations, including word knowledge, vocabulary, concepts, written expression, narrative skills, understanding grammar rules, and language use in various social situations.
5. Managing communication, including understanding hearing loss, developing assertiveness skills for various listening situations, managing communication breakdowns, and modifying situations to facilitate communication.
6. Managing hearing aids/assistive listening devices, including learning to clean, adjust, and troubleshoot aids/devices, and ultimately assuming responsibility for scheduling service provider appointments.

Treating Swallowing and Feeding Problems in Children

The main goals of pediatric dysphagia interventions are as follows: providing safe support for sufficient hydration and nutrition; ascertaining the best methods and techniques for making swallowing as safe, and feeding as efficient, as possible; incorporating children's preferred foods into their diets, through collaboration with parents/families; developing age-appropriate eating skills in the most normal manners and settings possible, e.g., eating meals in preschool with peers with normal chewing and swallowing; reducing the risks for pulmonary complications from aspirating liquids and/or foods; improving children's quality of life to the maximum extent

Copyright © Mometrix Media. You have been licensed one copy of this document for personal use only. Any other reproduction or redistribution is strictly prohibited. All rights reserved.
This content is provided for test preparation purposes only and does not imply an endorsement by Mometrix of any particular political, scientific, or religious point of view.

possible; providing positive feeding and oral experiences as much as possible given the child's medical circumstances in order to prevent future problems with eating and drinking; and helping children to eat and drink as safely and efficiently as possible. Overall health is the first consideration when treating pediatric swallowing problems. Intervention techniques and processes must never endanger a child's safety or their pulmonary or nutritional status.

Consider overall medical condition, mobility, cognition, swallowing abilities, and function and how these affect safe, efficient feeding. Can the child drink and eat safely? Considering efficiency, time duration, and fatigue, can the child obtain adequate hydration and nutrition orally alone? If not, what feeding tube/nonoral intake type, schedule and rate; oral supplements; calories should be recommended? How can treatment maximize functional abilities? Does the child have the potential for direct treatment to enhance swallowing function? This could include whether the child can eat an oral diet safely that fulfills nutritional requirements; need for dietary modifications or compensatory strategies needed for eating. Consider any fear the child has of eating, pleasure the child gets from eating, social interactions during meals, how long it takes to eat and family traditions and customs regarding food and mealtimes: How can treatment maintain or improve the child's quality of life? Consider whether sensorimotor and/or behavioral issues interfere with swallowing and feeding. Do such issues increase mealtime conflicts and/or parent/family frustration? Also, do these indicate a need for sensorimotor-based behavioral intervention?

The anatomical and physiological structures of the swallowing mechanism and their relationships are distinctly different in infants, young children, and adults. Also, infants and children, including those with chronic medical conditions, still continue to grow and develop; hence, their feeding and swallowing function can change with time. Clinicians must consider these differences when planning treatment. The age, physical abilities, cognitive abilities, and specific feeding and swallowing problems of the individual child determine treatment choices. Babies, young children, and older children with intellectual disabilities frequently require intervention methods not requiring them to follow simple verbal or even nonverbal directions. In these cases, indirect treatment approaches and/or changes in the environment can enhance safe and efficient feeding. Changing posture, position, pacing, timing, sensory input, and bolus characteristics such as taste, temperature, and texture can influence oral and pharyngeal transit. Depending on the results of assessments of an individual child, intervention can concentrate on ensuring hydration and nutrition; improving oral, pharyngeal, and respiratory coordination; reducing pulmonary complication risk; and/or modifying sensory and/or behavioral concerns.

Behavioral interventions aim to decrease maladaptive behaviors related to feeding and swallowing and increase appropriate behaviors. Studies show that behavioral interventions can significantly improve feeding behaviors. Environmental modifications to decrease noise levels and distractions, improve lighting, and promote social interaction can enhance mealtime experiences. Postural positioning techniques, which vary among infants and older children and among all individuals, protect the airway and enable safe liquid and solid food transit by centrally aligning and stabilizing the body. Research finds positioning helps children with cerebral palsy, for example, by reducing aspiration risks, making feeding safer; and increasing feeding efficiency. Dietary modifications make swallowing safer and easier by changing foods'/liquids' taste, temperature, texture, and/or viscosity by chopping/pureeing/softening solid foods/thickening liquids, incorporating preferences as possible. Adaptive/different utensils/equipment can optimize liquid flow rates; promote sucking, swallowing, and breathing coordination; and control bolus sizes. Biofeedback promotes physiological changes during swallowing for cognitively able children. Specific maneuvers, also requiring cognitive ability (effortful swallow, supraglottic and super-supraglottic swallow, Masako, Mendelsohn) modify certain swallowing movements' strength/timing. Oral-

Copyright © Mometrix Media. You have been licensed one copy of this document for personal use only. Any other reproduction or redistribution is strictly prohibited. All rights reserved.
This content is provided for test preparation purposes only and does not imply an endorsement by Mometrix of any particular political, scientific, or religious point of view.

motor treatments—passive, including vibration, stroking, tapping, and active, including chewing/swallowing, resistance, and range-of-motion exercises—stimulate and improve physiological eating/swallowing functions. Sensory stimulation, pacing, cue-based feeding strategies, appliances/prosthetics, and tube-feeding are additional treatments.

Chapter Quiz

Ready to see how well you retained what you just read? Scan the QR code to go directly to the chapter quiz interface for this study guide. If you're using a computer, simply visit the online resources page at **mometrix.com/resources719/priispedtssli** and click the Chapter Quizzes link.

Copyright © Mometrix Media. You have been licensed one copy of this document for personal use only. Any other reproduction or redistribution is strictly prohibited. All rights reserved.
This content is provided for test preparation purposes only and does not imply an endorsement by Mometrix of any particular political, scientific, or religious point of view.

Legal, Ethical, and Professional Aspects of the Job

Professional Practice

Wellness and Prevention

ASHA's Position on Prevention of Communication Disorders

The **American Speech-Language-Hearing Association (ASHA)** has traditionally emphasized the prevention of communication disorders as being among its main responsibilities. In ASHA's bylaws, Article II identifies promoting "investigation and prevention of disorders of human communication" as one of its purposes. The ASHA Legislative Council approved a policy statement, entitled "Prevention of Communication Problems in Children," in 1973. However, the perception of prevention for all age groups changed as national healthcare trends increasingly emphasized health promotion and disease prevention. This is a trend that is still continuing today. In response, SLPs and audiologists developed broader views regarding prevention of communication disorders, and ASHA revised its position statement in 1988 to reflect these changes in national perspective. Whereas SLPs and audiologists had historically focused on identifying and treating existing communication disorders, their roles have since expanded to include preventive efforts to promote the development and maintenance of optimal communication and to keep communication disorders from developing in the first place.

Duties of SLPs and Audiologists Relative

ASHA's official position relative to communication disorder prevention and communication wellness promotion is that SLPs and audiologists should use associated terminology consistently.

- **Primary prevention** is inhibiting/eliminating communication disorder onset and development by reducing exposure for vulnerable individuals/populations and/or changing their vulnerability.
- **Secondary prevention** is early identification and treatment of existing communication disorders. Disorder progression can be slowed, preventing additional complications, or disorders can be eliminated through detection and treatment as early as possible when primary prevention has not occurred/succeeded.
- **Tertiary prevention** is reducing disabilities through efforts to restore effective function. Its main approach is **rehabilitation** of individuals experiencing residual problems from disorders.
- **At risk** is the potential for developing a disorder based on biological, environmental, or behavioral variables. Populations without current disorders/symptoms can still be at risk.
- **Incidence** is rates of **new** occurrences of a given disorder within a population during indicated time periods.
- **Prevalence** is **total** percentage/proportion/rate of a given disorder's occurrences within a population during/at indicated times.
- **Epidemiology** is an observational science investigating causes and distribution of diseases/disorders in populations.
- **Wellness** is developing and maintaining optimal competency levels at any life stage.

In addition to correctly and consistently using prevention terminology, playing significant roles in developing and applying prevention strategies is another duty of SLPs and audiologists, according

Copyright © Mometrix Media. You have been licensed one copy of this document for personal use only. Any other reproduction or redistribution is strictly prohibited. All rights reserved.
This content is provided for test preparation purposes only and does not imply an endorsement by Mometrix of any particular political, scientific, or religious point of view.

to ASHA. For speech and hearing professionals to be competent in preventing communication disorders, they must demonstrate the ability to use prevention-related terms appropriately. They must understand the conditions that put individuals at risk of various communication disorders. Conversely, they must also understand the conditions that promote wellness, which is defined as the development and maintenance of optimal communication skills. They must be able to interpret prevention literature to enable appropriate application of the information. Presenting information on primary prevention of communication disorders to known at-risk and other groups and providing individual, family, and community primary prevention information and services are additional competencies. Providing early detection and intervention services for communication disorders to all ages is a secondary prevention competency. SLPs and audiologists must be able to make appropriate referrals for other prevention services; disseminate prevention information to healthcare and social service professionals, extended families, and other public sectors; and understand prevention-related methods for influencing public policy. Preparatory and continuing education should include prevention of communication disorders.

ASHA defines the responsibilities of SLPs and audiologists related to promoting communication wellness and preventing communication disorders as:

1. Using correct and consistent terminology relative to prevention
2. Being instrumental in developing and applying prevention strategies through demonstrating various competencies related to prevention
3. Expanding research into the etiologies of communication disorders and factors influencing the development and maintenance of communication skills
4. Educating the general public and colleagues about personal wellness strategies in relation to the prevention of communication disorders.

With regard to expanding research, ASHA points out that the promotion of communication wellness depends on knowledge about factors positively influencing communication skills and the prevention of communication disorders depends on knowledge about factors causing them. ASHA therefore recommends that to increase such knowledge, scientists should intensify their efforts in basic, clinical, and epidemiological research. Recommended epidemiological research includes:

- Specific communication disorder epidemiologies
- Causes and distributions of conditions leading to secondary communication disorders

Additional recommended prevention research includes causal model validity, early intervention model efficacy, prevention education material appropriateness, and family factors influencing vulnerability to communication disorders.

According to ASHA, to promote optimal communication and prevent communication disorders, SLPs and audiologists should:

1. Know and use correct, consistent prevention terminology
2. Acquire and use multiple identified competencies that contribute significantly to the development and application of preventive strategies
3. Extend research into variables affecting communication wellness and causing communication disorders
4. Function as educators regarding wellness and prevention strategies. SLPs and audiologists should inform their colleagues and the general public as well about personal wellness strategies that can help to prevent communication disorders from developing. ASHA identifies two areas of emphasis in prevention:

Copyright © Mometrix Media. You have been licensed one copy of this document for personal use only. Any other reproduction or redistribution is strictly prohibited. All rights reserved.
This content is provided for test preparation purposes only and does not imply an endorsement by Mometrix of any particular political, scientific, or religious point of view.

a. The identification of variables that cause communication disorders and the elimination of those variables
b. Promoting optimal functioning and increasing resistance to developing communication disorders, which together constitute wellness.

Referring to the accepted leadership principle that the best leaders teach and lead by example, ASHA advises that SLPs and audiologists should maintain their personal best communication performance levels by adopting personal wellness practices and endeavor to promote the general public's adoption of such wellness practices.

Collaboration in School Settings, with Parents, and with the General Public

SLPs who work in school settings can collaborate with classroom teachers to help identify students who are at risk of voice disorders. They can educate teachers about normal voice functions and voice disorders by providing classes for them. In middle schools and high schools, SLPs can give lectures and discussions about healthy voice use to biology and life choice classes. In addition to establishing, implementing, and managing school prevention programs, SLPs can extend these programs to include child care providers. SLPs can also support the prevention of communication disorders in schools by providing school administrators with information about their efforts and activities related to prevention. In addition to school administrators, SLPs can also inform the parents of students about the roles they can play in preventing and identifying communication disorders in their children. SLPs can engage in prevention activities with the general public as well as school personnel and parents. For example, they can develop information about vocal symptoms that represent early warning signs for laryngeal cancers and about the importance of medication assessment when symptoms emerge. They can then disseminate this information to educate the general public.

Activities to Perform with Clients

Unlike many members of the general public, school/workplace personnel, families, communities, and others who often have not developed communication disorders to whom SLPs contribute prevention activities, clients typically have communication disorders that SLPs are treating. However, SLPs can still promote prevention strategies with clients. For example, in addition to providing therapy to remediate voice disorders and teaching specific techniques for alternative vocal use, SLPs can inform clients how to avoid/limit vocal use in unhealthy circumstances and eliminate vocally destructive behaviors. They can teach clients who have had vocal nodules removed how to curtail/prevent further vocal abuse by changing specific lifestyle and communication habits. They can refer clients who smoke to smoking cessation programs as part of their voice disorder treatments and refer clients with alcohol/substance abuse disorders to treatment centers/programs. SLPs can refer clients showing early warning signs of laryngeal cancer to otolaryngologists. They can encourage clients to develop new ways of coping with environmental stressors and daily tensions. For clients whose conditions have improved, SLPs can encourage them to stop using prescription and nonmedicinal drugs that they no longer need.

Strategies

One way in which SLPs promote communication wellness and help to prevent communication and swallowing disorders is by encouraging and teaching preventive activities such as quitting smoking and not starting to smoke, which prevent oral, laryngeal, esophageal, and other cancers and vocal damage, and wearing helmets while riding bicycles to prevent brain and neck injuries that can result in communication and swallowing disorders. Another preventive SLP activity is educating groups and individuals known to be at risk of communication and/or swallowing disorders and other individuals and groups that work or otherwise interact with those at risk, by presenting them

Copyright © Mometrix Media. You have been licensed one copy of this document for personal use only. Any other reproduction or redistribution is strictly prohibited. All rights reserved.
This content is provided for test preparation purposes only and does not imply an endorsement by Mometrix of any particular political, scientific, or religious point of view.

with information about primary prevention measures. SLPs provide early identification and intervention services for communication and swallowing disorders. They serve as consultants to advise legislative and regulatory agencies about emergency response to people with communication and swallowing problems. They help to eliminate or reduce cultural, linguistic, and societal obstacles to communication, and they facilitate and increase access to full participation in communication through community awareness, education, health literacy, and training programs.

Prevention Services

According to ASHA Preferred Practice Patterns (2004), prevention services are designed to keep communication or swallowing disorders from developing in the first place, to minimize the sequelae and effects of existing disorders, and to facilitate normal development in both cases. ASHA's principles for prevention follow the International Classification of Functioning, Disability and Health framework developed by the World Health Organization. Both dictate that prevention is designed to delay or inhibit the onset of communication and swallowing disorders by addressing weaknesses in or associated with underlying structures and functions that can interfere with communicating or swallowing; capitalizing on the strengths of at-risk individuals and populations; facilitating normal development; minimizing the impacts of risk factors, related conditions, and sequelae to enhance individual participation levels and activities; decreasing exposure to context variables that can impede successful communication or swallowing, associated activities and participation; and furnishing appropriate supports, including accommodations and training people in the use of these supports. The expected outcomes of prevention include reduced risks for communication or swallowing disorders and their sequelae; recommendations for speech, language, communication, or swallowing follow-up or reassessment; and/or referral to other service providers.

Hearing Screening and Early Childhood Speech Dysfluencies

It is very important for all newborn infants to have hearing screenings for a number of related reasons. Hearing loss is one of the most common birth defects, affecting up to 3 of every 1,000 babies. The earliest possible detection enables the earliest possible intervention. Treatment can eliminate some types of early hearing loss, prevent others from becoming worse, and remediate others. Any degree of hearing loss at birth can lead not only to more significant loss or ultimately to deafness, but also to speech sound disorders and delayed language and speech development. Hence, universal newborn hearing screening can prevent speech and language disorders. Another consideration for parents with young children is not to overreact to occasional speech dysfluencies. These are normal as young children develop their speech skills. Sometimes misarticulating phonemes and even brief stuttering episodes can occur. The danger of focusing excessive attention on young children's normal dysfluencies is that parents can reinforce these, contributing to the formation of dysfluent speech patterns. However, if a young child consistently displays dysfluencies all or most of the time, prevention should include SLP consultation.

Preventing Voice Disorders in Children and Adults

Some congenital conditions always affect the voice. For example, cleft palate always affects the voice; when cleft accompanies it as is often the case, this additionally causes articulation disorders. Cleft palate and cleft lip must be surgically repaired as soon as possible. In addition to voice and speech problems, they cause facial disfigurement and associated social stigma. Vocal overuse and abuse are also frequent factors in voice disorders. Some children simply talk a great deal, straining their vocal cords. Some engage in frequent screaming, e.g., at sports events/games, music concerts, and during other recreational activities. Children may also use their vocal apparatus incorrectly without realizing it, e.g., applying excessive tension and causing vocal strain. SLPs can retrain phonation habits. This is not limited to children: Adult teachers, instructors, professors, public

Copyright © Mometrix Media. You have been licensed one copy of this document for personal use only. Any other reproduction or redistribution is strictly prohibited. All rights reserved.
This content is provided for test preparation purposes only and does not imply an endorsement by Mometrix of any particular political, scientific, or religious point of view.

speakers, and singers can easily overuse and strain their voices. Other adults may simply talk excessively. Some singers unwittingly use incorrect vocal techniques, causing vocal strain. SLPs can teach better techniques to reduce vocal cord pressure. Children and adults straining their voices can develop vocal cord polyps or nodules requiring surgical removal. Subsequent SLP therapy can prevent repeated damage.

Mechanisms in Primary Prevention of Communication and Swallowing Disorders

Primary prevention involves eliminating or decreasing conditions conducive to potential communication or swallowing disorders. SLPs practice this by:

- Changing someone's susceptibility to a condition, i.e., the odds of their remaining/not remaining healthy if exposed to it
- Decreasing exposure to avoid risk

For example, SLPs can help people working in noisy environments to:

- Change their susceptibility by teaching enhanced speech breathing. This enables them to speak above the noise without straining their voices.
- To help such clients decrease exposure to risk, SLPs can suggest that they change their work schedules if possible to allow vocal rest periods and/or work during less noisy times.

Some examples of simple, inexpensive, readily available tools to aid in prevention include kazoos and harmonicas to prevent oral-motor/motor speech disorders; learning to produce vocal sound effects, e.g., from books such as *Mouth Sounds* by Fred Newman (2005), videos, and choral reading to prevent fluency disorders; dental floss to remove interdental debris and plaque and mints to stimulate saliva production to prevent swallowing disorders; games/other leisure activities providing cognitive exercise; and healthy nutrition and physical movement to prevent speech and language disorders.

Delivering Culturally and Linguistically Appropriate Services

As is evident through observation and proven by US Census Bureau demographic data, the American population is steadily and rapidly increasing in diversity. SLPs are responsible for being knowledgeable about the impacts that these societal changes have on their clinical services and on the research needs of the profession. SLPs must be committed to providing culturally and linguistically appropriate services to all clients, and to considering diversity in scientific research investigating aspects of human communication and swallowing. As one example, a part of delivering culturally and linguistically appropriate SLP services includes determining whether the difficulties with communication English language learners encounter are consequences of learning a different language or symptoms of a communication disorder an individual already had when speaking the native language, which would affect any language spoken. Hence SLPs must assess strengths and weaknesses in communication and speech-language functioning in a client's L1, L2, or both. Included in bilingual assessment services are identifying the primary language used; proficiency in each/both language(s); possible impairments and related limitations in activity and participation; and contextual facilitators and obstacles.

Speech and Language Assessment of ELLs

SLPs' assessment of English language learners' (ELLs) speech and language should identify and describe any underlying structural and/or functional strengths and weaknesses in language and literacy knowledge and skills in the client's L1 that affect his/her communication with others speaking the L1, the effects of any such communication and speech-language impairments on the

Copyright © Mometrix Media. You have been licensed one copy of this document for personal use only. Any other reproduction or redistribution is strictly prohibited. All rights reserved.
This content is provided for test preparation purposes only and does not imply an endorsement by Mometrix of any particular political, scientific, or religious point of view.

client's capacity for and performance of everyday activities in communicative and curricular contexts and participation in the client's community, and any context variables that facilitate or impede successful communication and participation. Some outcomes of speech-language assessment of ELLs include identifying relative language proficiency, e.g., L1 proficiency but lack of English proficiency, similar proficiency in both languages, or limited proficiency in both; diagnosing a language disorder; clinically describing individual communication and speech-language strengths and needs in the L1 and English; identifying a communication difference that may coexist with a language disorder; evaluating the efficacy of previous interventions and supports; prognosis for any diagnosed disorder; estimating language learning capacity; a plan for dynamic/ongoing assessment of language learning capacity in L1 and/or English; recommendations for intervention, context modifications, or other follow-up procedures; and referral to other assessments/services.

ASHA requires comprehensive assessment of English language learners to be culturally and linguistically appropriate through sensitivity to cultural and linguistic diversity and consistency with the World Health Organization International Classification of Functioning, Disability and Health framework, including anatomical and physiological structures and functions, activities and participation, and contextual variables. Static assessment uses procedures designed for describing a client's current functioning levels in pertinent domains; dynamic assessment uses hypothesis-testing procedures to identify potentially effective interventions and supports. Some of the components included in both types of assessment include reviewing hearing, vision, motor, and cognitive status; collecting pertinent information for a case history, including profiling present and past exposure to specified languages, reports from parents, caregivers, teachers, others familiar with the client's speech/language community, and client perspectives when applicable; selecting, administering, and interpreting standardized assessment instruments and/or nonstandardized sampling such as observation and interviews in multiple activities and varied settings, recognizing unique characteristics of the client's linguistic community; and using a qualified interpreter if needed.

Among other things, the SLP's comprehensive assessment of English language learners (ELLs) should include examining the client's ability to use communication and speech-language skills. These include phonological development and grammatical development relative to the client's speech community's norms, client ability to understand and incorporate verbal information, and client ability to use verbal and nonverbal communication skills in interactions with people from different speech communities. The SLP should also examine the impacts of the client's linguistic strengths and needs in the L1 and English upon the client's participation in specific social, educational, and occupational activities that the assessment team has identified as problematic. The SLP additionally needs to investigate contextual factors that influence the client's relative degrees of success and/or difficulty with social, educational, and occupational activities. In selecting assessment procedures, the SLP must consider whether their ecological validity has been documented, which includes their relevance to client language proficiency, social and cultural experiences, educational curriculum, and/or occupational requirements. Assessment also includes follow-up services, e.g., monitoring cognitive and communication status and language-learning capacity and ensuring that ELL/bilingual individuals with speech-language disorders receive appropriate intervention and support.

Settings, Equipment, and Instrument Selection

To elicit a representative sample of client L1 and English language functioning, the SLP may conduct a comprehensive assessment of an English language learner in natural environments representative of the client's native or home speech community as well as in various clinical and/or educational settings. SLPs select assessment settings based on input from the client and others;

Copyright © Mometrix Media. You have been licensed one copy of this document for personal use only. Any other reproduction or redistribution is strictly prohibited. All rights reserved.
This content is provided for test preparation purposes only and does not imply an endorsement by Mometrix of any particular political, scientific, or religious point of view.

assessment goals; and the WHO's ICF framework. The SLP must collect data from both L1 and L2 settings and contexts to identify how contextual factors influence client activity and participation functioning. SLPs should assess deaf/hearing-impaired clients using optimal amplification and in their preferred communication mode. If clients use alternative/augmentative communication devices, these should be programmed in the applicable language(s). SLPs should select assessment instruments with consideration of their appropriateness for people from the client's linguistic and cultural community, their statistical validity and reliability, and their ecological validity. For example, SLPs may conduct curriculum-based assessment using education department standards and parts of a student's actual school curriculum for ecological validity.

Cultural Competence in Administration of Assessment Instruments

When SLPs select assessment instruments and tools to use for evaluating clients to determine speech, language, voice, or swallowing functions, differences, disorders, and therapy treatments, it is critical for them to have developed and applied cultural competence. Although standardized assessment instruments are more likely to have been found statistically valid and reliable and are uniform in their content as opposed to other measures, they may not apply to all racial, ethnic, linguistic, and cultural populations. The American Speech-Language-Hearing Association (ASHA) expects service providers who have ASHA certification in clinical competence to confirm that any assessments they administer are being used with the population(s) for which they were standardized. Many valid, reliable, standardized assessment instruments can still contain intrinsic linguistic and cultural biases. Such biases are commonly determined by the racial, ethnic, cultural, and linguistic backgrounds of the test authors. Assessments will not meet standards if they are administered to populations who were not part of the samples used to establish the norms. The results of assessments administered to these nonsampled, nonrepresented populations can be used only without standard scores, and only as information probes. Assessors should note any changes they make to the usual assessment process in their written reports.

Hearing, Speech, Voice, and Language Screenings in Early Childhood

Speech and language development are vital for communication with others and for learning. The earlier that delays and disorders in the development of children's speech and language are assessed and treated, the better their prognoses will be. Speech and language screenings are typically conducted prior to more thorough assessments or comprehensive evaluations. Screenings provide excellent tools for ascertaining whether a child's development is within the average or normal range in comparison to other children of the same age. Screening instruments help SLPs and others to identify conditions which could require additional assessment. Hence, screenings are important components of well-baby and well-child health care. Because hearing loss is relatively common among those with birth defects, universal newborn hearing screenings are vital for the earliest identification and intervention. In early childhood, developmental abilities that are often assessed in addition to hearing include receptive language, expressive language, phonology, articulation, speech fluency, voice, voice resonance, and pragmatic language skills.

Abilities and Skills Screened for in Babies and Young Children

Screenings for hearing, receptive language understanding, expressive language production; phonological awareness, perception, and production; the articulation of speech sounds; the pitch, loudness, resonance, and quality of voices; the fluency of speech production; and the understanding and social application of pragmatic language skills are important components of communicative wellness and the prevention or remediation of hearing, speech, and language disorders. Because research shows that earlier detection and intervention produce better results than later identification and treatment, well-baby and well-child health care include hearing, speech, and language screenings. Newborns can be screened for hearing loss; young infants can be screened for

Copyright © Mometrix Media. You have been licensed one copy of this document for personal use only. Any other reproduction or redistribution is strictly prohibited. All rights reserved.
This content is provided for test preparation purposes only and does not imply an endorsement by Mometrix of any particular political, scientific, or religious point of view.

receptive language response; and young children can be screened for both plus receptive language understanding, expressive language production, and speech production. Screenings use standardized assessment tools. Screening procedures are noninvasive, and children typically perceive the screening interactions favorably as play experiences. Screeners have children observe, think about, and verbally respond to stimuli presented and questions asked. Screenings are brief, usually taking roughly 20 minutes to complete. When children do not pass a screening, they are recommended for additional assessment.

Client Information Obtained During Screening for Speech-Language Therapy

On typical screening forms, SLPs record the following information: screening date; client name and birth date; facility name and room number, when applicable; admission/readmission date; client's physician's name; current client diet; previous functioning level; reason for screening, e.g., new admission/readmission, routine staffing, nursing/staff/family referral, incident report, restorative/rehabilitative programs, other; and previous speech-language therapy (yes/no)—if yes, last discharge date and functioning level at the time of discharge. A screening form may include a checklist of functional areas screened, which the SLP may mark with S for screened or D for deficit. Functional areas to screen include speech intelligibility; vocal weakness; confrontational naming; automatic speech; answering questions; auditory comprehension; simple conversation; oral-motor movements; swallowing; memory recall; orientation to time, place, and person as in mental status examinations; safety awareness; problem-solving abilities; attention; repetition; following directions; complex conversation; weight loss; and dehydration. The SLP may additionally record in a space provided on the screening form any problems or declines in abilities s/he has observed in the client during the screening. The screening form should have places to check whether evaluation for speech-language therapy is recommended or not; to write why if not recommending evaluation; and for the SLP's signature, credentials, and date.

Observations During Oral-Motor Screenings and Dysphagia Screenings

Oral-Motor

The SLP asks the client to stick out his/her tongue; move it laterally to each mouth corner; pucker the lips; say "ah"; smile; and repeat syllables as rapidly as possible that have initial unvoiced plosive stops: "puh, puh, puh.."; "tuh, tuh, tuh..."; "kuh, kuh, kuh..."; and "puh, tuh, kuh..." for mobility and rapidity of lip and tongue movements.

Dysphagia

As is appropriate for the individual client, give one-fourth of a cookie or cracker and/or one teaspoon of thin liquid and/or pureed food, and observe the client's swallowing functions for the following: breathing difficulties; residue/material pocketing in the oral cavity; coughing before, during, and/or after swallowing; increase in oral or laryngeal secretions; piecemeal swallowing, i.e., swallowing multiple times per bolus; inadequate awareness and control of oral or laryngeal secretions; lowered elevation of the larynx; significant signs of client fatigue from eating, drinking, and/or swallowing; frequent or repeated clearing of the throat; and changes in voice quality, particularly gurgling or wet sounds. The SLP marks each of these items yes/no to indicate that they were observed/not observed.

Copyright © Mometrix Media. You have been licensed one copy of this document for personal use only. Any other reproduction or redistribution is strictly prohibited. All rights reserved.
This content is provided for test preparation purposes only and does not imply an endorsement by Mometrix of any particular political, scientific, or religious point of view.

SCREENINGS OF COGNITION AND LANGUAGE WITH ADULT CLIENTS

The following are several of the items typically administered by SLPs during screenings of cognition and language with adult clients:

- **Orientation**: Time—ask the client the date, day of week, month, year, and season. Place—ask the client their current location or the facility name; room number, if applicable; and city and state. Person—ask the client his/her name.
- **Conversational speech**: Ask the client a "shotgun" (open-ended) question, e.g., what kinds of work s/he has done in the past. Take notes.
- **Immediate recall**: Say three simple monosyllabic words, e.g., "Ball, flag, tree," slowly and clearly, and ask the client to repeat them. Check or X these as correct or incorrect on the screening form.
- **Attention**: Ask the client to start counting backward from 100 by 7; stop after 5 numbers. Check or X the correct numbers 93, 86, 79, 72, and 65 on the screening form.
- **Immediate recall and reversal**: Ask the client to spell a word, e.g., "world", backwards. Check or X the box for each letter in correct sequence (D-L-R-O-W).
- **Delayed verbal recall**: Ask the client to recall the three short, simple words given earlier to screen Immediate recall (above).
- **Confrontational naming**: Present an object and ask the client to name it, e.g., "What do you call this?", e.g., hand, pen, pillow, ceiling, door. Automatic speech: Ask the client to tell you the days of the week and to count to ten.
- **Sentence completion**: Instruct the client to "Finish these sentences for me: I pledge allegiance to the ____. Three strikes and you're ___. The phone is off the ___. As you leave, close the ___. For fresh air, you raise the ____."
- **Repetition**: Instruct the client to repeat each word/phrase/sentence you say: "Book, home, spice, scarecrow, tornado, administration. Under the old wooden bridge. The silver moon hung in the dark sky."
- **Yes/No questions**: Instruct the client to answer "yes"/"no": "Is your name ____?" (first name); Is your name ____?" (last name). "Do you live in ____?" (US state name). "Am I touching my eye?" (touching your nose). "Do you wear gloves on your feet?" "Is a chicken bigger than a spider?" "Do you put your shoes on before your socks?"
- **Following directions**: "Point to your nose; open your mouth; point with your left hand to your right eye; point to the floor, then to your nose; before opening your mouth, touch your ear."

TEAM APPROACH TO ASSESSMENT OF SWALLOWING DISORDERS IN CHILDREN

Pediatric dysphagia includes a wide variety of diagnoses, and its management across childhood ages is complex. Therefore, a team approach, although it may not always be necessary, is frequently ideal. Involving the child's family and/or caregivers is the first step in forming the assessment team. Team members conducting comprehensive swallowing assessments of infants and young children are often multidisciplinary. These can include the following: an SLP with a clinical specialty in feeding and swallowing; physicians, who may include a neonatologist, pediatrician, physiatrist, otolaryngologist, neurologist, neurosurgeon, cardiac surgeon, pulmonologist, gastroenterologist, and/or endocrinologist; nurse/nurse practitioner; registered dietitian; psychologist; social worker; board-certified lactation consultant; occupational therapist; and physical therapist. In addition, the team might include other medical specialists and rehabilitation specialists. This depends not only on the individual child's case, but also on the specific population being served; the types of professional expertise that are required; and the type of facility in which the comprehensive assessment is being conducted.

Copyright © Mometrix Media. You have been licensed one copy of this document for personal use only. Any other reproduction or redistribution is strictly prohibited. All rights reserved.
This content is provided for test preparation purposes only and does not imply an endorsement by Mometrix of any particular political, scientific, or religious point of view.

School-Based Swallowing and Feeding Evaluation and Teams

The following are two reasons that SLPs working in schools are increasingly involved in evaluating students for swallowing and feeding disorders:

- More high-risk infants are surviving to school ages who have swallowing and feeding disorders that must be managed in school settings.
- Section 504 of the Rehabilitation Act and the Individuals with Disabilities Education Act both require services to students for medical disorders affecting their full access to and participation in educational programs.

Review Video: Development of the Individuals with Disabilities Education Act
Visit mometrix.com/academy and enter code: 100350

This is educationally relevant because:

- School systems are responsible for student safety while eating in school, including access to appropriate food, personnel, and procedures to minimize choking and aspiration risks.
- Full student access to school curriculum requires adequate student hydration and nourishment.
- Optimal school attendance depends on student health, without dehydration, malnutrition, aspiration, or aspiration pneumonia.
- Students need to develop efficient eating skills to eat and drink safely and timely with peers during school meal and snack times.

School-based swallowing and feeding teams include members who are school system employees, plus medical professionals such as doctors, dietitians, and psychologists from outside the school. Typical team core members responsible for dysphagia-related decisions include SLPs, family/caregivers, classroom teachers, school nurses, physical therapists, occupational therapists, and school administrators. School psychologists, school social workers, and cafeteria staff can also be team members.

When school-based dysphagia teams, which include SLPs, collaborate with physicians and other medical professionals, they consider factors such as whether they need to refer a student for medical assessment, medical clearance, or continuing medical care. Cases when such considerations occur typically involve students who have medically complex conditions rather than medically stable conditions and who require specialized care during the school day that has not been specified in the student's individualized education program, individual family service plan, individualized health plan, or 504 plan (based on provisions of Section 504 of the Rehabilitation Act). If the school dysphagia team finds that a student needs medical assessment, either before or during implementation of a school-based dysphagia program, they can recommend to the family that they obtain a medical consultation—for example, for a videofluoroscopic swallow study (VFSS) and/or other medical testing and evaluation. Although SLPs do not need a medical prescription or approval to conduct clinical assessments or interventions, in some cases, physicians/other healthcare providers may request prescriptions, medical clearance, or referral, e.g., for VFSS or fiber-optic endoscopic evaluation of swallowing or fiber-optic endoscopic evaluation of swallowing and sensory testing.

In some instances, when a public school has obtained approval to communicate directly with healthcare providers, the staff may ask a student's primary care physician or other healthcare provider(s) for medical clearance, a prescription, or a referral; for example, for instrumental evaluation such as a videofluoroscopic swallow study, fiber-optic endoscopy evaluation of

Copyright © Mometrix Media. You have been licensed one copy of this document for personal use only. Any other reproduction or redistribution is strictly prohibited. All rights reserved.
This content is provided for test preparation purposes only and does not imply an endorsement by Mometrix of any particular political, scientific, or religious point of view.

swallowing, or fiber-optic endoscopic evaluation of swallowing and sensory testing. The request for collaboration with medical practitioners may be made after discussing it with the family, directly of the provider, or through the family. Such requests for collaboration with medical care providers can include medical clearance or a prescription for clinical dysphagia assessment and/or intervention for students who receive all or part of their hydration and/or nutrition through parenteral or enteral tube feeding; students with medically complex conditions; and/or students whose medical status is a significant factor in choosing appropriate strategies for assessment and treatment. These requests can also include approval of a student's individualized health plan by the school physician or the student's primary care provider for a student whose needs are medically complex.

Any time a student is identified with any disability qualifying for special education services, the Individuals with Disabilities Education Act legally requires that public schools receiving federal funding must provide an individualized education program/plan (IEP) specifying which services are needed; educational goals and objectives; adaptive or assistive devices, or classroom modifications and accommodations needed. Schools form multidisciplinary teams to develop IEPs. If the student has any identified speech, language, and/or hearing disability—or other disability affecting speech, language, or hearing, SLP services will be included in the special education services the student will receive. In these cases, the SLP will be a member of the IEP team. The SLP collaborates with other IEP team members on developing the program; contributes the SLP therapy services components of the IEP; and works with other team members to coordinate SLP services, goals, objectives, and activities with other program components. For example, the SLP can offer classroom teachers ways to integrate activities supporting/reinforcing speech-language therapy goals into curriculum content lessons and daily classroom routines. SLPs may also coordinate their services with occupational therapy, physical therapy, behavioral/psychological, and other services for students with multiple special needs.

Review Video: 504 Plans and IEPs
Visit mometrix.com/academy and enter code: 881103

Review Video: Medical Conditions in Education
Visit mometrix.com/academy and enter code: 531058

Counseling Skills

According to ASHA researchers, graduate school programs for SLPs provide very little training in counseling. The majority of graduate students in SLP surveyed have expressed the need for more training in counseling methods and more practicum experiences in counseling. Additionally, very little research related to counseling issues in SLP exists. Experts observe the significance of this paucity of research considering that the clinical counseling relationship has profound impacts on positive client results. Although experts all agree that excellent counseling skills are important in SLPs, determining what to include in SLP counseling training and how to teach the skills is difficult. Although in-depth counseling services for clients with systemic and ongoing mental health problems are outside SLP qualifications, most speech-language-hearing clinic clients and/or their family members have psychological and emotional repercussions from communication disorders. Therefore, SLPs must be prepared for developing exemplary counseling skills and supporting the psychological and emotional issues of their clients relative to their communication disorders.

SLP graduate students usually receive basic information about the types of counseling services they will provide during the assessment and treatment processes they provide. Typically, their training will include explanation of information-getting, information-giving, and counseling interviews. During assessment, SLPs conduct information-getting interviews with clients about their

Copyright © Mometrix Media. You have been licensed one copy of this document for personal use only. Any other reproduction or redistribution is strictly prohibited. All rights reserved.
This content is provided for test preparation purposes only and does not imply an endorsement by Mometrix of any particular political, scientific, or religious point of view.

developmental, medical, and educational histories, communication disorders, etc. After completing an initial assessment, SLPs often conduct information-giving interviews to explain the assessment results, offer recommendations, answer questions, and describe the treatment plans they recommend. Counseling interviews, however, have different purposes than informational interviews: SLPs conduct them to encourage and support client acceptance of their communication disorders, and/or influence client behaviors. Counseling skills training for SLPs sometimes involves being given lists describing behaviors indicating effective counseling skills, e.g., making clients comfortable through appropriate nonverbal communication; limiting socially oriented conversations; and giving clients reflective, succinct feedback. Whereas informational interviews emphasize facts, counseling interviews and sessions emphasize feelings. Hence, SLPs must develop client-centered, not clinician-directed approaches. This includes learning to tolerate silence during client-SLP interactions; clarifying client self-perceptions; and reflecting client emotions.

Developing an effective therapeutic relationship is an important part of counseling. Humanistic psychological theories such as Maslow's and Rogers's find that client self-discovery and self-actualization are promoted best when clinicians do not proscribe but listen to clients, using a client-centered therapeutic approach. Clients and SLPs can too easily view the SLP as an expert who can solve clients' emotional problems; however, SLPs must resist adopting this role to be client-centered. Beginning SLPs can have great difficulty focusing on feelings, not facts, and listening, not talking. Previous student clinical experience often contradicts many client-centered counseling behaviors. Trainings for SLPs in client-centered counseling ask new clinicians to be reflective instead of directive and to give facilitating client personal growth priority above their own personal opinions and reactions. Experts characterize this client-centered relationship as nonreciprocal and unilateral. The client engages in self-expression, self-examination, and self-disclosure, and the SLP is the facilitator. To develop effective client-centered counseling, SLP students must attain comfort with various nonverbal communication behaviors including body posture, eye contact, head nodding, facial expressions, etc.

Nonverbal Communication

To communicate favorable affect and encourage clients to verbalize, SLPs should lean slightly forward and maintain relaxed postures, avoiding tightly crossed arms/legs; deliberately nod their heads and use appropriate facial expressions. Nonverbal behaviors typically support verbal behaviors and take place in combination sequences. Eye contact in counseling is typically longer than during ordinary communication. However, SLPs must also employ cultural sensitivity regarding eye contact. For example, whereas white Americans tend to listen using more direct eye contact and speak using less, black Americans conversely tend to listen using less eye contact and speak using more. SLP students also need to learn to tolerate "clinical silence." North Americans generally feel considerable discomfort with silence during conversation; SLP students frequently perceive silence during therapy as representing tension/other negativity. However, Native American, Middle Eastern, Asian, and other cultures conversely perceive silence as positive and appropriate. Allowing and tolerating silence is a powerful technique for client-centered therapeutic focus. Rather than simply absence of speech, silence can express empathy for client communication, agreement, and/or respect; enable clients to process information, and invite them to talk. One training technique teaches counting mentally to five before responding verbally to client communications.

Closed and Open Questions and SLP Responses

In counseling interviews, primary SLP interviewing behaviors include silence to increase client responses; questions are secondary interviewing behaviors. Closed questions are time efficient, eliciting factual information. Open questions communicate SLP interest in clients; encourage client

Copyright © Mometrix Media. You have been licensed one copy of this document for personal use only. Any other reproduction or redistribution is strictly prohibited. All rights reserved.
This content is provided for test preparation purposes only and does not imply an endorsement by Mometrix of any particular political, scientific, or religious point of view.

talking; and help uncover client perspectives, feelings, and knowledge. As examples, "How old was your child when you first noticed this?" and "Has your child already been diagnosed with stuttering?" are closed questions. "How are you feeling about the way things are going at school?" and "Tell me why you have come to the clinic today" are open-ended questions. Content-related SLP responses when restating/paraphrasing client communications encourage client elaboration about information, but not associated emotions. For example, a parent says, "He started stuttering around age three." SLP: (five-second pause) "About three years old..." This exemplifies content paraphrasing. The parent says, "I felt something was wrong. His doctor and teachers are supposed to be experts; they kept saying he'd grow out of it. Nobody said it could be this serious." SLP: "You feel angry nobody gave you more help understanding this earlier." Clients frequently avoid emotional expression. SLP affect-related responses are major components of empathic listening and building supportive clinical environments and relationships.

Paraphrasing, Summarizing, and Responding to Negative Client Emotions

During client counseling, the SLP should paraphrase what the client has expressed for the purposes of immediately and closely mirroring the informational content, and/or immediately capturing the client's underlying emotions, after the client expresses something. In contrast, the SLP should summarize the content and/or emotions of what the client has said over a longer time period, e.g., 10 to 12 minutes, in condensed form. Summarizing can be used for concluding interviews, and it give SLPs a way to obtain client denial, correction, or confirmation that the SLP has understood their messages correctly. SLP students normally have to practice to become effective at summarizing the "big picture" of client communication in as few words as they can. Clients with communication disorders or parents of children with communication disorders often experience sadness, anger, fear or other negative emotions. Many people feel uncomfortable hearing others' negative emotions and want to reassure them not to worry or that their situation is not that bad. However, effective SLP counseling skills require listening to, accepting, and reflecting back negative client emotions to enable clients to work through them.

SLPs can help clients work through negative feelings associated with communication disorders by inviting/encouraging, receiving, accepting, and reflecting them. Additionally, after reflecting client feelings, SLPs can follow by clarifying/interpreting client feelings to help clients understand their own emotions better. In one training technique, SLP students take turns role playing, saying things they imagine they would say/feelings they would express if they/their child/spouse/parent had a severe communication disorder; reflecting those messages; and adding interpretation. For example, the student as client says, "Sometimes I feel I could have prevented this; I'm the one who caused this problem." The student as SLP reflects emotion: "As her parent, you feel guilty" and adds an interpretation: "That is a very natural way to react." Or the client says, "I'm just at my wits' end. I simply can't deal with him anymore." The SLP reflects emotion: "You're feeling really frustrated" and adds interpretation: "It's good that you can recognize your limits." Allowing clients to express both positive and negative emotions has advantages: The first example could facilitate a discussion of problem causation; the second could enable an important respite care referral.

Documentation of Services

SLPs must prepare, sign, and maintain documentation reflecting the nature of their professional services within a designated time frame. They should report the results of their assessments and treatments, as is appropriate, to the clients they assessed and treated and/or their parents, family, or caregivers. With written consent and when it is appropriate, they distribute these reports to referral sources and other professionals. SLPs must comply with the regulations of the Family Education Rights and Privacy Act (FERPA), the Health Insurance Portability and Accountability Act (HIPAA), and other applicable federal and state laws. With the exception of screenings, SLPs should

Copyright © Mometrix Media. You have been licensed one copy of this document for personal use only. Any other reproduction or redistribution is strictly prohibited. All rights reserved.
This content is provided for test preparation purposes only and does not imply an endorsement by Mometrix of any particular political, scientific, or religious point of view.

address the type and severity of communication differences and disorders and related differences and disorders; associated medical or educational diagnoses or other associated conditions; and their impacts on social, educational, and occupational participation and activity in their documentation. In addition, SLPs should provide documentation that includes summaries of prior services according to all applicable legal and agency guidelines.

Elective Communication Modification Services

Elective communication modification services may be requested of SLPs by people who do not have any communication disorders, but who want help from the SLP in order to improve the efficacy of their communication. For example, some requests involve eliminating or modifying dialects or accents; receiving instruction to improve interpersonal communication skills; or instruction in public speaking techniques. These are within the scope of SLP services. To document their professional services to clients requesting elective communication modification, the SLP should include information indicating that the services provided were elective (voluntarily chosen by the client) and provide written records of the types of services provided, the dates of service provision, and the duration of services provided. The SLP should also include evaluations of the outcomes of the communication modification services and their effectiveness in application to contextual factors, participation, and activities. The client's progress toward the goals initially identified by the client and SLP should be included in the documentation. The SLP should also include his/her specific recommendations for the client.

Comprehensive Speech-Language or Swallowing Assessments

When conducting a comprehensive speech-language or swallowing assessment, the SLP should include at least (but not limited to) the following in the documentation: relevant background information; assessment results and interpretations; prognosis; and recommendations for additional assessment, follow-up, or referral as indicated. When recommending intervention, the SLP should also document the type of service and its frequency and estimate its duration. The type and severity of any cognitive-communication, speech, language, or swallowing disorder and associated medical diagnoses or other conditions should be addressed in the documentation. The SLP should also include summaries of previous services according to all pertinent legal and agency guidelines in the documentation of the comprehensive speech-language or swallowing assessment. SLPs must always safeguard the security and confidentiality of documents according to FERPA, HIPAA, and other federal and state regulations and laws. The SLP reports the documented assessment results to clients, families, and caregivers as indicated and distributes documents to referral sources and other professionals with written consent when appropriate.

Assessment of and Intervention with Speech Sounds

When the SLP assesses client speech sounds, i.e., phonological and articulatory functioning, s/he should document the relevant background information, assessment results and interpretation, prognosis, and recommendations. The SLP may include needs for additional assessment, follow-up, or referral to other professional services in the recommendations. For any intervention(s) the SLP recommends, s/he should include information in the documentation about the type, frequency, and estimated duration of service. The type and severity of the speech sound difference or disorder and any related conditions, such as medical or educational diagnoses, should be addressed in the SLP's documentation of the assessment. Summaries of any previous services the client received should also be included in the documentation according to pertinent legal and agency guidelines. SLP documentation of speech sound intervention services should include written records of the dates, type(s), and duration of interventions; progress toward identified goals; an updated prognosis; specific recommendations; and evaluation of the outcomes and effectiveness of the intervention

Copyright © Mometrix Media. You have been licensed one copy of this document for personal use only. Any other reproduction or redistribution is strictly prohibited. All rights reserved.
This content is provided for test preparation purposes only and does not imply an endorsement by Mometrix of any particular political, scientific, or religious point of view.

within the ICF framework of body structures and functions, context factors, and participation and activities.

Assessment of Spoken and Written Language in School-Age Children and Adolescents

When documenting assessment of school-age child and adolescent spoken and written language, the SLP should include relevant background information; observation and assessment results and interpretation; prognosis; and recommendations that can include additional assessment, follow-up, and/or referral. Treatment recommendations should include information about the service type, frequency, and estimated duration. The type and severity of the child/adolescent's spoken and/or written language difference/disorder and related conditions such as special education classification, medical diagnoses, etc., are documented. The SLP may include in the documentation a portfolio of the child/adolescent's communication samples, which can include written products; descriptions of writing processes; accounts of nonverbal interactions; transcripts of reading text aloud or spoken conversations, and audio and/or video recordings of the interactions. Complying with applicable legal and agency guidelines, SLPs should document any previous services. The SLP must adhere to FERPA, HIPAA, and other federal and state laws and regulations in protecting document security and confidentiality. The SLP may distribute records to referral sources and other professionals when indicated, given written consent. SLPs report/provide assessment results to clients and family or caregivers as is appropriate.

Interventions for Spoken and Written Language Skills

When SLPs document their intervention for spoken and written language skills with school-age children and adolescents, they should include a written record of the types of interventions they provided, including consultations, and their dates and durations. They should document any needs they identify for assistive technology, such as personal or classroom amplification systems or alternative/augmentative communication (AAC) systems, and a plan for the monitoring, maintenance, and upgrading of any needed technologies. The SLP's documentation of intervention should include the child/adolescent's progress toward goals identified in comparison to documented baseline levels and in relation to general education curriculum and/or vocational performance, an updated postintervention prognosis, and specific recommendations. In the documentation of spoken and written language intervention, the SLP should also include evaluation of the results and effectiveness of the intervention according to the WHO's ICF framework including contextual factors, body structures and functions, participation, and activities. The SLP's documentation of the intervention may be included in the child/adolescent's individualized education program if s/he receives special education services or in other collaborative and/or interdisciplinary treatment plans.

Assessment and Treatment of Severe Communication Impairments

When assessing clients with severe impairment in communication, SLPs should include any background information relevant to the disorder, all assessment results and the SLP's interpretation of them, the client's prognosis, and the SLP's recommendations for the client. The SLP may document strategies to replace challenging behaviors through self-regulation skills and more socially acceptable communicative behaviors; recommendations for interpretations of message and social interaction value; recommendations for AAC assessment and intervention and other communication supports; and any needs for additional assessment, referral, and/or follow-up activities. For any interventions the SLP recommends, s/he should document information about the service type (for example, individual, classroom, group, and/or home-based programs or consultations), recommended service frequency, and estimated service duration. Medical diagnoses or other associated conditions, as well as impairment type, should be included in the documentation of assessment. The SLP should also summarize previous services in the documents

Copyright © Mometrix Media. You have been licensed one copy of this document for personal use only. Any other reproduction or redistribution is strictly prohibited. All rights reserved.
This content is provided for test preparation purposes only and does not imply an endorsement by Mometrix of any particular political, scientific, or religious point of view.

as allowed. They should document intervention with written records of consultation and other intervention types, dates, and duration; progress toward identified goals related to reducing challenging behaviors and increasing conventional and functional communication compared to baseline measures; an updated post-treatment prognosis; specific recommendations; and treatment outcomes and effectiveness evaluations according to the International Classification of Functioning, Disability and Health (ICF) framework.

Assessment and Intervention Services Related to AAC Systems

After an initial alternative/augmentative communication (AAC) system assessment has been completed, the SLP should review the results of any trials conducted during dynamic assessment, identify and describe the AAC system components recommended and provide a rationale for their selection, give a description of the AAC intervention program s/he recommends for the client, and report the responses of the client and family and/or caregivers to the system and program recommended. For the intervention s/he recommends, the SLP should include the service type, frequency, and estimated duration. The SLP should also document any previous services with summaries as permitted by law and agency policy; relevant background information; assessment results and interpretation; prognosis; and additional recommendations for further assessment, referral, and/or follow-up. SLPs providing AAC intervention should document in writing the dates, types, and lengths of interventions; progress toward the client's identified goals; a post-treatment updated prognosis; specific recommendations; and an evaluation of the effectiveness of the AAC system and the results obtained from its use.

Assessment and Treatment of Fluency Disorders

For assessment of client fluency problems, the SLP should document the type and severity of stuttering dysfluencies and nonstuttering dysfluencies; secondary behaviors; and medical or educational diagnoses and other associated conditions, as well as relevant client background information; assessment results and interpretations; prognosis; and recommendations, including the need for other assessment, referral, and/or follow-up as indicated; and for intervention recommendations, the service type, frequency, and a treatment duration estimate. The SLP should document the impact of client fluency patterns on participation and activities and contextual factors that serve to facilitate or impede communication, activity, and participation. Previous services should also be documented within legal/agency parameters. When SLPs deliver fluency interventions, they should document the dates, durations, and types of interventions they provided; the client's progress toward identified goals of therapy; a revised or new post-treatment prognosis; and specific recommendations for the client. Documentation should additionally include the SLP's evaluation of the intervention's effectiveness and outcomes.

Public School Settings

For SLPs working in public school settings, documentation is a critical part of their jobs because it can influence the outcomes experienced by students who receive SLP services. Federal laws that include provisions related to documentation include; the Family Educational Rights and Privacy Act; Health Insurance Portability and Accountability Act; Individuals with Disabilities Education Act (IDEA); Elementary and Secondary Education Act, now expressed as the Every Student Succeeds Act; Americans with Disabilities Act; Section 504 of the Rehabilitation Act (504); and Medicaid requirements. IDEA, first passed in 1975 and reauthorized numerous times, most recently in 2004, guarantees all students with disabilities the right to a free, appropriate public education in the least restrictive environment possible. It therefore requires public schools receiving federal funds to provide special education and related services to students identified with eligible disabilities, with recourse for students/parents if they do not receive these services. Students with qualifying disabilities under IDEA become members of a protected class. This affords them procedural

Copyright © Mometrix Media. You have been licensed one copy of this document for personal use only. Any other reproduction or redistribution is strictly prohibited. All rights reserved.
This content is provided for test preparation purposes only and does not imply an endorsement by Mometrix of any particular political, scientific, or religious point of view.

safeguards, outlined in IDEA and realized through required special education procedures. The law includes safeguarding the privacy and confidentiality of special education student records.

The Family Educational Rights and Privacy Act (FERPA) and the Health Insurance Portability and Accountability Act (HIPAA) are two federal mandates that include provisions related to student records. FERPA determines who can have access to student records, gives parents opportunities to contest their children's school records and have them amended, and affords families some control over disclosure of student records. FERPA defines educational records as documents directly related to an individual student and maintained by an educational institution/agency/party acting on behalf of the institution/agency. FERPA clarifies parental access to student records, and by requiring consent, it limits student records transfer. HIPAA, another federal law, addresses protected health information. Passed in 1996, HIPAA was amended in 2003 to address electronic records transmission and increase restrictions on health records accessibility. Because school personnel frequently request information from healthcare providers, questions/confusion periodically arise about HIPAA applicability in schools. Most educational records are excluded from HIPAA and protected by FERPA. HIPAA permits certain uses/disclosures of PHI, usually including student IEPs, evaluations, health records, Medicaid claims, and other related school records.

Technology

Documenting information about their clients and services is vital to SLPs, yet it is also time consuming. Advances in computer technology have enabled the production of computer software programs that can save much time and effort by streamlining everyday chores associated with the profession. For example, the Columbus Speech and Hearing Center's Chart Links Rehabilitation Software (2012) improves the process of documenting and billing for SLP services. Not only can SLP facilities more efficiently conduct client registrations, manage referrals, process insurance claims, schedule appointments across disciplines, calculate fees, generate analytics and reports, and document therapy outcomes using this software, it also provides additional documentation features specific to the SLP including standardized SLP evaluation forms for speech-language, fluency, aphasia, cognition, and swallowing. SLPs can document while treating clients, fax evaluations to surgeons as clients depart, and customize many sections into forms and sets. They can print educational and instructional client handouts about oral-motor/feeding, fluency, articulation, hearing impairment, and home programs on demand; scan existing forms; create new forms; interface with third-party e-formats; monitor evaluation/follow-up visits; and receive client check-in notifications, facilitating time management. The software supports HIPAA, Commission for Accreditation of Rehabilitation Facilities, the Joint Commission on Accreditation of Healthcare Organizations, and Medicare compliance.

Clinical Documentation

As a critical part of their work functions, SLPs are responsible for preparing, signing, and maintaining documentation that provides accurate, detailed descriptions of the professional services that they have provided. In these documents, for each individual client they should include information about the client's background that is relevant, the results of the assessments the SLP conducted, the SLP's interpretation of the assessment results, the prognosis they assigned for the client, and their recommendations. The SLP's recommendations can include a need for additional evaluation for follow-up services after the SLP has provided the current services, and/or for referral to other practitioners for evaluation and/or treatment. When the SLP recommends intervention, s/he must specify the type of service (e.g., individual or group), frequency of treatment, and estimated treatment duration. The SLP's documentation should include the following: speech-language evaluation findings, objective and subjective measures of client functioning, measurable short-term and long-term therapy goals, the SLP's expectations for the

Copyright © Mometrix Media. You have been licensed one copy of this document for personal use only. Any other reproduction or redistribution is strictly prohibited. All rights reserved.
This content is provided for test preparation purposes only and does not imply an endorsement by Mometrix of any particular political, scientific, or religious point of view.

client's progress, the frequency of treatment sessions the SLP advises or expects, and a reasonable estimate of the length of time required for attaining identified therapy goals.

Four types of clinical documentation that SLPs provide are assessment documentation, treatment documentation, daily notes, and progress reports. Assessment documentation and treatment documentation are typically required; daily notes and progress reports may/may not be required depending on the setting. Regarding assessment documentation, the SLP determines the existence, type, etiology, and severity of speech, language, or swallowing disorders; contributing factors; and related factors by administering a variety of formal and informal assessment instruments, tools, and procedures. The SLP's initial assessment of the client supplies baseline data, i.e., the client's presenting and current levels of communication status and functioning. The SLP must establish baseline data before intervention to assess the client's expected rehabilitation/habilitation potential, form realistic therapy goals, and periodically measure treatment progress by comparing later status to baseline levels. Initial assessment documentation of baseline measures should include standardized and/or nonstandardized testing, objective and/or subjective diagnostic testing, the SLP's interpretation of test results, and clinical findings. If anything prohibits baseline testing, the SLP should document this, including the reason(s), in the initial assessment notes or progress notes. When clients demonstrate changes in functional communication, speech, and language skills, reassessment is indicated.

Review Video: Assessment Reliability and Validity
Visit mometrix.com/academy and enter code: 424680

Within the clinical documentation that SLPs typically provide, four types are assessment documentation, treatment documentation, daily notes, and progress reports. After completing and documenting the initial assessment of a client, once the SLP has planned and implements a treatment program, s/he must also document this treatment. A treatment program addressing a client's communication or swallowing disorder should be designed to incorporate ongoing evaluation of the client's progress in treatment. The treatment program should include professional analysis and documentation of the client's status, completed at regular time intervals. As s/he evaluates the client's status during therapy, the SLP will adjust the treatment when indicated. The SLP's treatment documentation should include measurable short-term and long-term therapy goals for the client. The SLP generally can choose the method for demonstrating client progress and the instruments or procedures for measuring it. However, once the SLP chooses these, the method and measures that are used must usually stay constant throughout treatment. If the SLP has to change the method to use for documenting client progress, s/he should document how the new and old methods are related and other reasons for the change.

The following are examples of how SLPs can document therapy goals in their treatment documentation:

- A therapy goal can represent a seemingly minor yet meaningful change in client communication that will enable more autonomous functioning within a reasonable time. For some clients, this could be communicating functional needs through short phrases or single-word utterances. For some, it could simply be conveying "yes/no" affirmative/negative responses consistently. For others, it could be going back to work and communicating effectively there.

Copyright © Mometrix Media. You have been licensed one copy of this document for personal use only. Any other reproduction or redistribution is strictly prohibited. All rights reserved.
This content is provided for test preparation purposes only and does not imply an endorsement by Mometrix of any particular political, scientific, or religious point of view.

- A goal underlying treatment for a client with apraxia could be decreasing the symptoms enough for the client to initiate brief, understandable phrases with minimal articulation errors. Within this goal, one short-term goal could be initiating easier phonemes before harder ones. This would give the SLP neurologically and linguistically solid ground for working on producing one phoneme before beginning another one.
- The SLP could select a set of phonemes with a common distinctive feature to work on before other groups. For instance, because the lip movements producing bilabial consonants are easy for the client to see, the SLP may work on these before working on less visible phonemes that are produced inside the mouth.

Delivering professional SLP services includes documenting those services for legal, insurance, accountability, and informational purposes. Four kinds of clinical SLP documentation are as follows: assessment documentation, treatment documentation, daily notes, and progress reports. Documentation may include daily notes that report the activities included in each therapy session with a client. One common charting format is SOAP notes, i.e., subjective, objective, assessment, and plan sections used to organize documentation among all practitioners involved in a client/patient's assessment and treatment. Daily notes are often recorded in the SOAP format. SLP documentation may also incorporate periodic progress reports or treatment summaries. These are typically short narratives that clearly and concisely present objective information about the client's progress in therapy to date. Reviewers can thus be informed of progress toward treatment plans and therapy goals, plus any changes in these. Progress reports/treatment summaries can include the client's initial functional communication level, the client's current functional communication level and progress/lack thereof within the specific reporting period, the client's expected potential for rehabilitation/habilitation, and any changes in the treatment plan. Electronic documentation systems, provided they are supported by suitable technology ensuring privacy, accessibility, and utility, are included and are becoming increasingly common.

Elements of Coverage Provided to Support Claims

For healthcare insurers to cover SLP services, these services must be deemed medically necessary. In other words, they must be necessary and reasonable to treat diseases, illnesses, disabilities, developmental conditions, or injuries. Fundamental elements of coverage that SLPs should provide to support claims for their services are based upon the *Model Medical Review Guidelines for Speech-Language Pathology Service* (ASHA, 2004b), available on the ASHA website. ASHA's guidelines reference and refine the original national review guidelines of Medicare regarding SLP services. These elements are that services be **Reasonable**, i.e., treatment meets current standards of practice in its frequency, duration, and amount; **Necessary**, i.e., suitable for the condition and diagnosis of the client; **Specific**, i.e., designed to achieve specific targeted therapy goals; **Effective**, i.e., expected to result in improvement for the client within a reasonable length of time; and **Skilled**, i.e., sophisticated, complex, and requiring the SLP's particular knowledge, skills, and judgment to implement them. In order to establish medical necessity for services, the SLP must furnish documentation of the client's status, assessment, diagnosis, referrals, treatment, and progress. Hence, documentation is required to demonstrate the medical necessity of SLP services.

Documentation to Establish Medical Necessity for Services

Health insurance companies require that covered services be medically necessary. Therefore, for the SLP and/or facility to be reimbursed for services, the SLP must provide documentation that establishes their medical necessity. Some examples of applicable documentation include the following: A client medical history that is relevant to the communication or swallowing disorder and influences the SLP therapy, including a brief account of client functional status and previous pertinent SLP treatment, should be documented. The SLP should record her/his diagnosis of a

Copyright © Mometrix Media. You have been licensed one copy of this document for personal use only. Any other reproduction or redistribution is strictly prohibited. All rights reserved.
This content is provided for test preparation purposes only and does not imply an endorsement by Mometrix of any particular political, scientific, or religious point of view.

speech, language, or related disorder, e.g., receptive aphasia, apraxia of speech, stuttering, dysarthria, or dysphagia. The SLP should document the date of the diagnosed disorder's onset. If a physician referral is required, this must be documented. The SLP should provide documentation of the date of the initial assessment and the procedures that the SLP used to diagnose the disorder(s). The SLP must also supply documentation of the chosen treatment plan or program, and the date this plan or program was produced. Progress reports or progress notes updating the client's current status must also be documented.

ASHA Code of Ethics

Preamble

In the Preamble to its Code of Ethics, the American Speech-Language-Hearing Association (ASHA) states in the first paragraph that for SLPs, audiologists, and scientists of speech, language, and hearing to perform their duties responsibly, they must preserve the highest ethical principles and standards of integrity. In order to fulfill this purpose, ASHA has established a Code of Ethics that defines the basic principles and rules that the organization finds most essential. The second paragraph of the Preamble to the ASHA Code of Ethics identifies the individuals who must adhere to this Code as including (a) every member of ASHA, whether or not they have certification, (b) any nonmember who has received the Certificate of Clinical Competence from ASHA, (c) anyone who has applied for membership in ASHA or certification by ASHA, and (d) any Clinical Fellows (e.g., individuals granted with research fellowships) who are endeavoring to meet certification standards. In the third paragraph, the Preamble states that ASHA will consider anything unethical if it violates the purpose and/or spirit of the Code of Ethics. It also stipulates that failing to state any specific practice or responsibility in the Code cannot be interpreted as denying such practices or responsibilities exist.

According to the fourth paragraph of the Preamble to the American Speech-Language-Hearing Association (ASHA)'s Code of Ethics, the Principles of Ethics and their accompanying Rules of Ethics describe the basics of ethical behavior as they relate to responsibilities to clients; the public; SLPs; audiologists scientists of speech, hearing, and language; and to conducting scholarly and research activities. In the fifth paragraph, the Code of Ethics Preamble describes the four main Principles of Ethics as "aspirational and inspirational in nature" and indicates that these principles provide the underlying moral structure for the ASHA Code of Ethics. In addition, this paragraph identifies the Principles of Ethics as "affirmative obligations" that all ASHA members, Certificate of Clinical Competence nonmembers, membership or certification applicants, and clinical fellows must follow under all circumstances of their professional undertakings. The final paragraph of the Preamble defines the Rules of Ethics as more specific descriptions of actions that they prohibit or the minimal accepted professional behavior and as applying to all individuals identified as bound by the Code of Ethics (see above).

Principles of Ethics and Rules of Ethics

The ASHA Principles of Ethics, which comprise the moral foundation for the ASHA Code of Ethics, have an inspirational and aspirational character. Rules of Ethics are more specific descriptions of prohibitions and the minimum professional conduct acceptable.

Principle of Ethics I

Principle of Ethics I requires members/other identified individuals to hold highest the welfare of people they serve and research participants and to treat research animals humanely. Under Principle I, Rule A requires competent service provision. Rule B requires using referrals when indicated and all resources to assure high-quality service provision. Rule C prohibits discrimination in service delivery or research/scholarly activities based on race, ethnicity, national origin, gender,

Copyright © Mometrix Media. You have been licensed one copy of this document for personal use only. Any other reproduction or redistribution is strictly prohibited. All rights reserved.
This content is provided for test preparation purposes only and does not imply an endorsement by Mometrix of any particular political, scientific, or religious point of view.

gender identity/expression, sexual orientation, age, disability, or religion. Rule D proscribes members/others' misinterpreting credentials of personnel they supervise and prescribes informing clients of names and professional credentials of service providers. Rule E states that members/others holding the ASHA Certificate of Clinical Competence must not delegate duties requiring the unique knowledge, skills, and judgment within the scope of their profession to support staff, technicians, assistants, or other nonprofessionals they are responsible for supervising.

In the ASHA Code of Ethics, the Principle of Ethics I states that members/other individuals identified must show the highest regard for the welfare of those they serve or who participate in research and scholarship, and it provides for humane treatment for animals used in research. Under this principle, Rule of Ethics F allows members/others with the ASHA Certificate of Clinical Competence (CCC) to delegate work to technicians, support staff, assistants, or others only with suitable supervision and realize that as certified professionals, they themselves retain responsibility for client welfare. Rule G adds that CCC members/identified others may only delegate clinical service provision-related duties within their scope of professional practice to students with fitting supervision, again with the certified individuals having responsibility for the welfare of clients. Rule of Ethics H requires members/others identified to inform clients fully of the nature of services rendered, products provided, and their potential effects and to apprise research participants about the potential effects of their participation.

ASHA's first Principle of Ethics requires members/others identified to place client and research participant welfare first and provide animals involved in research with humane treatment. Under this principle, Rule of Ethics I requires members/designated others to evaluate the effectiveness of the products and services they provide and to offer these only when they can reasonably expect clients to receive benefits from them. Rule of Ethics J prohibits members/others from guaranteeing any service or procedure's outcomes by either directly stating or implying such guarantees, but it allows them to offer reasonable statements of client prognoses. Rule of Ethics K proscribes delivering clinical services through correspondence only. Rule of Ethics L does allow members/others specified to include e-health/telehealth as part of their practice as long as it does not violate any law. Rule of Ethics M prescribes that members/others named must maintain professional service, research, and scholarly activity; dispense product records adequately and secure them appropriately; and only permit access to the records when it is legally required or authorized.

ASHA's Principle of Ethics I dictates that ASHA members/other individuals described must give the highest priority to client and research participant welfare and humane treatment to animals being used for research purposes. Under this principle, Rule of Ethics N prohibits members/designated others from unauthorized disclosure of any personal or professional information about identified clients or research participants unless so doing is legally required or necessary for protecting individual or community welfare. Rule of Ethics O proscribes members/others named from charging for services they have not delivered and misrepresenting products they have dispensed, services they have provided, or scholarly/research activities they have conducted. Under Principle of Ethics I, Rule of Ethics P prescribes that members/others covered will enroll people and include them as teaching demonstration or research participants only if they are not coerced and they have given their informed consent and are voluntarily participating. Rule of Ethics Q requires members/included others to seek professional help if substance abuse or other health-related conditions have adverse impacts on their professional services, and withdraw from affected practice areas when indicated. Rule of Ethics R prohibits members/specified others from terminating service to clients without giving reasonable notice.

Copyright © Mometrix Media. You have been licensed one copy of this document for personal use only. Any other reproduction or redistribution is strictly prohibited. All rights reserved.
This content is provided for test preparation purposes only and does not imply an endorsement by Mometrix of any particular political, scientific, or religious point of view.

Principle of Ethics II

In the ASHA Code of Ethics, Principle of Ethics II requires members/others included to maintain their professional competence and performance at the highest levels and to honor their responsibilities for achievement. NOTE: Under this principle, Rule of Ethics A restricting services to members/others holding the Certificate of Clinical Competence (CCC) or in the process of certification under a CCC member's supervision was deleted from the rules, effective June 1, 2014. Rule of Ethics B dictates members/others named must only participate in aspects of the professions within the scope of their professional competence and practice, taking into consideration their education, training, and experience levels. Rule of Ethics C directs members/specified others to participate in lifelong learning for the maintenance and improvement of their professional skills and practice. Rule of Ethics D prohibits members/applicable others designated from allowing or requiring their professional staff members to deliver services or conduct research activities that are beyond their levels of education, training, experience, and competency. Rule of Ethics E requires members/applicable others to assure the correct calibration and working order of all equipment used for delivering services or conducting research and scholarly activities.

Principle of Ethics III

ASHA Principle of Ethics III enjoins members/others specified to observe their public responsibilities through the promotion of understanding about the professions by the public; their support of developing services designed to meet public needs not addressed; and their provision of correct information in all communication related to any part of the professions, to include disseminating scholarly pursuits and research findings and advertising, promoting, and marketing services and products. Under this principle, Rule of Ethics A prohibits members/designated others from misrepresenting their education, training, experience, scholarly or research activities, competence, or credentials. Rule of Ethics B proscribes members/others named from conducting professional activities that represent conflicts of interest. Rule of Ethics C requires members/others included to refer clients only in the clients' interests and not in the members/others' own financial, personal, or other interests. Rule of Ethics D prevents members/others from misrepresenting any of the services they provide; the results of their services; the products they offer and the effects of those products, diagnostic information, or research.

Principle of Ethics III states that ASHA members/others covered by its terms must demonstrate their responsibility to the public by furthering the public's understanding regarding the ASHA professions, supporting service development for addressing public needs that have not been met, and accurately communicating all information about the professions, including marketing, advertising, and promoting products and services and disseminating research results and scholarly activities. Rule of Ethics E under Principle III prohibits members/others identified from scheming to defraud or committing fraud related to procuring reimbursement, payment, or grants for services they provide, products they dispense, or research they conduct. Rule of Ethics F requires members/others included to give accurate information about the nature of communication disorders and their management, the professions, professional services, salable products, and scholarly and research activities in public statements. Rule of Ethics G dictates that ASHA members/specified others' public statements to announce, market, and advertise their professional services; promote products; and report research findings must comply with professional standards and be free of misrepresentation.

Principle of Ethics IV

In the ASHA Code of Ethics, Principle of Ethics IV refers to the relationships of ASHA members and identified others with their colleagues, students, and members of other disciplines and professions; it describes member/other responsibilities to the ASHA professions; and it sets a standard for

Copyright © Mometrix Media. You have been licensed one copy of this document for personal use only. Any other reproduction or redistribution is strictly prohibited. All rights reserved.
This content is provided for test preparation purposes only and does not imply an endorsement by Mometrix of any particular political, scientific, or religious point of view.

members/others to honor these relationships and responsibilities. Under this principle, Rule of Ethics A enjoins members/designated others to stand by the autonomy and dignity of the professions, accept their self-generated standards, and keep their interprofessional and intraprofessional relationships harmonious. Rule of Ethics B requires members/included others to prevent anybody they supervise from violating the ASHA Code of Ethics through any of their practices. Rule of Ethics C prohibits members/others from misrepresentation, deceit, fraud, or dishonest words or deeds. Rule of Ethics D disallows members/specified others from unlawfully harassing anyone in any way, including the abuse of power or sexual harassment. Rule of Ethics E proscribes members/others named in the code from engagement in any other types of conduct that reflect adversely upon the member's/other's fitness to deliver professional services or upon the professions.

ASHA Principle of Ethics IV states that its members and others named in the Code of Ethics must respect the responsibilities they have to the ASHA professions and the relationships they share with students, colleagues, and members of other disciplines and professions. Under this principle, Rule of Ethics F bans members/specified others from engaging in any sexual behaviors with students, research participants, or clients over whom they have professional power or authority. Rule of Ethics G requires members/included others to give credit to only persons who have contributed to products, presentations, or publications;, to attribute credit only with the consent of the contributors;, and to assign credit proportionately to the contributions. Rule of Ethics H prescribes that members/others identified will refer to their sources in presentations or summaries they make orally, in writing, or in any other media that use other people's products, presentations, research, or ideas. Rule of Ethics I specifies that member/other statements about professional services, products, and research findings to colleagues must be free from misrepresentation and comply with current professional standards.

ASHA Principle of Ethics IV pertains to members/others identified in the Code of Ethics honoring their responsibilities to the professions and their collegial, supervisor-/instructor-student, interdisciplinary and interprofessional relationships. Under this ethical principle, Rule of Ethics J proscribes members'/others' professional service delivery, irrespective of prescriptions or referral sources, without applying their independent professional judgment. Rule of Ethics K prohibits members/others from discrimination in their collegial, teacher-/supervisor-student, interprofessional and interdisciplinary relationships based on race, ethnicity, national origin, age, gender, gender identity/expression, sexual orientation, disability, or religion. Rule of Ethics L restricts members/others from filing complaints or encouraging others to file complaints with disregard for facts that would refute them or from using the ASHA Code of Ethics as a vehicle for retaliating against others, expressing personal hostility, or enacting personal reprisals. Rule of Ethics M enjoins members/others to inform the ASHA Board of Ethics if they have reason to believe the ASHA Code of Ethics has been violated. Rule of Ethics N requires full member/other compliance with Board of Ethics policies for considering and adjudicating complaints of Code of Ethics violations.

Recent Legislation

According to Janet Deppe, director of state advocacy for ASHA, fewer laws pertaining to regulations for SLP and audiology practices and professionals were enacted by US states in 2012 than in 2011. Although more total bills passed in the 2011 2012 sessions than in the 2010-2011 sessions—1,528 in 2012 vs.1,091 in 2011, the proportion affecting SLPs and audiologists was much smaller—only 64 of 1,528 versus 85 out of 1,091. Thus, the proportion of laws passed affecting the SLP and audiologist professions in 2012 was little more than half that in 2011: compared to almost 8% (7.79%) of all laws enacted in 2011, bills affecting SLP and audiology were only 4% of all bills

Copyright © Mometrix Media. You have been licensed one copy of this document for personal use only. Any other reproduction or redistribution is strictly prohibited. All rights reserved.
This content is provided for test preparation purposes only and does not imply an endorsement by Mometrix of any particular political, scientific, or religious point of view.

passed in 2012. The director views this decline as reflective of economic concerns. However, she also sees reason for optimism regarding the future, predicting slow but steady economic recovery and resulting state budget improvements may enable reimbursements and programs to be restored and innovations in telepractice and other newer areas to continue. ASHA continues assisting members and state associations in advocating for services and programs to benefit consumers, the professions, and its members and in monitoring state regulatory and legislative proposals.

According to a report in *The ASHA Leader* by ASHA's director of state advocacy (Deppe, 1/1/2013), as the US Congress passed fewer bills during its 2012 session, presumably in reaction to slow economic recovery following a recession; individual US states were viewed as reflecting this federal trend by also passing fewer state regulations and laws. With specific respect to SLP and audiology services and professionals, the annual ASHA analysis of state legislation found that fewer bills were passed than in the years before. The ASHA analysts expressed the belief that because of budgetary constraints, state legislatures were less willing to pass laws whose implementations would incur additional expenses, or were perceived as being expensive. ASHA personnel reviewing 1,528 pieces of legislation enacted in 2012 found that only 64 of these concerned SLPs and audiologists. This represented a decrease from 2011, when out of 1,091 bills reviewed, 85 involved SLPs and audiologists. Additionally, only 115 regulatory proposals were adopted out of 365. State regulations and bills enacted involved scope of practice, licensure, insurance coverage, Medicaid, essential health benefits, autism, education, hearing aids, student loan forgiveness, truth and transparency, telehealth/telepractice, and licensure for music therapy.

Until 2012, South Dakota and Colorado were the only US states lacking SLP licensure regulations. That year, the South Dakota legislature passed a bill enabling SLPs and SLP assistants to attain state licensure. This law requires universal licensure across all practice settings. This state bill realized the endeavors of the South Dakota Speech-Language-Hearing Association and its members, who had campaigned for the past 30 years for SLPs in the state to be licensed. The Colorado Speech-Language-Hearing Association had also advocated for SLP certification regulation. A new Colorado bill passed in 2012 enables its Department of Regulatory Agencies' Division of Registration to certify SLPs practicing in all settings except for schools. These laws made state agency regulation of SLPs and audiologists unanimous across all 50 states and the District of Columbia. In addition, the state of Maine passed a new regulation in 2012 that permits SLPs and audiologists who hold state licenses to work in public schools in their states without requiring additional credentials from the state department of education.

In 2012, 10 US state legislatures passed regulations to make technical changes in their practice acts for SLPs and audiologists. In Missouri, legislation reduced the number of restrictions on the supervision of SLP assistants in all practice settings. In Kentucky, the state legislature enacted updates to its licensure forms pertaining to interim practice. In Florida, the state legislature changed the language regulating its disposition of disciplinary cases, and in both Florida and Iowa, the state legislatures passed amendments to their disciplinary guidelines. The continuing education requirements for maintaining licensure were amended by the Maryland and Missouri state legislatures. In Maine and Ohio, the state legislatures set up fee structures applying to biennial licensure. In the state of Oregon, the legislature approved some rules that would lower the fees for initial licensure applications, licensure renewals, and licensure delinquency fees back to the same amounts that were charged in 2011. Maryland, West Virginia, and several other states eliminated a specific number score for passing the Praxis audiology examination, substituting a "passing score" requirement.

Copyright © Mometrix Media. You have been licensed one copy of this document for personal use only. Any other reproduction or redistribution is strictly prohibited. All rights reserved.
This content is provided for test preparation purposes only and does not imply an endorsement by Mometrix of any particular political, scientific, or religious point of view.

ASDs

Several US state legislature passed laws in 2012 that required health insurance companies to cover services provided to children with autism spectrum disorders (ASDs). This affects SLPs because many children with ASDs have communication deficits that SLP services can address. The Arkansas state legislature passed a bill that requires autism-related services be covered by insurance without benefit limitations. In Alabama, the state legislature enacted a bill mandating health insurance coverage for autism-related services to children up to 9 years of age. A law in Louisiana's raised the age for insurance coverage of services to individuals with ASDs to 21 years old and removed its previous benefits cap. A Utah state law made it illegal for healthcare insurers to deny coverage because of ASD diagnosis. Massachusetts enacted regulations establishing insurance rates to charge for SLP, PT, OT, and other specialty services to children with ASD diagnoses. The Oregon state legislature placed a limit on the maximum health insurance benefit for ASD-related services of $36,000 annually per beneficiary. Laws were also passed stipulating required coverage amounts, which varied among states, for ASD-related services in Delaware, Michigan, New Jersey, Vermont, and West Virginia.

Medicaid

The expense of delivering services under Medicaid continues to present challenges to US state governments. States cut these costs in 2011 and 2012 by decreasing services, lowering rates of Medicaid reimbursement, and eliminating optional services, including SLP and audiological services for adults aged above 21 years. In 2012, for example, a state amendment adopted in Idaho, resembling Medicare restrictions, modifies copayments for SLP and other services and limits amounts of SLP, occupational therapy (OT), and physical therapy (PT) treatment per beneficiary annually. A bill enacted by Illinois' state legislature imposed a limit of 20 visits per year for SLP, OT, and PT services. The state of Colorado also established limits to case management, SLP, and other special services that Medicaid provides per year to each patient. Two rules enacted by Indiana state legislators mandate a 5% reduction in rates to SLPs, audiologists, optometrists, and other medical service providers. An amendment passed to a Texas state rule increased the limitations and reduced the benefits of hearing aid services covered by Medicaid. The State of Washington removed Medicaid coverage of hearing, dental, vision, and other optional medical services to clients aged 21 and above to aid in balancing its budget.

Education and Essential Health Benefits

As of 2012, the state of Minnesota revised the licensure of special education teachers by enacting new rules, including legislation addressing the new categories of academic strategist and behavioral strategist. The Minnesota Speech-Language-Hearing Association collaborated closely with the Board of Teaching in Minnesota to make sure that special educators in these categories were not being awarded credentials for providing speech and language therapy. The Virginia state legislature adopted new requirements for early intervention case managers and early intervention professionals, which specify the requirements for their certification as certified Medicaid providers and certification under the Department of Education. In Iowa, the state adopted substantial changes in its early access program, including the time lines for making referrals, conducting evaluations, monitoring, and general supervision. Additional legislation, affecting insurance coverage of SLP and other services, includes a Utah law authorizing its legislature to determine benchmarks for its essential health benefits plan and a California law requiring coverage of essential health benefits by individual and small group health insurance plans.

Military Personnel and Their Families

Regarding military personnel who hold SLP, audiologist, and other professional licenses, a 2012 state law enacted in Wisconsin extended the expiration date for licenses that would otherwise

Copyright © Mometrix Media. You have been licensed one copy of this document for personal use only. Any other reproduction or redistribution is strictly prohibited. All rights reserved.
This content is provided for test preparation purposes only and does not imply an endorsement by Mometrix of any particular political, scientific, or religious point of view.

expire while licensed personnel are on active duty, from 90 days to 180 days. This extension also includes professional licenses held by military spouses if they are not practicing while their military service member spouses are on active duty. Another state law, adopted by the Delaware State Legislature in 2012, permits military spouses to apply to have their professional licensure reinstated within two years of the expiration dates of their licenses, and it also grants them temporary licensure for up to six months while their licensure applications are being processed. In Oregon, a state bill was enacted in 2012 that requires licensure boards to accept military training and/or experience that is substantially equivalent to professional SLP, audiologist, or other education, training, and experience as a substitute for that professional education, training, and experience.

AMA's Role Regarding Legislation for Truth and Transparency

The American Medical Association (AMA) has established the Scope of Practice Partnership. This partnership is designed to identify professions that the AMA believes are conducting activities that are outside of their scope of practice and, through the legislation of state practice acts, to target these professions so identified. Legislation mandating "truth and transparency" is one of the major goals that the AMA's Scope of Practice Partnership has identified. Laws related to truth and transparency require that professionals who hold doctoral degrees in their professions must identify themselves as doctors of speech-language pathology, doctors of audiology, etc., to the general public. Healthcare professionals who are not physicians, however, are of the opinion that such truth and transparency legislation that the AMA supports is redundant and not necessary. They view the AMA's promotion of such legislation as reflecting AMA attempts to scrutinize and judge the professional competence of other healthcare professionals who are not physicians or AMA members. Massachusetts, Maryland, and a few other US states have enacted this kind of truth and transparency legislation.

Dispension of Hearing Aids and Student Loans for SLPs

During their 2012 sessions, three US states enacted changes to their laws that regulate the requirements for the licensure, credentialing, and governance of professionals for the dispensing of hearing aids. According to ASHA's director of state advocacy, a bill passed by the Iowa State Legislature requires that audiologists, SLPs, and other professionals applying for licenses to dispense hearing aids must demonstrate their knowledge of the functions of hearing aids, the anatomy and physiology of hearing, etc., instead of passing a written test. In North Carolina, legislators eliminated the previous state requirement of taking an examination preparation course as a prerequisite for taking the examination to become qualified to dispense hearing aids. And in Virginia, a new state law dictated that the board for dispensers of hearing aids and the board for opticians would be merged. Since many professionals begin their careers with crushing student loan debts incurred to finance their education and professional preparation, a number of lobbyists and activists have recently been calling for student loan forgiveness. In keeping with this trend, a 2012 Mississippi law established a student loan forgiveness program for SLPs employed in Mississippi schools.

Telehealth and Telepractice

The state legislature of Maryland passed legal measures in 2012 that require health insurance companies to provide the same coverage for health care services whether they are delivered via telehealth or in person and that prohibit health insurance companies from denying coverages for services based only on the fact that they are remotely delivered. In Michigan, state legislation also prohibits health care insurers from denying coverage for remotely delivered services. And in New York State, a bill also passed in 2012 provides for health care practitioners who deliver services via telehealth to be awarded professional credentials. That same year, several US states considered

Copyright © Mometrix Media. You have been licensed one copy of this document for personal use only. Any other reproduction or redistribution is strictly prohibited. All rights reserved.
This content is provided for test preparation purposes only and does not imply an endorsement by Mometrix of any particular political, scientific, or religious point of view.

proposals for licensure of music therapy. ASHA opposed these proposals because of the broad scope of practice the bills contained, including the assessment and treatment of communication disorders. In Georgia, a revised bill for music therapy licensure was signed into law after ASHA worked closely with the Georgia state association to limit the scope of practice defined in the bill.

EBP

Evidence-based practice (EBP) has the purpose of integrating expert opinion and clinical expertise with external scientific evidence and the perspectives of clients and/or their caregivers for delivering quality services addressing the needs, choices, values, and interests of those served. Four main steps in the EPB process are formulating a clinical question, locating evidence, assessing that evidence, and making a clinical decision. One commonly used approach to defining a specific clinical question is called population, intervention, comparison, outcome (PICO). Addressing all four PICO areas in the clinical question helps assure the relevance of evidence obtained to the clinician's specific situation. For example, if population = stroke patients, intervention = initiating aphasia treatment early, comparison = initiating aphasia treatment following time for initial spontaneous recovery, and outcome = functional communication skills, the clinical question might be "Are early SLP interventions more likely to facilitate functional communication skills for stroke patients with aphasia than later SLP interventions?" Framing clinical questions typically takes trial and error to arrive at their ultimate forms; experts note that this process is not a science but an art. The biggest challenge in determining applicable clinical questions is deciding how specific the information should be within each PICO area.

PICO

PICO stands for population, intervention, comparison, and outcome. As an example, suppose the population consists of kindergarteners having articulation disorders, intervention involves individual pull-out therapy, comparison is with group pull-out therapy, and outcome is kindergarteners' producing the /s/ phoneme consistently. For Population, the SLP must decide whether to obtain evidence only about kindergarteners or to include children one/two years older and/or younger and/or older students, e.g., sixth graders, for comparison. If the evidence search is motivated by receiving a new ELL client, the clinician should consider whether to seek evidence about ELLs only, or both ELLs and native English speakers. Under intervention and comparison, the clinician should consider whether comparing individual versus group pull-out therapy is sufficiently specific, e.g., whether more information about therapy session content is necessary, or overly specific, e.g., individual versus group is less germane than pull-out versus classroom-based or collaborative consultation approaches as the primary issue. An alternative to the outcome of /s/ articulation could be a functional outcome, e.g., how much better kindergarteners could participate in classroom activities involving speech. Each outcome would require different kinds of evidence.

Framing a Clinical Question and Obtaining Evidence

The final form of a clinical question that a clinician develops in EBP is influenced by two main factors. The first factor is which theoretical model informing the SLP's thinking concerning the particular communication disorder in question. For example, if the population involved is stroke patients with aphasia, the SLP will use her/his expertise to decide how much weight to accord patient age as an influencing factor or whether differentiating left- versus right-hemisphere strokes is important to answer the clinical question. Therefore, true EBP requires clinician experience and expertise. The second factor is evidence availability. Addressing the question as defined depends on how much evidence can be obtained in reality. For example, the SLP may have originally posed a question regarding elementary-grade students with articulation disorders, but then s/he discovered a large amount of evidence specific to ELL and/or kindergarten students. This would inform focusing the question more on these populations to increase its pertinence to the clinical

Copyright © Mometrix Media. You have been licensed one copy of this document for personal use only. Any other reproduction or redistribution is strictly prohibited. All rights reserved.
This content is provided for test preparation purposes only and does not imply an endorsement by Mometrix of any particular political, scientific, or religious point of view.

conditions initiating it. However, scarce evidence is usually more common. Then clinicians must rely on their expertise to ascertain how much to loosen their criteria, yet still preserve relevance.

SYSTEMATIC REVIEWS AND INDIVIDUAL STUDIES

Four evidence-based practice (EBP) steps are posing a clinical question, finding evidence, assessing evidence, and making a clinical decision. Sometimes existing clinical EBP guidelines will apply to certain clinical questions, which is ideal. However, if not, SLPs must help inform their treatment decisions by looking for scientific evidence. Two main kinds of useful evidence are systematic reviews and individual studies. Systematic reviews are the foundations of clinical EBP guidelines. These are formal evaluations of the existing scientific evidence relative to a clinical question. Although they describe whether the evidence supports different diagnostic and/or treatment approaches, and if so, to what degree, systematic reviews do not actually offer specific clinical practice recommendations. Clinicians can use systematic reviews to help them make treatment decisions, because these reviews identify the characteristics of existing evidence about a clinical question in systematic ways. Some sources for locating systematic reviews include the following: ASHA Evidence Maps, ASHA/National Center for Evidence-Based Practice in Communication Disorders Compendium of Guidelines and Systematic Reviews, the Campbell Collaboration, the Cochrane Collaboration, the US Department of Education's What Works Clearinghouse, the Psychological Database for Brain Impairment Treatment Efficacy, the speechBITE™: Speech Pathology Database for Best Interventions and Treatment Efficacy, and the *Evidence-based Communication Assessment and Intervention* journal.

When systematic reviews of the literature relevant to a clinical question are unavailable, individual studies can provide evidence for informing treatment decisions. Online bibliographic databases are the first source to look in for studies. MEDLINE is the biggest online bibliographic database of healthcare-related studies in the world, citing 4,000 peer-reviewed journals with more than 12 million articles. However, scientific quality is not guaranteed by publication in a peer-reviewed journal. Also, English-language journals, especially American publications, less often contain studies with negative findings than European journals and other non-English-language publications. To review both positive and negative research evidence comprehensively, the Cumulative Index to Nursing and Allied Health Literature is a useful European database. Although it publishes more studies with negative findings than MEDLINE, it still publishes more with positive findings. "Gray" literature—i.e., research not published in peer-reviewed literature, e.g., unpublished evidence, conference proceedings, technical reports, or testimony—contains more negative as well as positive findings. Finding gray literature is challenging: internet searches, professional organizations, and consulting content experts are some ways to look for it.

ASSESSING SYSTEMATIC REVIEW EVIDENCE

When assessing systematic review evidence, one factor important to consider is whether the review is relevant to the specific clinical question the clinician poses. For example, if the SLP's clinical question is about treating a client with a brain injury who belongs to a linguistic/cultural minority group, the SLP must determine how useful is a systematic review on brain injury that omits linguistic/cultural minority populations or fails to mention them specifically. Or if the SLP's question is about treatment for an adolescent with an autism spectrum disorder (ASD), the SLP must decide whether reviews mainly concerning studies of younger children with ASDs are pertinent. These examples illustrate the absolute necessity of individual clinician experience and expertise to evidence-based practice. Another important factor is the author and publisher of the review. Although academic institutions and interdisciplinary collaboratives publish many reviews, so do payors and advocacy groups. The SLP must consider these sources' objectivity and how much

Copyright © Mometrix Media. You have been licensed one copy of this document for personal use only. Any other reproduction or redistribution is strictly prohibited. All rights reserved.
This content is provided for test preparation purposes only and does not imply an endorsement by Mometrix of any particular political, scientific, or religious point of view.

positive or negative findings would influence them. However, reviews from less objective sources are not guaranteed to be flawed any more than reviews from trustworthy sources are guaranteed to be of high quality: Critical judgment is essential.

Assessing Individual Research Studies

To evaluate the quality of an individual published study, two dimensions are generally assessed: the quality of the study and the level of evidence. Regardless of the type of research design used, study quality involves assessing how suitably a study was designed and implemented. No one group of criteria is universally accepted for defining studies of high quality. ASHA recommends the Scottish Intercollegiate Guidelines Network (SIGN) as a source to consult for examples of criteria for establishing study quality. Assessing the level of evidence entails establishing a hierarchy of research study designs according to their relative ability for protecting against research bias. Although, as with study quality, no single hierarchy is universally accepted, the design generally viewed as least subject to bias is that of randomized controlled trials (RCTs). One example adapted by ASHA from the SIGN of a hierarchy of levels of evidence follows: Ia: A well-designed meta-analysis of more than one RCT; Ib: a well-designed randomized, controlled study; IIa: a well-designed controlled, non-randomized study; IIb: a well-designed quasi-experimental study; III: well-designed nonexperimental studies, such as case studies and correlational studies; IV: an expert committee's report, a consensus conference, or a respected expert's clinical experience.

Factors to Consider for Applying Established Evidence-Based Clinical Guidelines

After asking a clinical question, finding evidence, and assessing the evidence, the SLP must combine that evidence with the client's perspective and the SLP's clinical expertise to make a specific clinical decision for an individual client. Evidence-based clinical guidelines have already been developed in some cases that apply to the SLP's specific question. To decide whether or how much to follow these guidelines, the SLP should consider several important factors. The first of these factors is whether the clinical guideline is relevant to the SLP's particular clinical question. For example, if the SLP has posed a clinical question regarding which intervention to choose for treating a client with childhood schizophrenia, the SLP must consider whether guidelines developed based mainly on evidence obtained from adults with schizophrenia are relevant. Or if the SLP formulated a clinical question about the treatment of an English language learner (ELL) client with aphasia, the SLP must then consider the usefulness of clinical guidelines developed regarding only native English-speaking aphasia patients. In evidence-based practice, these decisions require individual clinician experience and expertise.

When evidence-based clinical practice guidelines already exist that apply to a specific clinical question the SLP has posed, the SLP must consider whether to follow these guidelines and if so, to what extent. In addition to a guideline's relevance to the question, a second factor important to consider is whether and to what degree the guidelines are really evidence-based. Experts develop many guidelines via nonsystematic methods, such as consensus processes, etc. Although the consensus of experts is a valuable information source, without systematic methodology, expert conclusions are especially susceptible to the biases of the experts involved. Many such conclusions are actually incorrect, as evidenced by plentiful historical instances. With truly evidence-based guidelines, the methodology for obtaining and assessing evidence should be transparent to the clinician. However, quality is not guaranteed by transparency alone. Clinicians can find it challenging to ascertain whether evidence-based practice guidelines are of high quality. Hence, authorities have developed systems to evaluate practice guidelines, which can be helpful tools to decide whether to apply guidelines. The Appraisal of Guidelines Research and Evaluation II framework developed by the European Union and endorsed by the US Agency for Health Research and Quality is the preeminent tool.

Copyright © Mometrix Media. You have been licensed one copy of this document for personal use only. Any other reproduction or redistribution is strictly prohibited. All rights reserved.
This content is provided for test preparation purposes only and does not imply an endorsement by Mometrix of any particular political, scientific, or religious point of view.

In addition to guideline relevance to the clinical question and whether guidelines are truly evidence-based, SLPs should consider the source, i.e., guideline authorship and publisher. Although many guidelines are developed objectively, some sources have vested interests in methods recommended, outcomes, etc. and may be more subjective/biased. SLPs must consider who produced guidelines and how much any positive/negative recommendations would likely influence them. Clinicians cannot assume guidelines from less objective sources are necessarily deficient, or guidelines produced by accepted/trusted sources are necessarily of higher quality. In addition to their own informed judgment, SLPs can consult objective criteria such as the Appraisal of Guidelines Research and Evaluation II framework. Sources for evidence-based practice guidelines include the Scottish Intercollegiate Guidelines Network, ASHA/National Center for Evidence-Based Practice in Communication Disorders' Compendium of Guidelines and Systematic Reviews, the American Academy of Pediatrics, the National Guideline Clearinghouse, the US Department of Veterans Affairs, the Academy of Neurologic Communication Disorders and Sciences, the Royal College of Speech-Language Therapists, and the National Health Service of the UK's Electronic Library for Health. In lieu of available applicable guidelines, clinicians must consider factors including alternative treatment availability, potential harm, cost-effectiveness, client preference, etc. in treatment decisions.

Chapter Quiz

Ready to see how well you retained what you just read? Scan the QR code to go directly to the chapter quiz interface for this study guide. If you're using a computer, simply visit the online resources page at **mometrix.com/resources719/priispedtssli** and click the Chapter Quizzes link.

Copyright © Mometrix Media. You have been licensed one copy of this document for personal use only. Any other reproduction or redistribution is strictly prohibited. All rights reserved.
This content is provided for test preparation purposes only and does not imply an endorsement by Mometrix of any particular political, scientific, or religious point of view.

Praxis Practice Test

Want to take this practice test in an online interactive format?
Check out the online resources page, which includes interactive practice questions and much more: **mometrix.com/resources719/priispedtssli**

1. Which theory/theories of language acquisition emphasize(s) nature over nurture?

a. Relational frame theory
b. Generativist theories
c. Emergentist theories
d. Empiricist theories

2. Which of the following is NOT a part of Chomsky's transformational grammar?

a. Embedded structure
b. Structural changes
c. Surface structure
d. Hidden assumptions

3. MacWhinney's Competition Model falls into which category of language development theory?

a. Emergentist
b. Empiricist
c. Behavioral
d. Nativist

4. Which of the following has most recently been determined to be the most important factor in Piaget's cognitive development theory?

a. Nature
b. Nurture
c. Learning processes
d. Inherent structures

5. At approximately what age do children begin to give names to things?

a. Between four and six months of age
b. Between six months and one year old
c. Between one year and eighteen months
d. Between eighteen and twenty-four months of age

6. Which of the following observations does NOT support Chomsky's theory?

a. Children learn a probabilistic model of word sequences through experience.
b. Children in different countries go through similar stages of language development.
c. Children overregularize irregular verbs without having heard any examples of this.
d. Children invent unique languages in the absence of exposure to standard language.

Copyright © Mometrix Media. You have been licensed one copy of this document for personal use only. Any other reproduction or redistribution is strictly prohibited. All rights reserved.
This content is provided for test preparation purposes only and does not imply an endorsement by Mometrix of any particular political, scientific, or religious point of view.

7. A unit of sound is a:

a. Morpheme
b. Grapheme
c. Phoneme
d. Chereme

8. The International Phonetic Alphabet symbol /ʌ/ corresponds to:

a. The vowel sound in "book"
b. The vowel sound in "buck"
c. The vowel sound in "back"
d. The vowel sound in "beck"

9. The International Phonetic Alphabet symbol / ʃ/ represents the initial consonant sound in:

a. "Sass"
b. "Foe"
c. "Cha"
d. "She"

10. People in the southern United States tend to pronounce the words "pin" and "pen" the same way while people in the northern United States do not because:

a. Southerners were unable to differentiate between their meanings.
b. Nasality often obscures similar vowel sounds.
c. Southern speech has fewer overall vowel sounds.
d. Homophony within a nasal environment can occur in some dialects

11. Mary Ellen has diagnoses of both cerebral palsy and spastic dysarthria. What does spastic dysarthria indicate?

a. She cannot hear speech.
b. She cannot produce speech.
c. She cannot understand words.
d. She cannot sort speech sounds.

12. The study of sentence structure and word order is called:

a. Syntax
b. Semantics
c. Pragmatics
d. Morphology

13. Which of the following is NOT a psychogenic voice disorder?

a. Conversion muteness
b. Spasmodic dysphonia
c. Conversion aphonia
d. Mutational falsetto

Copyright © Mometrix Media. You have been licensed one copy of this document for personal use only. Any other reproduction or redistribution is strictly prohibited. All rights reserved.
This content is provided for test preparation purposes only and does not imply an endorsement by Mometrix of any particular political, scientific, or religious point of view.

14. Which of the following is unlikely to be observed in a preschool-aged child with delayed phonological development?

a. Delayed morphological development
b. Delayed syntactic development
c. Delayed discourse structure development
d. Delayed muscular development

15. Which of the following is NOT a phase of effective coughing behavior?

a. Inspiratory
b. Compressive
c. Depressive
d. Expiratory

16. Which scientific principle explains the decrease in air pressure in response to an increase in airflow as found in the myoelastic aerodynamic theory of phonation?

a. Bernoulli effect
b. Coanda effect
c. Boyle's law
d. Charle's law

17. While the anatomy and physiology of speech production is more than the sum of its parts, for the sake of convenience the speech mechanism can be divided into four phases. Which of the following is NOT one of these?

a. Respiration
b. Phonation
c. Modulation
d. Articulation

18. The parts of the body associated most closely with speech production obviously include the oral cavity, including the lips, tongue, and teeth. Which of the following is NOT one of the body parts *normally* most closely involved?

a. The larynx
b. The trachea
c. The esophagus
d. The nasal cavities

19. Which extrinsic muscle of the larynx is NOT a suprahyoid muscle?

a. The stylohyoid muscle
b. The mylohyoid muscle
c. The geniohyoid muscle
d. The sternohyoid muscle

20. Which of these theories of voice production was NOT first proposed in the 19th century?

a. Myoelastic-aerodynamic theory
b. Neurochronoaxic theory
c. Cavity-tone theory
d. Harmonic theory

Copyright © Mometrix Media. You have been licensed one copy of this document for personal use only. Any other reproduction or redistribution is strictly prohibited. All rights reserved.
This content is provided for test preparation purposes only and does not imply an endorsement by Mometrix of any particular political, scientific, or religious point of view.

21. Which of the five senses sends nerve impulses to the cerebral cortex without going through the thalamus?

a. Vision
b. Hearing
c. Gustation
d. Olfaction

22. How many cranial nerves are there in the human central nervous system?

a. Eight
b. Ten
c. Twelve
d. Fourteen

23. Of the following cranial nerves, which does NOT have sensory functions?

a. I
b. II
c. VIII
d. VI

24. Of the following cranial nerves, which has explicitly motor functions?

a. V
b. III
c. X
d. IX

25. Which of the following cranial nerves is NOT necessary for speech?

a. V
b. VII
c. XI
d. XII

26. Echolalia is:

a. Repeating oneself over and over
b. Repeating what other people say
c. Hearing echoes when others speak
d. The inability to control the volume of one's speech

27. Marco's first language is Castilian Spanish. His English is fluent, but his teacher refers him to the speech-language pathologist for what she calls a "lisp." Upon testing it is found that this feature of his articulation is systematically used only in words with the letter "c" followed by a vowel. The most likely explanation is:

a. Marco's first language is influencing his second language.
b. Marco is demonstrating a systematic articulation disorder.
c. Marco has developed Broca's aphasia.
d. Marco has an undiagnosed case of CAS.

Copyright © Mometrix Media. You have been licensed one copy of this document for personal use only. Any other reproduction or redistribution is strictly prohibited. All rights reserved.
This content is provided for test preparation purposes only and does not imply an endorsement by Mometrix of any particular political, scientific, or religious point of view.

28. Jason is a bright, happy, active four-year-old whose IQ scores are above average. He is healthy and his audiological testing is normal. His mother reports that 2-3 days after birth he was observed to have jaundice and lethargy, which resolved in an equally short time. These symptoms were recorded at the hospital but not diagnosed or treated as they resolved so quickly. Jason is referred to an SLP because his speech is fluent but characterized by substitution of glottal stops for many consonants, which he seems unable to produce by using the normal configurations of tongue, teeth, and shape of the oral cavity. The most likely reason for this is that:

a. Jason is simply lazy about using his mouth and is using his throat instead.
b. Jason's development is normal; his speech will correct without treatment.
c. Jason formed this habit in his early speech and did not grow out of it.
d. Jason probably sustained minimal neurological damage when a newborn.

29. When you make the sounds /t/, /d/, /s/, or /z/, normally your tongue is in contact with:

a. Your upper teeth.
b. Your alveolar ridge.
c. Your soft palate.
d. Your hard palate.

30. Arlene was born blind and deaf. Which maternal condition was most likely to have caused this?

a. Her mother contracted rubella while in her first trimester.
b. Her mother ate fish contaminated by mercury while pregnant.
c. Her mother regularly smoked cigarettes throughout her pregnancy.
d. Her mother regularly drank alcohol throughout her pregnancy.

31. Jane is a native speaker of American English. She is seven years old. She is lisping this year whereas she was not doing so last year. What is the most likely cause of this?

a. She lost all of her front baby teeth this year.
b. She picked up a bad habit from her friends.
c. It is a late-developing articulation disorder.
d. She is reacting to social or academic stress.
e. Her vocabulary has grown and contains words that are more difficult to pronounce.

32. Tommy is diagnosed with Broca's aphasia. What is NOT true related to this diagnosis?

a. Tommy probably has trouble with spoken word retrieval.
b. Tommy should be able to understand what is said to him.
c. Expressive and receptive language are equally impacted.
d. This is a neurological and language problem, rather than a speech problem.

33. Clara has a diagnosis of Wernicke's aphasia. What is NOT true about this disorder?

a. Clara can speak fluently but cannot understand what others say.
b. Clara's speech makes sense but will deteriorate without feedback.
c. Clara's words all have meaning but are not arranged in proper order.
d. Clara will probably develop compensatory strategies like stock phrases.

Copyright © Mometrix Media. You have been licensed one copy of this document for personal use only. Any other reproduction or redistribution is strictly prohibited. All rights reserved.
This content is provided for test preparation purposes only and does not imply an endorsement by Mometrix of any particular political, scientific, or religious point of view.

34. If a child is able to form words correctly but unable to string them together correctly to form a sentence, the child's issue is with:

a. Morphology
b. Syntax
c. Semantics
d. Memory

35. Which of these tests analyzes both receptive and expressive language?

a. The TACL
b. The ACLC
c. The NSST
d. Peabody

36. Which test assesses knowledge of the meaning of both English and Spanish words?

a. TOLD: Picture Vocabulary subtest
b. Peabody Picture Vocabulary Test
c. Toronto Tests of Receptive Vocabulary
d. Assessment of Children's Language Comprehension test

37. Which of these semantic intervention tasks is most similar to Sentence Completion?

a. Cloze format
b. Using riddles
c. 20 Questions
d. Role playing

38. Which of these intervention formats would be least applicable to learning synonyms and antonyms?

a. Identification, differentiation, and elaboration of meaning
b. Semantic classification and categorization
c. Judgment of consistency of meaning
d. Lexical paraphrasing

39. What is NOT a characteristic or tendency that would cause difficulty with semantics?

a. Concrete thinking
b. Limited imagery
c. Divergent thinking
d. Narrow perception

40. Which test does NOT assess immediate recall of digit series *both* forward and backward?

a. McCarthy Scales: Numerical Memory
b. ITPA: Auditory Sequential subtest
c. WISC-IV: Digit Span subtest
d. WAIS-IV: Digit Span subtest

41. In audiology, what does MCL stand for?

a. Maximum Comfort Level
b. Minimum Clarity Locutions
c. Medial Cochlear Ligaments
d. Most Comfortable Loudness

Copyright © Mometrix Media. You have been licensed one copy of this document for personal use only. Any other reproduction or redistribution is strictly prohibited. All rights reserved.
This content is provided for test preparation purposes only and does not imply an endorsement by Mometrix of any particular political, scientific, or religious point of view.

42. A "notch" audiogram (sometimes called "cookie-bite") with a sharp dip in acuity around 4,000 Hz typically represents what kind of hearing?

a. A normal curve of hearing
b. Noise-induced hearing loss
c. Conductive hearing losses
d. Age-related hearing losses

43. Which of the following is NOT one of the ossicles?

a. The stapedius
b. The stapes
c. The malleus
d. The incus

44. What would NOT cause a conductive hearing loss?

a. Obstruction by a foreign body in the ear
b. Perforation of the tympanic membrane
c. Exposure to excessively loud noises
d. Damage to one or more ossicles

45. What is NOT a source of sensorineural hearing loss?

a. Destruction of hair cells in the cochlea
b. Damage to one or more of the ossicles
c. Exposure to excessively loud noises
d. A common progression of old age

46. Which of the following is a bilabial consonant?

a. /f/
b. /r/
c. /v/
d. /m/

47. In audiology, what is UCL?

a. Ultimate comfortable level
b. Usual communication losses
c. Uncomfortable loudness level
d. Upper confidence limit (or level)

48. What does recruitment mean in audiology?

a. Reduced range between threshold, MCL, and UCL
b. Recruiting other nerves to supplant damaged nerves
c. Recruiting hearing acuity for barely audible sounds
d. Abnormally wide range between threshold and MCL

Copyright © Mometrix Media. You have been licensed one copy of this document for personal use only. Any other reproduction or redistribution is strictly prohibited. All rights reserved.
This content is provided for test preparation purposes only and does not imply an endorsement by Mometrix of any particular political, scientific, or religious point of view.

49. Antoine is a second-grader whom Glenda the SLP is evaluating at the beginning of the school year. His IQ and achievement tests are below average, but not profoundly so. When she tests his hearing, he initially responds normally, following the directions to raise his left or right hand when he hears a tone in his left or right ear. But after a couple of minutes he stops responding. Glenda keeps increasing the intensity of the tones but still gets no response. She tests the machine again by listening to the earphones herself and they work. She can get Antoine's attention easily by tapping him on the shoulder, standing in front of him, or talking to him, and he understands and answers questions. Even stranger, his teacher also reports he seems to hear and understand what is said to him. Glenda runs into her predecessor in the SLP position, who was promoted and still visits the school as part of her new job. She reports having the exact same experience with Antoine last year. So does the audiologist when she makes her periodic visit. While the school team will need neurological/psychological/psychiatric consultations for this phenomenon, which of the following is the most likely explanation for it?

a. Antoine is faking a hearing loss to receive special education or attention.
b. Antoine is suffering from conversion hysteria or psychogenic deafness.
c. Antoine is demonstrating the classic symptoms of organic hearing loss.
d. Antoine is likely to have some attentional or neurological deficiencies.

50. Presbycusis is most often characterized by:

a. More hearing loss at lower frequencies
b. More hearing loss at middle frequencies
c. Uniform hearing loss at all frequencies
d. More loss at higher frequencies

51. Dysarthria is:

a. A neurologically caused articulation disorder
b. A learning disability affecting reading ability
c. A neurologically caused swallowing disorder
d. An articulation disorder of the speech organs

52. Which of the following malocclusions is *most* likely to cause distortion of sibilants?

a. Overbite
b. Open-bite
c. Underbite
d. Cross-bite

53. Willie is a man in his 50s who sustained brain damage due to head injuries from multiple motor vehicle accidents. He now has motor apraxia. This means that:

a. When he walks, he appears to be drunk.
b. He can use his upper but not lower body.
c. He cannot control external speech organs.
d. He can speak but not understand speech.

Copyright © Mometrix Media. You have been licensed one copy of this document for personal use only. Any other reproduction or redistribution is strictly prohibited. All rights reserved.
This content is provided for test preparation purposes only and does not imply an endorsement by Mometrix of any particular political, scientific, or religious point of view.

54. Mrs. Stokes is an elderly woman who suffered a cerebrovascular stroke. She now has difficulty swallowing solid foods. She is most likely to have a diagnosis of:

a. An esophageal dysphagia
b. Oropharyngeal dysphagia
c. An esophageal achalasia
d. A case of odynophagia

55. Therapy for dysphagia includes all of these EXCEPT?

a. Lip exercises
b. Tongue exercises
c. Mental exercises
d. Swallowing exercises

56. Among exercises to improve swallowing ability in cases of dysphagia, not all involve actually swallowing. One of these is the Shaker exercise, which involves lifting the head but not the shoulders while lying flat on the back. Which of the following is another swallowing exercise that does NOT involve swallowing?

a. The Mendelsohn maneuver
b. The hyoid lift maneuver
c. The effortful swallow
d. The supraglottic swallow

57. In Piaget's stage theory of cognitive development, which of the following is NOT a stage?

a. Sensorineural
b. Sensorimotor
c. Preoperational
d. Concrete operations

58. What did the psychologist Lev Vygotsky mean by "private speech?"

a. Talking to oneself as a pathological symptom
b. Talking privately between two close friends
c. Talking to oneself to direct one's behavior
d. Talking privately among several intimate friends

59. How many stages of expressive language development do children go through according to Brown?

a. 4
b. 3
c. 5
d. 2

60. On which of the following does learning theory focus?

a. Unconscious impulses
b. Internal mechanisms
c. Social relationships
d. Observable behaviors

Copyright © Mometrix Media. You have been licensed one copy of this document for personal use only. Any other reproduction or redistribution is strictly prohibited. All rights reserved.
This content is provided for test preparation purposes only and does not imply an endorsement by Mometrix of any particular political, scientific, or religious point of view.

61. Which of these techniques does systematic desensitization use?

a. Exposure to excessive amounts of the stimulus found aversive
b. Successive approximations of exposure to an aversive stimulus
c. Extinction of the undesirable response to the aversive stimulus
d. Exchanging the aversive stimulus for a more desirable one

62. Wendy is a five-year-old who substitutes /w/ for /r/ in her speech. She is referred to you, the speech-language pathologist for her school, because her mother and her teacher are concerned about her articulation. Of the following things you could tell them, which would be correct?

a. Wendy has an articulation disorder and must have speech therapy.
b. Wendy has an idiolectal pronunciation that is unusual but normal.
c. Wendy must have hearing loss, as /r/ is most often affected by it.
d. Wendy is normal as the norm for correct /r/ production is 8 years.

63. Elise is a fourth-grader who palatalizes her /tʃ/sound (i.e., her tongue is pressed up against her hard palate), noticeably distorting it. Glenda the SLP mentions this student to her predecessor Linda, who was Elise's SLP last year, and Linda affirms she was completely unsuccessful in remediating this articulation error. Glenda hits upon the idea of giving Elise a tongue depressor, instructing her to use it initially to keep her tongue from touching her palate while producing the target phoneme. Once Elise has become accustomed to the feeling of this tongue position and the sound she produces, Glenda has her phase out the tongue depressor until eventually she is pronouncing the sound correctly without it. Which of the following conclusions about this episode is most likely?

a. Elise's success this year is due to maturation alone and the treatment was superfluous.
b. Glenda's solution of the tongue depressor was entirely responsible for Elise's success.
c. Elise's success is most likely due to a combination of the therapy and her maturation.
d. Elise's success was due to her choice to change her speech, not therapy or maturation.

64. You would expect to use Melodic Intonation Therapy (MIT) for a client with which of the following diagnoses?

a. Transcortical sensory aphasia
b. Wernicke's aphasia
c. Broca's aphasia
d. Conduction aphasia

65. Which is the most common form of stuttering?

a. Neurogenic stuttering
b. Psychogenic stuttering
c. Developmental stuttering
d. Profound stuttering

66. Stuttering involves disorders with all of these EXCEPT?

a. Rate
b. Rhythm
c. Fluency
d. Volume

Copyright © Mometrix Media. You have been licensed one copy of this document for personal use only. Any other reproduction or redistribution is strictly prohibited. All rights reserved.
This content is provided for test preparation purposes only and does not imply an endorsement by Mometrix of any particular political, scientific, or religious point of view.

67. Which of the following is NOT true about stuttering?

a. Approximately 3 million Americans stutter.
b. Stuttering happens in individuals of all ages.
c. It is most frequent between the ages of 2-5.
d. In children it always lasts for several years.

68. Which of these statements is NOT true of stuttering?

a. Boys are twice as likely to stutter as girls are.
b. As they age, fewer boys are likely to stutter.
c. The majority of children outgrow stuttering.
d. Around 1% or fewer of adults are stutterers.

69. Which of the following is true in regards to stuttering?

a. Three genes attributed to stuttering have been identified.
b. All stuttering is genetic in nature.
c. Developmental stuttering is not found to run in families.
d. Familial stuttering is attributed to environmental factors.

70. Jane has cerebral palsy characterized by poor balance, lack of muscle tone, and a slight reoccurring tremor. Which type of cerebral palsy does Jane have?

a. Diplegic
b. Ataxic
c. Dyskinetic
d. Spastic

71. In Starkweather's (1987) demands/capacity model of stuttering, what is NOT true?

a. Some individuals have a predisposition for their speech to break down.
b. When demands exceed capacity, speech breaks down into dysfluency.
c. Stressors in the social environment do not influence speech demands.
d. Most stutterers report that their speech is "just fine" a lot of the time.

72. Which of these is NOT an overt feature of stuttering?

a. Blocks
b. Repetitions
c. Avoidances
d. Prolongations

73. What is the only unpaired muscle in the larynx?

a. Cricothyroid
b. Oblique arytenoid
c. Transverse arytenoid
d. Superior thyroarytenoid

74. "When reading aloud, John will raise his hand to signal 90% of his stuttering occurrences without cueing." This is an example of a behavioral objective for:

a. Speech awareness
b. Speech description
c. Speech modification
d. Speech preparation

Copyright © Mometrix Media. You have been licensed one copy of this document for personal use only. Any other reproduction or redistribution is strictly prohibited. All rights reserved.
This content is provided for test preparation purposes only and does not imply an endorsement by Mometrix of any particular political, scientific, or religious point of view.

75. "John will identify three physical signs of his anxiety right before introducing himself to a group." This is an example of a behavioral objective for:

a. Emotional exploration
b. Emotional awareness
c. Emotional modification
d. Emotional understanding

76. "He bad." "Where was you?" "That Renee toy." "She don't drive." "I knowed that." These expressions are most likely attributed to:

a. Delayed language development
b. Disorders of articulation
c. Non-standard English
d. Stage V of early expressive language development

77. Which of the following is NOT a component of a lesson plan for speech-language therapy?

a. Goals for the semester
b. Behavioral objectives
c. Describing activities
d. Medical history

78. What have researchers NOT found regarding articulation with cleft lip and cleft palate?

a. Individuals with cleft lip only have essentially normal articulation.
b. Differences in articulation between repaired and unrepaired clefts are very large.
c. Unilateral clefts allow better articulation than bilateral ones.
d. Articulation is better with incomplete rather than complete clefts.

79. Research has found which of the following types of consonants to have the highest rates of correct production in people with cleft palates?

a. Nasal consonants
b. Consonant glides
c. Plosive stops
d. Fricatives

80. Who of the following speech-language pathologists is/was NOT a specialist in the field of stuttering?

a. George H. Shames
b. Charles G. Van Riper
c. Martin F. Schwartz
d. Daniel R. Boone

81. Which of the following conditions affecting the voice is NOT responsive to voice therapy?

a. Thickening of vocal cords
b. Vocal nodules or polyps
c. Laryngeal contact ulcers
d. Acute infectious laryngitis

Copyright © Mometrix Media. You have been licensed one copy of this document for personal use only. Any other reproduction or redistribution is strictly prohibited. All rights reserved.
This content is provided for test preparation purposes only and does not imply an endorsement by Mometrix of any particular political, scientific, or religious point of view.

82. Which of the following is NOT a traditional symptom of laryngeal trauma?

a. Dysphagia
b. Wheezing
c. Hoarseness
d. Hemoptysis

83. Which is the least common feature of functional dysphonias?

a. Breathy voice
b. Loud voice
c. Weak voice
d. Harsh voice

84. Of the following voice disorders, which is *most* likely to result in no voice at all?

a. Spastic dysphonia
b. Functional aphonia
c. Vocal cord paralysis
d. Laryngeal web/synechia

85. What is NOT a variable typically rated in a voice screening for school children?

a. Rate
b. Pitch
c. Quality
d. Resonance

86. Cleft palate is known to cause hypernasality. Among other organic etiologies, which does NOT cause a hypernasal voice?

a. An elongated palate
b. Surgical trauma
c. Soft palate injury
d. Neurological impairment

87. When determining the "incidence" of a disorder, what is being measured?

a. The number of newly diagnosed cases of the disorder within a given time frame
b. The proportion of the population that currently has the disorder
c. The number of cases of the disorder that were successfully treated
d. The distinct cause of the disorder

88. Which of the following treatments is NOT used for denasality?

a. Ear training
b. Target voice models
c. Establishing new pitch
d. Explanation of problem

89. What is NOT true about nasal emission?

a. It is a type of nasal resonance problem.
b. It can often accompany hypernasality.
c. It can be due to palatal insufficiency.
d. It rarely exists for functional reasons.

Copyright © Mometrix Media. You have been licensed one copy of this document for personal use only. Any other reproduction or redistribution is strictly prohibited. All rights reserved.
This content is provided for test preparation purposes only and does not imply an endorsement by Mometrix of any particular political, scientific, or religious point of view.

90. Which is NOT a characteristic of voice differences in the deaf?

a. Overly high pitch before puberty
b. Pharyngeal focus of resonance
c. Severe denasality of the voice
d. True hypernasality with some

91. Which of the following reinforcement types has the highest resistance to extinction?

a. Variable-ratio
b. Variable-interval
c. Fixed-ratio
d. Fixed-interval

92. What does the abbreviation NPO stand for?

a. Once a night by mouth
b. Unable to perform plosives
c. New phonetical orientation
d. Nothing by mouth

93. What is NOT an advantage of electrolarynx devices?

a. The quality of the voice tone produced
b. Their use is quickly and easily learned
c. They are able to produce a loud voice
d. No interference with other methods

94. Tympanometry is an acoustic test designed to assess the condition of which portion of the ear?

a. Outer
b. Inner
c. Middle
d. Auditory nerve

95. After total laryngectomy, some patients may use a device called an HME. This is:

a. Used to prosthetically produce a voice tone
b. Used to protect the airway for respiration
c. Used to electromechanically produce voice
d. Used to highlight, mitigate, and evaluate any respiratory insufficiencies

96. Which of the following is NOT one of the seven subscales measured by the Adolescent Language Screening Test (ALST)?

a. Expressive vocabulary
b. Pragmatics
c. Rate
d. Phonology

Copyright © Mometrix Media. You have been licensed one copy of this document for personal use only. Any other reproduction or redistribution is strictly prohibited. All rights reserved.
This content is provided for test preparation purposes only and does not imply an endorsement by Mometrix of any particular political, scientific, or religious point of view.

97. What is NOT a disadvantage of silicone prostheses inserted via the tracheoesophageal puncture (TEP) technique for a postoperative total laryngectomy patient?

a. Prosthesis maintenance
b. Time between replacement of the device
c. Low resistance to the flow of air
d. Total expense

98. An effective and desirable voice prosthetic should include all of the following features EXCEPT?

a. Safe and reliable use
b. A loose-fitting fistula capable of expansion
c. Frontloading insertion
d. Semipermanent fixation

99. In second language acquisition, what is Stage II also called?

a. Speech Emergence Stage
b. Receptive Stage
c. Intermediate Proficiency Stage
d. Early Production Stage

100. Who described the Acquisition-Learning, Monitor, Natural Order, Input, and Affective Filter hypotheses?

a. Swain
b. Cummins
c. Gregory
d. Krashen

Copyright © Mometrix Media. You have been licensed one copy of this document for personal use only. Any other reproduction or redistribution is strictly prohibited. All rights reserved.
This content is provided for test preparation purposes only and does not imply an endorsement by Mometrix of any particular political, scientific, or religious point of view.

Answer Key and Explanations

1. B: Generativist theories (B) of grammar such as those of Noam Chomsky and Eric Lenneberg emphasize nature over nurture. They posit the existence of innate abilities (nature) such as a language acquisition device as being more fundamental to language development than environmental influences (nurture). Relational frame theory (A) is based on operant conditioning and therefore emphasizes the role of the environment in language learning. Emergentist theories (c) and empiricist theories (D) of language development both focus more on the interactions between nature and nurture rather than emphasizing either one over the other.

2. A: Deep structure (A) is what Chomsky said was the original form in which we conceive a linguistic expression, which often does not follow traditional rules of grammar. Compliance with those rules involves structural changes (B) or transformations. Surface structure (C) is the expression following those transformations, which does observe grammatical rules. For example, a deep structure might be something like "me + go." The mind performs transformations to reflect the subject of a sentence rather than the object, and the tense of a verb, to produce a surface structure like "I went." Transformations also change statements into questions ("why you not go" becomes "why didn't you go?"), add "-'s" to make a proper noun possessive ("Tommy ball" becomes "Tommy's ball", etc. With the elements "John" + "kiss" + "Mary," two different surface structures such as "Mary kissed John" and "John was kissed by Mary" have the same deep structure and the same meaning. Hidden assumptions (D) or biases are knowledge that nativist theorists like Chomsky believe are inherent and allow children to ascertain rapidly what is/is not possible in their language's grammar, and to achieve mastery of the grammar by the age of three.

3. A: MacWhinney's Competition Model is an (A) emergentist theory of language development. Such theories claim that language acquisition is a cognitive process emerging from the interactions of biology and the environment. Empiricist (B) theories arose as a reaction against nativist theories which emphasized the innate nature of language acquisition. These include relational frame theory, social interactionist theory, statistical learning theories, and functional linguistics. Empiricism recognizes the interaction between nature and nurture, but puts more emphasis on the role of learning, or nurture, and finds that the inherent, or nature, part is a general cognitive learning mechanism. Behavioral (C) theories such as Skinner's find language acquisition to be a form of operant conditioning in which linguistic behavior is shaped by the consequences of verbal responses. Nativist (D) theories include Chomsky's transformational grammar or generative grammar and the theories of Jerry Fodor and Eric Lenneberg. These theories view the acquisition of language as being based more on inherent abilities or mechanisms than on environmental influences.

4. C: Those influenced by Piaget's theory of cognitive development (C) have found the role of learning processes to be more important than previously thought. Piaget believed that children learn by interacting with and acting upon their environments, and that in so doing, they construct knowledge (constructivism). These beliefs are compatible with placing more importance on learning processes than on inherent structures (D), such as a language acquisition device (LAD) and a universal grammar, which are emphasized by nativist theories. While most theories recognize the interaction of nature and nurture (A & B) to some degree, those subscribing to Piaget's models have come to feel since the 1980s that learning processes play a more important role than previously realized.

Copyright © Mometrix Media. You have been licensed one copy of this document for personal use only. Any other reproduction or redistribution is strictly prohibited. All rights reserved.
This content is provided for test preparation purposes only and does not imply an endorsement by Mometrix of any particular political, scientific, or religious point of view.

5. C: Children begin naming things (C) between the ages of one year and eighteen months, most commonly around the age of one year. In addition to naming things, children also begin to use symbolic gestures (e.g., shrugging to indicate "I don't know" or spreading the arms wide to indicate "big" or "a lot") at the end of the first year. Between four and six months (A), babies begin to distinguish the main vowel and consonant sounds of their native languages in speech they hear. Between six months and one year (B), children can recognize words within the flow of speech that they hear. At seven months, a baby may recognize and remember individual words, but may not recognize the same word uttered by different speakers. Between eighteen and twenty-four months (D), children start speaking in two- and three-word phrases, often called telegraphic speech, and can understand the meanings of verbs based on the contexts in which they are used.

6. A: The observation that (A) children learn a probabilistic model of word sequences through experience supports statistical learning theories of language development, not Chomsky's theory. In statistical learning theory, children develop an understanding of the probability of how words will likely appear in a sequence through experience and generalize their learning to patterns and categories of word order. The observation that children with different languages go through similar developmental stages in learning language (B) supports Chomsky's theory of universal grammar. Overregularization of irregular verbs, such as "goed" or "taked," reflects a basic understanding of how regular verbs conjugate. Children applying the rule to irregular verbs without having heard such constructions supports Chomsky's theory of inherent linguistic structures. The observation that children may invent unique languages when not exposed to a standard language (D) supports Chomsky's theory of innate devices enabling language development. Researchers found a group of deaf children in Nicaragua who could not hear spoken Spanish and were never taught any standard sign language. These children invented their own sign language, which was grammatically complex and was not related to Spanish or to any standard sign language.

7. C: A phoneme (C) is a single unit of sound. A morpheme (A) is a unit of semantic meaning, which may be a word or a syllable (such as "un" or "-s"). A grapheme (B) is a unit of written language as opposed to spoken language. A chereme (D) is the sign-language equivalent of a spoken-language phoneme, i.e., a single unit of gestural language.

8. B: The symbol /ʌ/ corresponds to the sound in "buck" (B). The sound in "book" (A) is represented by the symbol /ʊ/. The sound in "back" (C) is denoted by the symbol /æ/ (called "ash"). The sound in "beck" (D) is represented phonetically by the symbol /ɛ/.

9. D: The symbol /ʃ/ represents the first sound in (D) "She," the "sh" sound. The "s" sound in "sass" (A) is /s/ in the International Phonetic Alphabet. The "f" sound in "fist" (B) is given the symbol /f/. The sound in "cha" (C) as in "cha-cha" is actually a combination of a /t/ sound and the /ʃ/ sound in "she" (D). As such it is represented by the symbol /tʃ/.

10. D: The "pin"/"pen" phenomenon is an example of (D) homophony in a nasal environment which occurs in some dialects, such as Southern American English. The nasality of the /n/ following the vowel in both words causes the vowels to sound the same in this regional dialect. The idea that the nasal /n/ sound obscures the distinction between /I/ and /ɛ/ (B) sounds plausible but is untrue. Southern speech does not have fewer vowel sounds (C) than Northern speech; many vowels are pronounced as diphthongs or triphthongs in the South, suggesting more vowel sounds. It is wholly untrue that Southerners do not know the meanings of these words (A), as evidenced by a common response in Southerners when hearing either word without sufficient context to distinguish the meaning; i.e. "Do you have a pen/pin?" will often be met with the response, "Do you mean an ink pen or a safety pin?" Linguists have demonstrated the homophony phenomenon with native

Copyright © Mometrix Media. You have been licensed one copy of this document for personal use only. Any other reproduction or redistribution is strictly prohibited. All rights reserved.
This content is provided for test preparation purposes only and does not imply an endorsement by Mometrix of any particular political, scientific, or religious point of view.

Southerners by asking them to make a conscious effort to pronounce each vowel differently in isolation while nasalizing their speech; most cannot, producing the same vowel sound each time.

11. B: Spastic dysarthria means Mary Ellen (B) cannot produce speech sounds. She can vocalize but not verbalize. Her spasticity is a rigidity and incoordination of the muscles used to produce meaningful speech sounds due to damage to the parts of the brain that control these muscles. This term does not mean she is unable to hear speech (A). It does not mean that she cannot understand words (C) or spoken language; this would be a definition of Wernicke's aphasia or receptive aphasia, a neurological disorder that interferes with processing receptive language. It does not mean that she cannot sort or differentiate among speech sounds (D); she can understand what she hears but cannot reproduce it herself.

12. A: Sentence structure and word order and/or their study are called syntax (A). Semantics (B) refers to the study of meaning in language. Pragmatics (C) refers to the study of how context contributes to meaning. Morphology (D) refers to the study of the structure of words.

13. B: Spasmodic dysphonia (B) is a voice disorder caused by involuntary muscular movements in the larynx. Because this disorder is physiological in nature, rather than psychological, it is not considered a psychogenic voice disorder. Conversion muteness (A), conversion aphonia (C), and mutational falsetto (D) are all psychogenic in origin, meaning they are not specific to any underlying organic cause.

14. D: There is no evidence to suggest a correlation between phonological development delays and muscular development delays (D). However, according to research findings, preschool-aged children with delayed phonological development are likely to also have delayed morphological (A), syntactic (B), and discourse structure development (C). In addition, young children typically demonstrate better phonological performance when uttering individual words and verbal labels for pictures than connected conversational speech and organized, syntactically complex narratives.

15. C: There is no depressive coughing phase (C). Coughing behavior has three phases: inspiratory (A), compressive (B), and expiratory (D). Effective coughing requires all three phases to work in conjunction.

16. A: According to the myoelastic-aerodynamic theory of phonation, the adducted vocal folds create resistance against the exhaled air. Air pressure below the glottis then builds up, opening the vocal folds. The subglottic pressure is then immediately released as airflow. This increased air velocity causes air pressure to drop relative to the vocal folds' medial (inner) borders, which brings the vocal folds back together again. This air pressure decrease corresponding to the increased air speed that causes the vocal folds' approximation is known as the Bernoulli effect (A). All of the other principles are unrelated.

17. C: Modulation (C) is not one of the four phases of the speech mechanism. Modulation can mean varying the pitch, tone, or intensity of one's voice, which will determine the prosody of a person's speech, but is not one of the actual phases of producing speech. The phases are respiration (A) or breathing, which is required to provide a stream of air; phonation (B) or producing sound by using the air to vibrate the vocal folds and/or other parts of the vocal tract; articulation (D) or altering the specific qualities of phonation to produce various specific vowel and consonant sounds, mainly by changing the shape of the oral cavity as well as manipulating the tongue, teeth, lips to block or release airflow; and resonance, or the natural frequency of vibration of the vocal apparatus.

18. C: The esophagus (C) is not *normally* most closely involved in speech production. The exception is when a person has had a laryngectomy, i.e. the removal of the larynx, usually in cases of laryngeal

Copyright © Mometrix Media. You have been licensed one copy of this document for personal use only. Any other reproduction or redistribution is strictly prohibited. All rights reserved.
This content is provided for test preparation purposes only and does not imply an endorsement by Mometrix of any particular political, scientific, or religious point of view.

cancer. In these cases, the individual cannot phonate normally. Such individuals often learn esophageal speech, wherein they swallow air and then burp, using their other speech production parts to shape this belched air into speech sounds. However, most individuals have intact larynxes and do not use esophageal speech. The body parts most closely involved are the lungs, larynx, trachea, and nasal cavities. The larynx (A) is at the top of the trachea and creates a valve to open and close the air stream. It is used in producing speech and also in coughing, vomiting, urinating, moving the bowels, and heavy lifting. The trachea (B), commonly known as the windpipe, lies vertically between the larynx and the bronchi and in front of the esophagus. It is made up of cartilage rings, fibrous tissue, and smooth muscle, giving it the flexibility to accommodate changes in air pressure within the chest. The nasal cavities (D) are involved in inhaling and exhaling air, producing nasal speech sounds, and contributing to resonance, as well as controlling temperature, humidity, and inhaled particles.

19. D: The sternohyoid muscle (D) is not a suprahyoid muscle but an infrahyoid muscle. It originates in the sternum as its name implies, specifically in the manubrium sterni, and inserts on the hyoid bone. The stylohyoid (A) originates in the styloid process and inserts on the hyoid bone. The mylohyoid (b) is a sheet of muscle fibers forming the muscular floor of the mouth. Its fibers run along a bony ridge called the mylohyoid line on the inner surface of the mandible. The geniohyoid (C) muscle fibers originate via a short tendon in the lower mental spine at the mandibular symphysis and insert on the anterior surface of the hyoid bone. The suprahyoid muscles are all laryngeal elevators, i.e. they lift up the larynx. Infrahyoid muscles such as the sternohyoid (D) are, along with the omohyoid muscles, the "strap muscles" of the neck. The sternohyoid pulls the hyoid bone down, and keeps it fixated in place when the mandible is opened against resistant force.

20. B: Neurochronoaxic theory (B) was proposed by Raoul Husson in 1950 and is the only theory listed here that was formulated in the 20th century. The myoelastic-aerodynamic theory (A) was proposed by Johannes Müller in 1843 and has been very popular ever since. It states that the vocal folds are subject to well-known aerodynamic and physical principles. According to this theory, the frequency and mode of vibration of the vocal folds depend on their length related to tension and mass and their boundaries, and on the properties of mucus, mucous membranes, connective tissue, and muscle tissue, which properties in turn are regulated by the interaction of the laryngeal muscles. The cavity-tone theory (C) was proposed by Willis in 1830. In this theory, vowel sounds depended on the length of the resonating tube and were independent of the "reed" tone, based on the analogy with early "talking machines" consisting of an air supply, a reed, a resonator, and a cover. The harmonic theory (D), proposed by Charles Wheatstone in 1837, postulated that the "reed" tone described by Willis was not a pure tone but a complex tone with many harmonics or overtones and that vowel sounds resulted from augmentation of some harmonics. Accordingly, the harmonic theory is also called the overtone theory or the steady state theory.

21. D: Olfaction (D) or the sense of smell is the only sense which does not make a synapse in the thalamus before proceeding to the cerebral cortex. Visual information (A) travels via the optic nerve to the superior colliculus, the thalamus, and the visual cortex in the occipital lobe at the rear of the cerebral cortex. Auditory information (B) travels from the cochlea via the auditory nerve to the inferior colliculus of the side of the midbrain opposite the hearing ear, through the medial geniculate nucleus inside the thalamus, then to the auditory cortex, to the cochlear branch of cranial nerve VIII (acoustic), to the cochlear nucleus of the brain's medulla. Gustatory information (C) travels via cranial nerves VII (facial nerve), IX (glossopharyngeal nerve) and X (vagus nerve) to the nucleus solitarius in the medulla, through the ventral posterior medial nucleus of the thalamus, and then to the gustatory cortex. In contrast, olfactory sensations (D) are received by olfactory receptor neurons which pass through the cribiform plate and make a synapse in the olfactory bulb. From the

Copyright © Mometrix Media. You have been licensed one copy of this document for personal use only. Any other reproduction or redistribution is strictly prohibited. All rights reserved.
This content is provided for test preparation purposes only and does not imply an endorsement by Mometrix of any particular political, scientific, or religious point of view.

olfactory bulb the impulses go straight to the cerebral cortex. Olfactory centers are connected to structures that process memories and emotions such as the amygdala and hippocampus. This may explain why certain smells will trigger vivid, emotionally charged memories.

22. C: There are twelve (C) cranial nerves in the human CNS. They are: I – olfactory; II – optic; III – oculomotor; IV – trochlear; V – trigeminal; VI – abducent; VII – facial; VIII – auditory or acoustic; IX – glossopharyngeal; X – vagus; XI – accessory; and XII – hypoglossal. There are not eight (A), ten (B), or fourteen (D) cranial nerves, so these answers are all incorrect. A helpful mnemonic that many medical students use to remember these nerves is: "On Old Olympus' Towering Top, A Finn And German Viewed A Hop." The initial letters of each word correspond to the initial letters of each nerve.)

23. D: The abducent (D) nerve, CN VI, innervates the lateral eye muscles. The olfactory (A) nerve, CN I, transmits sensory impulses of smell. The optic (B) nerve, CN II, transmits sensory impulses of vision. The auditory (C) nerve, CN VIII, transmits sensory impulses of hearing.

24. B: The oculomotor (B) nerve, CN III, has the motor functions of visual convergence and accommodation, allowing binocular vision. The trigeminal (A) nerve, CN V, transmits sensations in the eye, nose, and face and also innervates muscles of the tongue and muscles used in chewing. The vagus (C) nerve, CN X, transmits sensations in the ears, pharynx, larynx, and viscera and also innervates muscles of the pharynx, larynx, tongue, and the viscera's smooth muscles. The glossopharyngeal (D) nerve, CN IX, transmits sensations in the tonsils, pharynx, and soft palate and also innervates muscles of the pharynx and stylopharyngeus.

25. C: The accessory (C) nerve, CN XI controls the motor function of the muscles needed to shrug the shoulders and turn the head. The trigeminal (A) nerve, CN V, transmits sensations in the eye, nose, and face and also innervates muscles of the tongue and muscles used in chewing. The facial (B) nerve, CN VII, transmits sensations in the tongue and soft palate and also innervates muscles in the face and the stapedius muscle, which connects to the stapes (stirrup) in the middle ear. The glossopharyngeal (D) nerve, CN IX, transmits sensations in the tonsils, pharynx, and soft palate and also innervates muscles of the pharynx and stylopharyngeus.

26. B: Echolalia is (B) repeating what other people say. People who display this behavior may only repeat what others say exclusively and never make any original utterances of their own, or they may be able to both engage in purposeful speech and in repetition at times. Echolalia is not repeating oneself (A). It is not hearing echoes of speech (C). Difficulty with voice modulation (D), the ability to control the volume of one's speech, can be a symptom of various voice disorders; however, echolalia specifically refers to the repetition of other people when they speak.

27. A: The most likely explanation for this example is (A): Marco's first (native) language is influencing his second language. In Castilian, one dialect of Spanish, the letter "c" when followed by a vowel is not pronounced as /s/ as it is in English and in Catalan, South American, and other dialects of Spanish, but as /θ/ or theta, represented in the English alphabet as "th" (devocalized as in "thin" or "math," not vocalized as in "this" or "that"). With the similarities between Spanish and English, Marco is transferring his Spanish pronunciation to his English pronunciation. If the SLP does not find any physiological or possible neurological deficits in testing Marco, it is likely he is not showing a systematic articulation disorder (B) in which a person regularly mispronounces a certain phoneme or phonemes. Broca's aphasia (C) is a language disorder that is typically secondary to some form of traumatic brain injury. This is a speech issue, not a language issue; and there is nothing in the question to give the impression that Marco has any sort of injury, which makes this answer unlikely. Considering Marco is now able to speak two languages fluently and the passage

Copyright © Mometrix Media. You have been licensed one copy of this document for personal use only. Any other reproduction or redistribution is strictly prohibited. All rights reserved.
This content is provided for test preparation purposes only and does not imply an endorsement by Mometrix of any particular political, scientific, or religious point of view.

gives no indication that he has any other articulation or phonological speech errors, an undiagnosed case of CAS (D) is very unlikely.

28. D: The most likely reason for Jason's substitution of glottal stops for many consonants normally shaped in the mouth with the aid of the tongue and teeth is that (D) the newborn's jaundice and lethargy were most likely symptoms of a virus which caused minimal neurological damage. This kind of damage can slightly impair specialized functions such as motor functions related to the oral apparatus. He may have sustained subtle damage to the glossopharyngeal nerve (CN IX), the vagus nerve (CN X), the accessory nerve (CN XI), and/or the hypoglossal nerve (CN XII) involved with the muscles of the pharynx, larynx, tongue, and soft palate. It is not likely that he is merely being lazy (A) as it is developmentally normal for a child to use the apparatus best suited to imitate the sounds he hears. The fact that Jason substitutes glottal stops for *many* consonants means it is not likely that this speech dysfunction will correct itself without treatment (B). Glottal stops are not features of many consonants in English, making Jason's substitution for many consonant sounds unusual. It is not likely that Jason simply formed a habit he did not grow out of (C) as making this substitution is not natural. He would be more likely to employ the usual oral structures. The glottal stops take more effort even though he is fluent.

29. B: The normal way a /t/ or /d/ is produced in English is by pressing the tip of the tongue against the alveolar ridge (B). In some American regional dialects, such as in working-class populations in areas of New York, Massachusetts or Connecticut, these sounds may be made with the tongue touching the upper teeth (A), but this is a dialect or what many people call an "accent." When pressing the tongue against the alveolar ridge, no other sounds but /t/ or /d/ are possible. (The only difference between the two is that /t/ is unvoiced while /d/ is voiced.) When the tongue is in close contact with the alveolar ridge but not pressed against it, allowing some air through, the unvoiced or voiced fricatives /s/ or /z/ are produced. Pressing the back of the tongue against the place where the soft palate (C) meets the hard palate (D) produces the sounds /k/ or /g/ in the case of plosives, and by not pressing firmly produces /ʃ/ or /ʒ/ in the case of fricatives. (Affricates combine an alveolar stop with a fricative, such as /tʃ/as in "cha-cha" or /dʒ/ as in "judge.")

30. A: The most likely cause for congenital blindness and deafness is maternal rubella (A) or German measles during pregnancy, especially in early pregnancy. Maternal mercury exposure via contaminated fish (B) is more likely (as is lead exposure) to cause lower IQ scores and attentional deficits in the infant than to cause blindness and deafness. Smoking cigarettes throughout pregnancy (C) is more likely to lead to miscarriages or abnormal fetal heartbeats, premature births, and low birth weights than to blindness and deafness. Drinking alcohol regularly while pregnant (D) is more likely to impair the child's attention span, IQ, cognitive abilities, and school achievement than to result in blindness and deafness. Moreover, consuming more than two drinks per day is likely to result in fetal alcohol syndrome, which includes low birth weight, reduced brain size, facial abnormalities, lack of motor coordination, and intellectual disabilities, but not blindness and deafness.

31. A: The most likely reason Jane is lisping at seven when she did not at six is (A): she lost her front baby teeth this year. Without the barrier of the front teeth, fricatives like /s/ and /z/ easily become /θ/ or /ð/ as the tongue protrudes. It is unlikely that her friends were deliberately lisping and she joined in (B). It is unlikely to be a late-developing articulation disorder (C); articulation disorders producing lisps are more likely to develop as the child learns to speak. Absent any other physiological or psychological changes, an articulation disorder would not suddenly appear at age seven. A reaction to academic or social pressures (D) manifested in a speech disorder would more likely appear as stuttering. A child's growing vocabulary can cause mispronunciation of certain new words learned, but not of a specific phoneme she could already produce (E). Typically, children

Copyright © Mometrix Media. You have been licensed one copy of this document for personal use only. Any other reproduction or redistribution is strictly prohibited. All rights reserved.
This content is provided for test preparation purposes only and does not imply an endorsement by Mometrix of any particular political, scientific, or religious point of view.

mispronounce words they have read but not heard, especially children who are advanced readers. This does not involve distorting or substituting "th" sounds for "s" or "z" sounds, but is more likely to involve omitting or adding sounds to the word, mispronouncing vowel sounds, putting stress on the wrong syllable, and similar errors.

32. C: What is not true is that (C) expressive and receptive language will be equally impacted. Broca's aphasia is thought to result from damage to Broca's area in the inferior frontal gyrus of the brain. New research suggests it may involve other areas as well, but it is known for causing problems with expressive language more than with receptive language. Certain aspects of receptive language processing are affected in some patients, but these seem related to more difficult retrieval processes. It is common for those suffering from Broca's aphasia to have difficulty recalling words they want to use when speaking (A). Other aspects of spoken and written expression of language may be affected as well. Tommy should be able to understand what is said to him (B). There is a different type of aphasia associated with damage to a different area of the brain, which interferes with receptive language. This is a neurological problem affecting language development and linguistic expression rather than a speech problem (D). Though difficulty with recalling words, arranging them in grammatical order, and other expressive language problems will certainly seem to disrupt the individual's speech, speech problems by definition disrupt the physical production of speech, whether they are neurological, physiological, or psychological in origin. For example, articulation disorders and stuttering are speech problems while aphasias and delayed language development are language problems.

33. C: Clara's words will all very likely be in the correct order and meaningful within the context of her own sentence; (C) however, their meaning within the context of a conversation will be tenuous or nonexistent. People with Wernicke's aphasia often speak fluently and with correct syntax. However, while they can express themselves in speech, their ability to process and understand the speech of others is significantly impaired (A). Therefore, though Clara's speech makes sense, eventually its meaning will break down due to the lack of feedback (B) from other people's speech which she cannot understand. Clara is likely to develop strategies, as most Wernicke's aphasia patients do, to compensate for and hide her lack of comprehension (D). For example, if asked "Where did you go yesterday?" and she cannot understand what you said, she may respond with something like, "Oh my, what a pretty dress you have on!" in an attempt to hide the fact that she doesn't know what you asked her, and to divert attention in the hope of having a successful social interaction. Clara's disorder is thought to be caused by damage to Wernicke's area, in the posterior of the superior temporal gyrus in the cerebral cortex, around the auditory cortex, on the Sylvian fissure where the temporal and parietal lobes of the brain meet. New research suggests that functions traditionally attributed to Wernicke's area take place more widely in the temporal and frontal lobes as well.

34. B: Problems with syntax (B) involve difficulty forming sentences. Problems with morphology (A) will appear as difficulty forming words. Semantics problems (C) manifest as difficulty understanding words and word relationships. Problems with memory (D) will be evidenced by difficulty with retention, such as remembering spoken messages, and retrieval, such as word finding, fluency, and speech flexibility. Fluency is shown by having words, phrases, and sentences readily available. Flexibility is the ability to shift from one set of words, phrases, and sentences to another set or type, either adaptively in response to external changes or limits, or spontaneously. Other criteria for assessing language ability include creativity and elaboration.

35. C: The NSST (C) or Northwestern Syntax Screening Test has two sections, Receptive and Expressive. The TACL (A), or Test for Auditory Comprehension of Language, contains sections on Vocabulary, Morphology, and Syntax, but only tests the receptive side of language. Its format

Copyright © Mometrix Media. You have been licensed one copy of this document for personal use only. Any other reproduction or redistribution is strictly prohibited. All rights reserved.
This content is provided for test preparation purposes only and does not imply an endorsement by Mometrix of any particular political, scientific, or religious point of view.

requires a child to point to one of several pictures that best illustrates the meaning of the word, phrase, or sentence spoken by the tester. The ACLC (B), or Assessment of Children's Language Comprehension, also assesses basic receptive language skills. It includes a section of vocabulary words and three sections of syntactic sequences (phrases or sentences). It also requires the child to point to the correct choice among several. The Peabody (D) Picture Vocabulary asks the child to point to one of several pictures to identify which word (or occasional short phrase) the examiner has spoken as well.

36. C: The Toronto Tests of Receptive Vocabulary (C), or TTRV, assesses knowledge of word meaning with both English and Spanish words. These tests contain an equal number of words (40) in each language. English and Spanish word choices are not identical. The Picture Vocabulary subtest of the TOLD (A), or Test of Language Development, does not include Spanish words. Neither does the Peabody Picture Vocabulary Test (PPVT) (B) or the Assessment of Children's Language Comprehension (ACLC) test (D).

37. A: The semantic intervention most similar to Sentence Completion is the cloze format (A). This format can be oral or written. The only difference is that the missing word the child must supply can be in any part of the sentence, while in Sentence Completion the missing word is always at the end of the sentence. Therefore, Sentence Completion is better for learning semantic rules for choosing words, relationships, or concepts that come at the end of a phrase or sentence, while cloze has a wider range of application. Examples of sentence completion using prototypical contexts are "I take my coat __ (off/on/over); I put my shoes ___ (in/on/over)." Examples of sentence completion using verbal analogies are "Trees have leaves and birds have _______ (feathers); John is my uncle and Mary is my ___ (aunt); you drive a car and you fly a ____ (plane)." Cloze may use a paragraph in which certain parts of speech such as prepositions, as used in the first sentence completion example, are left blank throughout: "Billy has a green rug _ on the floor _ his room. There is a poster of a tiger _ the wall ____ his bed and a desk ___ to the window. He has an aquarium ___ fish _ them." Riddles (B) are good for teaching the consolidation of labels or names of things, animals, or people, i.e., teaching referential vocabulary. 20 Questions (C) is good for teaching verbal specificity by narrowing down groups of words according to their semantic class or to their shared features of meaning. Role playing (D) is good for teaching appropriate word, phrase, or sentence choices according to the social context.

38. B: Semantic classification and categorization (B) would be least applicable to learning synonyms and antonyms. This format is for classifying and categorizing objects, events, or words illustrated in pictures, and for identifying the semantic class to which they belong. Identification, differentiation, and elaboration of meaning (A) is for identifying similarities and differences in word meanings, so it is good for learning antonyms and synonyms. Judgment of consistency of meaning (C) is for identifying words, phrases, or clauses that violate the context (e.g., "The girl washed *itself*. Does this sentence make sense? Can you correct this?" or "The cat was sitting *in* the table. Does this make sense? Can you correct it?"), so it is good for teaching the rules of selection for antonyms and synonyms, as well as pronouns, prepositions, etc. Lexical paraphrasing (D) involves restating sentences by substituting one or more words, so it is also a good format for teaching synonyms (e.g., "Give me another word for…." after presenting a sentence) and antonyms.

39. C: Divergent thinking (C) is not a tendency or characteristic that would cause difficulty with semantics. Being able to generate a greater variety of alternatives would facilitate ease with semantics. Concrete thinking (A) would contribute to difficulty with semantics as the ability to think abstractly is important to interpreting meanings. Limited imagery (B) would interfere, as would limitations in the ability to use symbols and to conceptualize, since these all require some degree of abstraction and imagination. Narrow perception (D) would interfere with semantic ability

Copyright © Mometrix Media. You have been licensed one copy of this document for personal use only. Any other reproduction or redistribution is strictly prohibited. All rights reserved.
This content is provided for test preparation purposes only and does not imply an endorsement by Mometrix of any particular political, scientific, or religious point of view.

in that sticking to only one referent for words or concepts, retaining narrow meanings for words, and not shifting from one semantic-grammatical category to another would all prevent someone from identifying multiple and alternative meanings. Another thing that would interfere with semantics is a limited ability to accomplish simultaneously the logical operations, analyses, and syntheses needed for interpreting spatial, temporal, and other relationships among words, phrases, and clauses.

40. B: The Auditory Sequential subtest of the Illinois Test of Psycholinguistic Abilities (B), or ITPA, tests immediate recall of digit series forward *only.* The Numerical Memory scale of the McCarthy Scales (A) and the Digit Span subtest of the Wechsler Intelligence Scales for Children (C) or WISC-IV both test immediate recall of spoken digit series *both* forward and backward. The Digit Span subtest of the Wechsler Adult Intelligence Scale or WAIS-IV assesses recall in both directions as well.

41. D: In audiology, MCL stands for Most Comfortable Loudness (D). This is the volume at which sound is neither too loud nor too quiet. In audiological examinations, the measure in decibels (dB) assigned to an individual's hearing threshold reflects a loudness at which that person can hear a pure tone *half* of the time. Therefore, we may still be able to hear sounds at a quieter level than we prefer, yet we feel uncomfortable with that level. Conversely, some sounds may not be loud enough to damage our hearing, yet we are still uncomfortable if we find them too loud. Maximum Comfort Level (A) and Minimum Clarity Locutions (B) are invented choices. Medial Cochlear Ligaments (C) is an invented choice as well.

42. B: An audiogram with a sharp "notch" or "bite" showing a drop in acuity around 4,000 Hz, with the other frequencies above and below 4,000 showing a higher, flat line, indicates noise-induced hearing loss (B) in its early stages. Exposure to loud noise destroys nerve fibers that receive the 4,000-Hz frequency. A normal hearing curve (A) would show a relatively flat line across all frequencies, with the dB level close to 0, within a range from -10 dB to 25 dB, the standard for normal hearing. Conductive hearing losses (C) tend to show an audiogram curve that is relatively flat, similar to a normal hearing curve except that the dB level is not within normal range (for example, it could be 50 or 80 dB instead of 0 dB). Age-related hearing losses (D) or presbycusis are the most common form of hearing loss. Their audiograms are often described as "ski-slope loss" for their resemblance to a downhill curve, with hearing being best at the low frequencies and dropping at higher frequencies. The downward curve from left to right may be gradual with smaller decreases in acuity from one frequency to the next (higher) frequency; or it may be very steep in cases of the most extreme loss at the highest frequencies; or it may be anything in between.

43. A: The stapedius (A) is not one of the ossicles, though it is attached to one. "Ossicles" means "little bones." These tiny bones in the middle ear perform the function of conducting sound from the external auditory meatus to the inner ear. They are the stapes (B) or stirrup, the malleus (C) or hammer, and the incus (D) or anvil. When sound enters the ear, the malleus strikes the incus, vibrating the stapes. The stapedius (A) is a muscle that attaches to the stapes. In the event of a sudden, very loud sound, the stapedius muscle pulls the stapes away from the incus, keeping the middle and inner ear from registering the full loudness and protecting against sustaining noise-induced hearing loss. This action by the stapedius muscle is called the stapedius reflex.

44. C: Exposure to excessively loud noises (C) would not cause a conductive hearing loss but a sensorineural hearing loss. Conductive hearing losses are caused when something interferes with the conduction of sound waves to the inner ear where they are converted to electrical energy and sent along the auditory nerve to the brain. Conductive hearing loss is due to any dysfunction of the outer or middle ear while the inner ear is intact. Obstruction by a foreign body (A) such as wax is one cause of conductive hearing loss. Perforation of the tympanic membrane (B) or eardrum would

Copyright © Mometrix Media. You have been licensed one copy of this document for personal use only. Any other reproduction or redistribution is strictly prohibited. All rights reserved.
This content is provided for test preparation purposes only and does not imply an endorsement by Mometrix of any particular political, scientific, or religious point of view.

prevent it from vibrating and cause a conductive hearing loss. Rupture would have the same effect as perforation. Damage to one or more of the ossicles (D) that prevents vibration would also stop the conduction process, causing conductive hearing loss. Conductive losses can usually be remedied, either improving the hearing or completely restoring it. Sensorineural losses have until recent years been permanent and irreversible, but the cochlear implant now replaces permanently destroyed hair cells for people with profound sensorineural hearing loss and a functioning auditory nerve.

45. B: Damage to one or more ossicles (B) is not a source of sensorineural hearing loss but a source of conductive hearing loss. Damage to any of the middle ear's tiny bones, stopping them from vibrating and sending sound through the oval and round windows to the inner ear, will impede conduction of sound and cause conductive hearing loss. Destruction of hair cells in the cochlea (A) is a source of sensorineural hearing loss. It can also be caused by sudden or ongoing exposure to excessively loud noises (C), by disease or infection, or as a result of aging (D).

46. D: Bilabial consonants are created using both lips. In this case, /m/ (D) is the only consonant that is bilabial. /f/ and /v/ (A & C) are labiodental, and /r/ (B) is palatal.

47. C: UCL in audiology refers to uncomfortable loudness level (C). This is the level of intensity (loudness) at which a sound becomes uncomfortable to an individual. Answers (A) and (B) are invented choices. Upper confidence limit and upper confidence level (D) are terms used in inferential statistical analysis. Confidence levels have to do with margins of error in statistics, not audiology.

48. A: In audiology, recruitment means (A) reduced range between an individual's hearing threshold, most comfortable loudness (MCL) and uncomfortable loudness level (UCL). In individuals with normal hearing, the hearing threshold, MCL and UCL are spread far enough apart to tolerate a wide range of loudness levels without discomfort and still hear the stimulus. People with sensorineural hearing loss are more likely to experience recruitment, so there is a much smaller range within which they hear without uncomfortable loudness. Someone who asks a speaker to speak louder and then becomes irritated because the speaker is 'shouting' actually has a very small difference between sounds too soft to here and those so loud they hurt. Recruitment is frustrating for both speaker and hearer as the hearer needs a narrow range of loudness in order to understand what is said without discomfort. The term recruitment does not refer to the phenomenon that at times, nerves or brain tissue can be substituted to serve the same function as the usual tissues when these are damaged (B). It does not refer to the ability of normal hearing acuity to focus well enough to capture barely audible sounds (C). And it does not refer to a wider than normal range between threshold and MCL (D).

49. D: Antoine is likely to have some attentional or neurological deficiencies. The fact that he always starts out responding normally to the sound stimuli indicates that he can hear them, which eliminates symptoms of organic hearing loss (C). It may be that his attention wanders after a few minutes, or some neurological abnormality may cause him to cease noticing sound stimuli after a few minutes. Though malingering (A) is not impossible, it is unlikely due to Antoine's young age and the absence of complaints that he can't hear when spoken to. From interviews and other measures, Antoine also does not demonstrate the knowledge, understanding, sophistication, or initiative to try to manipulate adults or the system this way. He does not display any other attention-seeking behaviors. He is not suffering from hysterical conversion deafness (B) because he does not display any hearing loss with others' speech or other auditory stimuli, and responds normally for the first few minutes of the hearing tests. Deafness by conversion hysteria would result in a uniform failure to respond to auditory stimuli.

Copyright © Mometrix Media. You have been licensed one copy of this document for personal use only. Any other reproduction or redistribution is strictly prohibited. All rights reserved.
This content is provided for test preparation purposes only and does not imply an endorsement by Mometrix of any particular political, scientific, or religious point of view.

50. D: Presbycusis, or age-related hearing loss, is most often characterized by (D) more hearing loss at higher frequencies. More loss at lower frequencies (A) is not typical of hearing loss associated with aging and is unusual in general. More loss at middle frequencies (B) is also unusual. While early noise-induced hearing loss can cause a sharp drop in acuity around 4,000 Hz, this is not so much a middle frequency as a medium-high frequency. Uniform loss at all frequencies (C) is not characteristic of presbycusis specifically or of sensorineural losses in general, but is more often found with conductive hearing losses. With presbycusis, the higher the frequency, the more loss is seen. This accounts for the difficulty people with age-related hearing loss have with discrimination of words containing high-frequency consonant sounds such as /s/, /t/, /f/, etc.

51. A: Dysarthria is a neurologically caused articulation disorder (A). Damage to the parts of the central nervous system controlling the muscles used for speech is the origin of dysarthria. A learning disability affecting reading (B) is dyslexia. A neurologically caused swallowing disorder (C) is dysphagia. An articulation disorder due to dysfunction of the speech organs (D) rather than of the brain is called dyslalia.

52. B: Open-bite (B) in which the upper and lower teeth do not meet is the *most* likely cause of distorted sibilant consonants /s/, /z/, / ʃ/, and /ʒ/. Overbite (A) or supraclusion does not usually cause consonant distortion. Underbite (C) or mandibular protraction, also called mesioclusion, causes no speech distortions when mild. Even when severe, the tongue and lips can usually adjust to accommodate it. A protruding mandible can sometimes cause sibilant distortion, but it is not as frequent. This type of malocclusion can also cause distortion of /f/ and /v/ consonants. Cross-bite (D) can make it harder to produce sibilants by placing the tongue in a poor position for it, but is not as likely to cause distortion except when it co-exists with other problems such as open-bite, motor problems with the tongue, or malformed dental arches.

53. C: The best definition of motor apraxia among the choices given is that (C) he cannot control his external speech organs. For example, when asked to make an /m/ sound, someone with motor apraxia is unable to. When the SLP models using thumb and forefinger to pinch the lips together, Willie will be able to imitate, but he cannot voluntarily press his lips together without the aid of his hand. If he walked as if he were drunk (A), it is a sign of *ataxia* rather than apraxia. If he used his upper but not lower body (B), it is hemiplegia. If he can speak but not understand speech (D), it indicates Wernicke's aphasia or receptive aphasia. None of these other conditions exist in this case. Apraxia means loss of ability to make simple voluntary acts, *especially* loss of ability to perform simple units of action in expressive language.

54. B: This patient is most likely to have oropharyngeal dysphagia (B). Dysphagia is difficulty swallowing. Oropharyngeal is a type of dysphagia most often caused by cerebrovascular strokes or other neurological etiologies such as MS, MG, ALS, Parkinson's disease or Bell's palsy. It can also be caused by radiation, neurotoxins, neck tumors, and other medical conditions. Esophageal dysphagia (A) is not caused by strokes. It can have functional or mechanical etiologies, and is most often caused by cancers in or near the esophagus, or by cancers in the pharynx or stomach. Esophageal achalasia (C) differs from dysphagia in that there is more difficulty with swallowing liquids than solids. It is characterized by failure of peristalsis along the entire length of the esophagus, by failure of the lower esophageal sphincter to relax sufficiently, and by functional narrowing of the lower esophagus. Though primary achalasia, the most common type, is due to failure of esophageal neurons, the cause of this failure is not known. Odynophagia (D) is pain upon swallowing and is often a symptom of carcinoma.

55. C: Mental exercises (C) are not part of the traditional set of dysphagia therapies. Lip exercises (A) increase strength and coordination of the lips, which are important for moving food around the

Copyright © Mometrix Media. You have been licensed one copy of this document for personal use only. Any other reproduction or redistribution is strictly prohibited. All rights reserved.
This content is provided for test preparation purposes only and does not imply an endorsement by Mometrix of any particular political, scientific, or religious point of view.

mouth and for creating a tight seal when swallowing. Tongue exercises (B) are helpful because the tongue also moves food around the mouth as the lips do, plus the tongue helps create a bolus of food to be more easily swallowed. Also, the tongue transports the food bolus backward to the pharynx where it can be moved into the esophagus. It is not unusual for a stroke to impair the tongue's mobility. Swallowing exercises (D) obviously are indicated for swallowing difficulty, especially when this is the result of a stroke.

56. B: Like the Shaker exercise, the hyoid lift maneuver (B) does not involve swallowing. In this exercise, a sheet of paper placed on a towel is picked up by sucking on a straw and moved to a container into which it is dropped by the release of suction. The goal is to move several sheets of paper into the container in each session. The Mendelsohn maneuver (A) involves consciously keeping the larynx lifted, while swallowing. This exercise is to be repeated several times a day. The effortful swallow (C) involves swallowing while squeezing the swallowing muscles as hard as possible. Three sets per day are done, with each set consisting of 5-10 attempts. The supraglottic swallow (D) involves holding the breath while swallowing, then coughing (to clear anything that went down past the vocal cords). It is to be done first without food and can be done with food later as proficiency increases.

57. A: In Piaget's theory of cognitive development, sensorineural (A) is not one of the stages. Sensorineural is most often an adjective used to describe a type of hearing loss. Piaget's first stage of cognitive development is the sensorimotor (B) stage. In this stage the infant learns about the environment through sensory input received and motor outputs made to act upon the environment. A milestone during this stage is the achievement of object permanence, the understanding that something exists even when it is not in your presence. Piaget's second stage is the preoperational (C) stage. In this stage the young child cannot yet perform mental operations, but the child's use of symbols and language is accelerated. In Piaget's third stage, concrete operations (D), the child can perform mental operations with concrete objects, such as conservation and class inclusion tasks. The child gains in logical thinking and being able to understand another's point of view, but cannot think abstractly.

58. C: Vygotsky formulated a theory of cognitive development based on sociocultural influences. What he termed "private speech" is when children talk to themselves to direct their own behavior (C). He said that once children have acquired language and learned the rules of their culture, they start using private speech. When they are young, we often hear them talking to themselves aloud as they guide themselves through cognitive activities. Vygotsky said that as children grow older, they continue "private speech," but it becomes silent as they internalize it. Even adults talk to themselves aloud, a sign that "private speech" never goes away but is just internalized. "Private speech" is not a sign of psychological disturbance (A). It does not refer to private discussions between two close friends (B) or among several intimate friends (D).

59. C: According to Brown (1973), children go through five stages in expressive language development: Stage I typically takes place between 12 and 26 months. Stage II typically occurs between 27 and 30 months. Stage III typically occurs between 31 and 34 months. Stage IV typically occurs between 35 and 40 months. Finally, Stage V occurs between 41 and 46 months.

60. D: Learning theory focuses only on observable behaviors (D). This is why learning theory is also called behavioral theory. B. F. Skinner, a pioneer of learning theory and behavior modification, maintained that what was going on internally in a subject did not matter, not because internal processes and states did not exist, but because they could not be observed or measured and therefore could not be changed in a reliable, measurable way. Unconscious impulses (A) were the focus of Freud's psychoanalytic theory and neo-Freudian theories. Freud believed that the majority

Copyright © Mometrix Media. You have been licensed one copy of this document for personal use only. Any other reproduction or redistribution is strictly prohibited. All rights reserved.
This content is provided for test preparation purposes only and does not imply an endorsement by Mometrix of any particular political, scientific, or religious point of view.

of the personality was internalized and hidden, even to oneself. Attempts to understand the unconscious were made through "talk" therapy or analysis of patient interviews, including introspection, free association, slips of the tongue, and dream analysis and interpretation. Internal mechanisms (B), such as Freud's ego defense mechanisms, Chomsky's language acquisition device, and other mechanisms described by other theories, are disregarded in learning theory as they are not outwardly demonstrated or observable. Social relationships (C) are the focus of Erikson's psychosocial theory of development, Vygotsky's theory of sociocultural learning, Bandura's social-cognitive theory and others, but not of learning theory. Behavioral theorists like Skinner would assert that social relationships could be changed in practice by the application of behavior modification principles, but the focus of the theory itself is behavior, not social relationships.

61. B: Systematic desensitization uses the technique of (B) successive approximations of exposure to an aversive stimulus. By introducing controlled exposure in small increments or steps, the aversive stimulus is more tolerable to the individual. As the individual becomes less sensitive to a small amount of the stimulus, the next step is taken or increment is added. When the client is allowed to become comfortable with each small step before continuing, this procedure can do much to help overcome, for example, phobias (and may be combined with anti-anxiety medication). It can also be useful in cases of stuttering with strong psychological components. Shaping and chaining are behavioral methods that use successive approximations. Exposure to excessive amounts of the aversive stimulus (A) is a technique called flooding and is the opposite of systematic desensitization. Extinction of an undesirable response (C) is the technique of ignoring the response until the individual no longer engages in it. This typically only works with attention-seeking behaviors. If attention does not reinforce a given behavior, ignoring that behavior will not extinguish it. Exchanging the aversive stimulus (D) is an invented answer choice.

62. D: The mother and teacher should be told that (D) Wendy is normal developmentally, because norms for correct consonant articulation vary depending on the specific consonant, and the norm for consistently producing /r/ correctly is around eight years of age. Wendy is only five, so she should not be expected to be able to say /r/ correctly yet. Therefore, it cannot be assumed that she has an articulation disorder needing speech therapy (A). Wendy's /w/ for /r/ substitution is not idiolectal because she is not the only child to do this; it is not unusual but quite common (B). It is one of the most common errors by children in this age group, as /r/ is one of the most difficult consonants to produce correctly, which is why it has one of the highest age norms. While it is true that in those with hearing impairment, /r/ is also one of the most common sounds to be produced incorrectly, this does not automatically mean that Wendy has a hearing loss (C). A speech-language pathologist would test her hearing as part of her evaluation, so any hearing loss would be identified, but her developmentally normal articulation error does not mean that she *must* have hearing loss.

63. C: Elise's success is most likely due to a combination of Glenda's therapy and Elise's maturation. From third to fourth grade, Elise's vocal apparatus and central nervous system have matured, making her speech more amenable to correction. Additionally, last year's SLP did not try using a physical aid to help interrupt Elise's habitual palatalization (which could have been an incorrect learned behavior, a physiological reflex, or both) and reposition her tongue, nor help her become familiar with how the correct position felt until she could reproduce it. Thus, it is not likely that Elise's correction is due only to maturation or that the treatment did not help (A). She continued to produce the distorted sound until Glenda tried the tongue depressor; thereafter her articulation improved quickly. While Glenda's idea deserves credit, it cannot be said that it was entirely responsible for the results (B) as maturation probably enhanced Elise's ability to respond to the treatment. To say that success was due to a choice Elise made (D) is unfounded; there is much evidence to the contrary.

Copyright © Mometrix Media. You have been licensed one copy of this document for personal use only. Any other reproduction or redistribution is strictly prohibited. All rights reserved.
This content is provided for test preparation purposes only and does not imply an endorsement by Mometrix of any particular political, scientific, or religious point of view.

64. C: Individuals with Broca's aphasia (C) have better linguistic comprehension than expression, and it does not remove their ability to employ repetition. Melodic Intonation Therapy (MIT) can be useful for the SLP in this case. MIT is a process where the SLP sings or hums a phrase to the affected individual. The individual then tries to sing, hum, or tap the phrase back to the SLP. MIT would not be an effective treatment for an individual with transcortical sensory aphasia (A) because they have severely impaired auditory comprehension skills, and MIT requires the ability to understand not only what the speaker is saying, but to understand and appreciate their own productions in order to try to repeat them. An individual with Wernicke's aphasia suffers from the same difficulty with comprehension, and would therefore not likely be effectively treated by MIT. Conduction aphasia (D) causes significant impairment of an individual's capacity for repetition, making MIT ineffective.

65. C: The most common form of stuttering is (C) developmental stuttering. When young children are still developing speech and language skills, they may stutter. Some scientists believe that this is due to a child's cognitive and verbal development outpacing that child's speech and language development. Neurogenic stuttering (A) is not as common as developmental stuttering but more common than psychogenic stuttering (B). Neurogenic stuttering is a result of a neurological problem. This can be caused by head trauma, cerebrovascular stroke, or other brain injuries. The stuttering arises from an impaired ability of the brain to coordinate speech actions by properly controlling the muscles and/or nerves involved. Psychogenic stuttering (B) is a result of emotional trauma, emotional problems, mental disorders, and/or cognitive impairments. In the past, stuttering was believed to be always psychogenic in origin. However, now that more research has been done, it has been found that psychogenic stuttering is actually not common. Profound stuttering (D) is a label of severity rather than a category of form and is therefore incorrect.

66. D: Volume (D) is not a variable that is assessed in stuttering disorders. Rate (A) refers to the speed at which one speaks. Many stutterers speak too fast. Others slow or stop their speech in their struggle to get the words out. Slowing down can often help stutterers in combination with other strategies. However, when some stutterers struggle too hard to get a word out without repetition or prolongation, the tension can cause blocking, i.e., their speech is completely stopped, which is counterproductive. Many stutterers also show disordered speech rhythms (B), alternately speeding up and slowing down, prolonging vowel or consonant sounds, or having parts—words, phrases, or sentences—within their overall speech flow that are faster or slower than what sounds normal. Fluency (C) refers to the speaker's ability to speak easily without undue effort and with normal rate and rhythm. There is a class of stutterers known as "fluent stutterers" who do stutter but without interrupting, slowing, or stopping their speech. These are usually mild stutterers.

67. D: It is not true that (D) stuttering always lasts for several years in children. It is true that about 3 million Americans stutter (A) and that they may be of any age (B). It is true that stuttering occurs most frequently between the ages of 2 and 5 years (C) when children's speech and language abilities are still developing.

68. B: It is not true that fewer boys are likely to stutter as they age (B). In fact, boys are twice as likely to stutter as girls are (A), and the numbers of boys who continue to stutter as they get older is three to four times as many as girls who continue to stutter as they get older. It is true that the majority of children outgrow stuttering (C), and that only around 1% or fewer of adults stutter (D).

69. A: The only true statement is that (A) three genes causing stuttering have now been identified and isolated. This was done for the first time by researchers at the National Institute on Deafness and other Communication Disorders (NIDCD) in 2010. Stuttering can occur as a result of acute stroke or TBI and is therefore not specifically genetic in natrure (B). It is not true that developmental stuttering is not found to run in families (C); researchers have found that

Copyright © Mometrix Media. You have been licensed one copy of this document for personal use only. Any other reproduction or redistribution is strictly prohibited. All rights reserved.
This content is provided for test preparation purposes only and does not imply an endorsement by Mometrix of any particular political, scientific, or religious point of view.

developmental stuttering is more frequent in members of the same family. It is also not true that stuttering that runs in a family is attributed to environmental factors (D) such as reinforcement. Developmental stuttering running in families is attributed to genetic factors, which is supported by the recent isolation of genes causing some cases of it (A).

70. B: Ataxic cerebral palsy (B) is distinguished by problems with balance and coordination, unsteady gait, and impaired fine motor control. These are typically accompanied by low muscle tone and tremors. Diplegic cerebral palsy (A) is a type of spastic cerebral palsy usually marked by rigidity or stiffness in the legs, with the arms mildly affected or unaffected. They will typically have trouble walking and their legs will "scissor" together. Dyskinetic cerebral palsy (C) is characterized by uncontrollable movement of the hands, arms, feet, or legs. This will typically present as slow or writhing movements, but can also be rapid or jerky. Their muscle tone can vary from day to day or multiple times a day. Spastic cerebral palsy (D) is associated with increased muscle tone and rigidity that makes movement awkward or difficult. Depending on which parts of the body are affected, further classification is given e.g., diplegic, hemiplegic, and quadriplegic.

71. C: It is not true in Starkweather's model that (C) stressors in the social environment do not influence speech demands. Social stressors are an important factor according to Starkweather. Speech is a social behavior. Starkweather states that stressors, or demands, in the social environment can trigger stuttering when those demands exceed the capacity of the individual to speak fluently and continuously (B). These demands trigger the stuttering rather than causing it; Starkweather believes that some people have a predisposition for speech breakdowns (A). These predispositions are thought to be genetic in some people, while in others they may not be hereditary but are results of weaknesses in the speech process involving muscular control, motor coordination, word finding, sentence formation, or auditory monitoring. It is true that most stutterers report that their speech is "just fine" a lot of the time (D), but they will stutter in stressful situations such as talking to a superior, talking on the phone, making a presentation, or in a job interview.

72. C: Avoidances (C) are not overt or core features of stuttering; they are covert. Avoidances include substituting another word in place of one with an initial sound that is difficult for the speaker. Pausing before beginning a difficult word is another form of avoidance. Circumlocution, i.e., paraphrasing or "talking around" a difficult word or phrase by describing it in other terms is another type of avoidance. Blocks (A) are overt features of stuttering. These occur when the speaker's larynx, vocal folds, lips, and/or tongue become so tense that airflow is stopped or blocked. The speaker appears "stuck." Repetitions (B) involving a single phoneme, syllable, or word ("P-p-p-p-p-person," "wha-wha-wha-wha-what," and "It would be impossible to-to-to-to-to" respectively) are overt features of stuttering. Prolongations (D) are drawing out the length of a sound, (e.g., "Mmmmmother" or "ssssssister") and they are also overt features of stuttering.

73. C: The transverse arytenoid (C) is the only unpaired muscle in the larynx. The intrinsic paired laryngeal muscles are the cricothyroid (A), lateral cricoarytenoid, oblique arytenoids (B), transverse arytenoid, posterior cricoarytenoid, superior thyroarytenoid (D), thyroarytenoid-muscularis, and thyroarytenoid-vocalis.

74. A: This is an example of a behavioral objective written for speech awareness (A). If met, it will demonstrate that John is aware of his dysfluencies 90% of the time. An example of a behavioral objective written for speech description (B) would be: "When asked by the therapist, John will correctly identify the type and place of dysfluency eight out of ten times." This goes beyond awareness to being able to describe the dysfluencies specifically. An example of a behavioral objective written for speech modification (C) would be: "John will implement Speech Target X in

Copyright © Mometrix Media. You have been licensed one copy of this document for personal use only. Any other reproduction or redistribution is strictly prohibited. All rights reserved.
This content is provided for test preparation purposes only and does not imply an endorsement by Mometrix of any particular political, scientific, or religious point of view.

three out of four dysfluencies without cueing." (In reality the X would be replaced by the number or letter identifying one of the listed targets developed for that individual client.) This goes beyond awareness and description to independently using a learned technique to modify, or change, one's speech when dysfluency occurs. An example of a behavioral objective written for speech preparation (D) would be: "John will implement Speech Target X without cueing before initiating words he expects to stutter on three out of four times." This goes beyond modifying speech when it becomes dysfluent to preventing the dysfluency by implementing a strategy in advance of stuttering.

75. B: This is an example of a behavioral objective written for a stutterer in the area of (B) emotional awareness. If met, it will show that John is aware of his anxiety and the associated symptoms in this type of situation. An example of a behavioral objective for emotional exploration (A) is: "When asked by the therapist, John will describe in detail three childhood experiences that triggered negative emotions." Once he is aware of his emotions related to stuttering, John can explore them to see how they may have developed and been compounded over time. An example of emotional modification (C) is: "On three separate occasions, before speaking to a group, John will pause, take a deep breath, slowly exhale, and attend to the release of muscle tension in one part of his body." This is a part of progressive relaxation practice. Once John recognizes his emotional reactions, he can practice changing them by focusing on the physical tension they cause and releasing it. The effects are reciprocal; just as anxiety causes muscular tension, releasing that tension reduces the anxiety. An example of a behavioral objective written for the area of emotional understanding (D) is: "With the therapist's assistance, John will form one plausible reason for his stuttering and will express it to someone outside of therapy." This reflects gaining insight into reasons for stuttering.

76. C: Non-standard English. In Vernacular Black English, Southern White non-standard English, and other non-standard English dialects, these are all common utterances. "He bad" demonstrates the absence of the copula "is" whenever it can be a contraction in Standard English and is common in Black and White non-standard English. "Where was you?" demonstrates lack of subject-verb agreement with respect to person number and is used by Black and White non-standard English speakers. "That Renee toy" demonstrates omission of the possessive [*'s*] when word order indicates possession. This is common in Vernacular Black English and tends to be consistent in Southern speakers, while northern urban speakers may alternate between using the [*'s*] ending or relying on word order. "She don't drive" uses the plural form of the auxiliary verb "do" in Standard English instead of the singular "does" when the construction is negative ("don't" instead of "doesn't"). This is common in both Black and White non-standard English. "I knowed that" is using the regular "-ed" past tense ending with irregular verbs instead of, for example, the correct vowel change ("know-knew," "freeze-froze," "drink-drank," etc.) and is a feature of non-standard English. These expressions are not due to delayed language development (A). Delayed language development typically results in incorrect word order; incorrect prepositions; incorrect pronouns; limited vocabulary; and misuse of synonyms and antonyms. They are not attributable to disorders of articulation (B) as they are differences in morphology, not in speech sound production or pronunciation. Stave V of early expressive language development (D) involves the use of third-person irregular verb forms such as "she *does*" or "he *has*," and the use of the verb *to be* in most standard forms which is contrary to the phrases described by the question.

77. D: A medical history (D) may be consulted when developing a lesson plan, but it is not contained within the lesson plan itself. A student will usually have about three goals (A) to work on over the semester. These may be revised during the semester as needed, for example, if the student makes such great progress that they no longer apply or if new information is discovered. Behavioral

Copyright © Mometrix Media. You have been licensed one copy of this document for personal use only. Any other reproduction or redistribution is strictly prohibited. All rights reserved.
This content is provided for test preparation purposes only and does not imply an endorsement by Mometrix of any particular political, scientific, or religious point of view.

objectives (B) are ways to achieve the goals. They specifically describe what behaviors the student is expected to perform during a given activity. They can often be changed or adjusted as often as weekly according to the student's performance. The activities the student is to engage in should be described (C) briefly in a lesson plan to give an idea of what you are planning, but not in great detail. You should also list the materials to be used (D) during each separate activity in your lesson plan.

78. B: Researchers did not find that (B) differences in the articulation of those with surgically repaired clefts and those with unrepaired clefts were very large. While those with unrepaired cleft palates did have worse articulation than those with surgical repair, the differences were not large. One study found a difference of only .17 between the mean ratios of obtained scores to norms for subjects with and without surgical repair of cleft palates. Another study found a difference of 25%, i.e., 54% correct articulation for subjects with unrepaired clefts and 79% correct articulation for subjects with repaired clefts. Researchers did find that those with cleft lip only but not cleft palate have essentially normal articulation (A). They found that unilateral clefts (clefts on only one side) allowed better articulation of speech sounds than bilateral or two-sided clefts (C). They also found that those with incomplete clefts had better articulation than those with complete clefts (D).

79. A: Research has found that people with cleft palates consistently have the highest rates of correct production of (A) nasal consonants like /m/, /n/, and /ŋ/. This makes sense when one considers that one of the byproducts of cleft palate is hypernasality. It would follow that it is easier for people whose speech is already nasal to produce nasal consonants correctly. The second highest ranking of correct articulation for those with cleft palate was (B) glides or semivowels like /r/, /l/, /j/, or /w/; the third was (C) plosives or stops like /p/, /b/, /t/, /k/; ranked fourth highest were (D) fricatives like /θ/, /ð/, /s/, /z/, /f/, /v/.

80. D: Daniel R. Boone (D) of the University of Arizona specializes in voice disorders and voice therapy, not stuttering. George H. Shames (A), professor emeritus of the University of Pittsburgh, was director of the university's speech clinic for 40 years and a licensed clinical psychologist, and specialized in stuttering. He developed "Stutter-Free Speech" and invented three biofeedback devices for stuttering. Shames was influenced by Charles G. Van Riper (B), a lifelong severe stutterer himself, who founded the speech clinic at Western Michigan State Normal School in Kalamazoo, and was the first chair of the school's speech pathology and audiology department. Martin F. Schwartz (C) from NYU Medical Center was a researcher in cleft lip and cleft palate surgery who stumbled on neck constriction in stutterers in 1974. Schwartz had been using ultrasound imaging on stutterers and found they had laryngeal spasms, ultimately discovering that the physical origin of stuttering was a reflexive locking of the vocal cords. He then created the passive-inhalation airflow technique of stuttering therapy. He directs the National Center for Stuttering.

81. D: Acute infectious laryngitis (D) is not responsive to voice therapy. The infection must be treated then the patient must rest the voice until phonation feels and sounds normal again. Thickening of the vocal cords (A) can result from long-term abuse or misuse of the voice or from chronic infections of the vocal folds. Voice therapy focuses on reducing voice abuse and misuse and reducing or eliminating sources of irritation, such as allergies, smoking, etc. Vocal nodules and vocal polyps (B) are both treated first by surgery, then by complete voice rest, and finally by voice therapy. The same is true of laryngeal contact ulcers (C).

82. B: Wheezing is not a common symptom of laryngeal trauma. Common signs of laryngeal trauma include dysphagia (A), hoarseness (C), and hemoptysis (D). Wheezing (B) tends to indicate an issue with the lungs rather than the structures of the neck.

Copyright © Mometrix Media. You have been licensed one copy of this document for personal use only. Any other reproduction or redistribution is strictly prohibited. All rights reserved.
This content is provided for test preparation purposes only and does not imply an endorsement by Mometrix of any particular political, scientific, or religious point of view.

83. B: The least common feature of a functional dysphonia would be (B) an overly loud voice. It is more common in disorders of loudness to find an overly weak, soft, or quiet voice (C). This is thought by some clinicians to reflect shyness, insecurity, and poor interpersonal interactions. Nonetheless, voice therapy to improve respiration and loudness is found more effective than trying to improve the patient's self-esteem and social relationships. Common features of functional dysphonia not related to loudness include breathiness (A), caused by lax approximation of the vocal folds, which may be consistent or only occur with fatigue from overuse; and harshness (D), caused by hard vocal attack, over-approximation of the vocal folds, or by a resonance disorder featuring tongue retraction, pharyngeal constriction, and sometimes nasality.

84. B: The disorder most likely to result in no voice at all is (B) functional aphonia because underadducted vocal folds do not touch and will permit only whispering. The most common form of spastic dysphonia (A) involves overadduction of the vocal folds, bringing them together tightly so air cannot easily escape, resulting in a strained, choked or creaky voice. A less common form of spastic dysphonia features abduction and causes sudden moments of breathiness or momentary loss of voice in the midst of phonation when the glottis widens. Vocal cord paralysis (C) can cause hoarseness, breathiness, loss of intensity, and loss of pitch range. Laryngeal web or synechia (D) can grow between the vocal folds, usually triggered by mucosal surface irritation or laryngeal trauma (injury). It can cause severe dysphonia and shortness of breath, but not a total absence of voice. Treatment is surgery followed by voice therapy to normalize phonation as much as possible.

85. A: A variable not typically rated in a voice screening for school children is (A) rate, or speed of the child's speech. This would be a variable more likely to be evaluated in screening or testing for stuttering, expressive aphasia, or possibly delayed language development. The variables typically rated in voice screenings include (B) pitch, or frequency—how high or low the voice is relative to norms for the child's sex and age; (C) Quality of phonation, or whether the voice is hoarse, breathy, etc.; and (D) resonance, or whether the voice sounds too nasal (hypernasality), not nasal enough (denasality), or has assimilative nasality (i.e., vowel sounds become more nasal when next to nasal consonants).

86. A: A *short* palate (A) can lead to inadequate velopharyngeal closure, which results in a hypernasal voice. Surgical trauma (B) can also cause velopharyngeal insufficiency and hence hypernasality, as can accidental injury to the soft palate (C). Some diseases can impair the innervation of the soft palate, and such neurological impairment (D) will also result in velopharyngeal insufficiency and hypernasality.

87. A: Incidence (A) is the measure of newly diagnosed cases of a particular disorder within a specified time frame. Prevalence is the proportion of the population that currently has the specified disorder (B). A measure of successful treatments (C) is typically known as a success rate or cure rate. The distinct cause of a disorder (D) is the etiology.

88. C: Establishing new pitch (C) is used for hypernasality but not denasality. Some people with hypernasal voices speak with overly high pitches, which increases nasality. Speaking at a lower pitch can contribute to greater oral resonance instead of greater nasal resonance. People with denasalized voices sound congested all of the time. The other four therapy approaches listed can be used with both hypernasality and denasality. Ear training (A) focuses on increasing the patient's ability to hear the differences between oral resonances and nasal resonances, so it can be used for either decreasing or increasing nasality. The target voice models approach (B) consists of recording the patient's voice whenever it has a good balance of oral and nasal resonance, and playing this back for the patient to hear. The patient's own phonation, when its resonance is closest to ideal, becomes the patient's own model and can be used equally for hypernasality and denasality. The

Copyright © Mometrix Media. You have been licensed one copy of this document for personal use only. Any other reproduction or redistribution is strictly prohibited. All rights reserved.
This content is provided for test preparation purposes only and does not imply an endorsement by Mometrix of any particular political, scientific, or religious point of view.

explanation of problem approach (D) involves explaining to the patient before beginning any therapy exactly what the patient's speech problem is—overly nasal or not nasal enough (the latter especially with nasal consonants)—and is used with either type of problem.

89. A: It is not true that nasal emission is a nasal resonance problem (A). Nasal emission is nasal noise caused by air escaping through the nose when there is incomplete velopharyngeal closure. Though it is not a disorder of nasal resonance per se, it often accompanies hypernasality (B) when the etiology is structural. In addition to weakened movement of the velum and pharynx, a short palate can cause nasal emissions, so these can be symptomatic of palatal insufficiency (C). It is true that nasal emission rarely occurs for functional reasons (D). It is nearly always related to some structural inadequacy.

90. A: Deaf children around the ages of seven or eight years old have not been observed to speak with higher pitches than hearing children. However, children with hearing develop lower-pitched voices after puberty, while deaf children do not (A). Researchers have concluded this is because they do not have the auditory feedback that hearing children do and thus cannot acoustically monitor their voices. It has been found that deaf individuals without voice training tend to focus their resonance in their pharynx (B), caused by poor tongue positioning, especially retraction toward the pharyngeal wall, leading to "cul de sac resonance." Severe denasality (C) often results from pharyngeal resonance focus, but there are also some deaf people who display true hypernasality (D) in their voices.

91. A: Variable-ratio (A) reinforcement yields the highest response rate as well as the highest resistance to extinction because reinforcement occurs after an unpredictable number of responses. Variable-interval (B), fixed-ratio (C), and fixed-interval reinforcement (D) all produce a lower resistance to extinction because reinforcement occurs more frequently.

92. D: NPO refers to the medicinal order of nothing by mouth (D) or *nil per oris*. Once a night by mouth (A) would typically be written out in full or with some mix of QHS and PO. The other choices are invented.

93. A: The quality of the voice tone produced (A) is not an advantage of electrolarynx devices. Being electromechanical, they produce a robotic-sounding voice which is perceived as unnatural and distracting to listeners. It is an advantage of these devices that laryngectomy patients can quickly and easily learn to use them (B). This contrasts with the time and effort it takes to learn esophageal speech, for example. Therefore, they are a good choice for being able to communicate more immediately while learning other methods, as they do not interfere with or delay this (D). Another advantage of electrolarynx devices is that they produce a loud voice (C) which can be easily heard, which other methods like esophageal speech may not.

94. C: A tympanogram evaluates the eardrum and conduction bones by subjecting it to variations of air pressure in the ear canal to test the condition of the tympanic membrane located within the middle ear (C). Otoacoustic emission (OAE) tests are employed when determining inner ear functioning (B), and inspection and palpation of the outer ear (A) are components of a full ear exam. An auditory brainstem response (ABR) test is used in conjunction with OAE tests to determine any infirmities of the auditory nerve (D).

95. B: The HME device is (B) used to protect the airway for respiration. HME stands for Heat and Moisture Exchanger. It is a filter installed to the tracheostoma which captures heat and moisture from the air exhaled through it. Then, when the patient inhales, some of this captured heat and moisture are picked up so the patient is not breathing cool, dry outside air. This protects the airway.

Copyright © Mometrix Media. You have been licensed one copy of this document for personal use only. Any other reproduction or redistribution is strictly prohibited. All rights reserved.
This content is provided for test preparation purposes only and does not imply an endorsement by Mometrix of any particular political, scientific, or religious point of view.

Total laryngectomy patients have lost the air moisturizing and warming functions of their noses because they now breathe through their necks via a tracheostoma instead of through the nose. This causes mucus to become more viscous, reducing escalator transport. It can also result in excessive phlegm production. The simple HME device restores some of the air conditioning and filtration. The HME is not used to produce a voice, either prosthetically (A) or electromechanically (C). It is only used to condition and filter the air inhaled by the patient. Choice (D) is an invented choice.

96. C: Rate (C) is measured when determining speech fluency when diagnosing stuttering, but it is not measured by the ALST. The Adolescent Language Screening Test (ALST; Morgan and Guilford, Pro-Ed, 1984) is designed for ages 11 to 17 years. It takes 10 to 15 minutes to administer. The ALST screens the adolescent's language content, form, and use. It includes seven subscales that respectively measure phonology (D), morphology, sentence formulation, receptive vocabulary, expressive vocabulary (A), concepts, and pragmatics (B).

97. C: Low resistance to the flow of air (C) is not a disadvantage of TEP-inserted prostheses, but an advantage in that it makes vocal production easier than working against higher airflow resistance. Major disadvantages of this treatment include required daily maintenance (A); the need to replace the prosthesis periodically (B); and the expenses associated with this method (D). Another disadvantage is that most patients have to use one hand to block the tracheostoma, similarly to the need to use one hand with an electrolarynx. Other less frequent complications that can occur with TEP prostheses are the formation of granulomatous tissue at the site, which has been reported in about 5% of cases; and aspiration of the prosthesis itself, which is more serious but occurs in only about 1% to 5% of cases.

98. B: A fistula that is loose-fitting and capable of expansion (B) is not a desirable characteristic of a good voice prosthesis. When a tracheoesophageal fistula (TEF) is surgically created for the insertion of the prosthesis, it should fit snugly around the inserted device. If the fistula becomes larger with time, this leads to leakage around the prosthesis. According to voice rehabilitation specialists, the characteristics that today's best voice prostheses should have are: (A) safe and reliable use; (C) frontloading insertion, meaning insertion through the tracheostoma rather than the mouth; low resistance to airflow; and (D) semi-permanent fixation, also known as indwelling fixation, whereby the prosthesis has an additional flange to keep it fixed in place so it is not aspirated and does not migrate or move around. This was developed by Panje as a variation of previous prostheses and was refined by Groningen.

99. D: In the Early Production Stage, ELLs begin to use words that they learned in the Pre-production Stage. One word and yes/no responses are common. Conversation is initiated with gesture or one or two words. Children in this stage will verbally respond to an increasingly wider variety of linguistic stimuli.

100. D: Krashen. Acquisition-Learning, Monitor, Natural Order, Input, and Affective Filter hypotheses are central to Steven Krashen's highly respected theory of second language acquisition. Language Acquisition is subconscious and requires meaningful communication, while Language Learning is conscious and involves formal instruction; the Monitor is concerned with editing and correcting errors in speaking or writing; Natural Order finds there is a predictable natural order in which grammatical structures are absorbed; Input refers to the hypothesis that language is ultimately acquired and not learned, and the Affective Filter hypothesis explores ways in which positive and negative factors such as motivation, self-esteem, and anxiety help or hurt the acquisition of language.

Copyright © Mometrix Media. You have been licensed one copy of this document for personal use only. Any other reproduction or redistribution is strictly prohibited. All rights reserved.
This content is provided for test preparation purposes only and does not imply an endorsement by Mometrix of any particular political, scientific, or religious point of view.

How to Overcome Test Anxiety

Just the thought of taking a test is enough to make most people a little nervous. A test is an important event that can have a long-term impact on your future, so it's important to take it seriously and it's natural to feel anxious about performing well. But just because anxiety is normal, that doesn't mean that it's helpful in test taking, or that you should simply accept it as part of your life. Anxiety can have a variety of effects. These effects can be mild, like making you feel slightly nervous, or severe, like blocking your ability to focus or remember even a simple detail.

If you experience test anxiety—whether severe or mild—it's important to know how to beat it. To discover this, first you need to understand what causes test anxiety.

Causes of Test Anxiety

While we often think of anxiety as an uncontrollable emotional state, it can actually be caused by simple, practical things. One of the most common causes of test anxiety is that a person does not feel adequately prepared for their test. This feeling can be the result of many different issues such as poor study habits or lack of organization, but the most common culprit is time management. Starting to study too late, failing to organize your study time to cover all of the material, or being distracted while you study will mean that you're not well prepared for the test. This may lead to cramming the night before, which will cause you to be physically and mentally exhausted for the test. Poor time management also contributes to feelings of stress, fear, and hopelessness as you realize you are not well prepared but don't know what to do about it.

Other times, test anxiety is not related to your preparation for the test but comes from unresolved fear. This may be a past failure on a test, or poor performance on tests in general. It may come from comparing yourself to others who seem to be performing better or from the stress of living up to expectations. Anxiety may be driven by fears of the future—how failure on this test would affect your educational and career goals. These fears are often completely irrational, but they can still negatively impact your test performance.

Elements of Test Anxiety

As mentioned earlier, test anxiety is considered to be an emotional state, but it has physical and mental components as well. Sometimes you may not even realize that you are suffering from test anxiety until you notice the physical symptoms. These can include trembling hands, rapid heartbeat, sweating, nausea, and tense muscles. Extreme anxiety may lead to fainting or vomiting. Obviously, any of these symptoms can have a negative impact on testing. It is important to recognize them as soon as they begin to occur so that you can address the problem before it damages your performance.

The mental components of test anxiety include trouble focusing and inability to remember learned information. During a test, your mind is on high alert, which can help you recall information and stay focused for an extended period of time. However, anxiety interferes with your mind's natural processes, causing you to blank out, even on the questions you know well. The strain of testing during anxiety makes it difficult to stay focused, especially on a test that may take several hours. Extreme anxiety can take a huge mental toll, making it difficult not only to recall test information but even to understand the test questions or pull your thoughts together.

Copyright © Mometrix Media. You have been licensed one copy of this document for personal use only. Any other reproduction or redistribution is strictly prohibited. All rights reserved.
This content is provided for test preparation purposes only and does not imply an endorsement by Mometrix of any particular political, scientific, or religious point of view.

Effects of Test Anxiety

Test anxiety is like a disease—if left untreated, it will get progressively worse. Anxiety leads to poor performance, and this reinforces the feelings of fear and failure, which in turn lead to poor performances on subsequent tests. It can grow from a mild nervousness to a crippling condition. If allowed to progress, test anxiety can have a big impact on your schooling, and consequently on your future.

Test anxiety can spread to other parts of your life. Anxiety on tests can become anxiety in any stressful situation, and blanking on a test can turn into panicking in a job situation. But fortunately, you don't have to let anxiety rule your testing and determine your grades. There are a number of relatively simple steps you can take to move past anxiety and function normally on a test and in the rest of life.

Physical Steps for Beating Test Anxiety

While test anxiety is a serious problem, the good news is that it can be overcome. It doesn't have to control your ability to think and remember information. While it may take time, you can begin taking steps today to beat anxiety.

Just as your first hint that you may be struggling with anxiety comes from the physical symptoms, the first step to treating it is also physical. Rest is crucial for having a clear, strong mind. If you are tired, it is much easier to give in to anxiety. But if you establish good sleep habits, your body and mind will be ready to perform optimally, without the strain of exhaustion. Additionally, sleeping well helps you to retain information better, so you're more likely to recall the answers when you see the test questions.

Getting good sleep means more than going to bed on time. It's important to allow your brain time to relax. Take study breaks from time to time so it doesn't get overworked, and don't study right before bed. Take time to rest your mind before trying to rest your body, or you may find it difficult to fall asleep.

Along with sleep, other aspects of physical health are important in preparing for a test. Good nutrition is vital for good brain function. Sugary foods and drinks may give a burst of energy but this burst is followed by a crash, both physically and emotionally. Instead, fuel your body with protein and vitamin-rich foods.

Also, drink plenty of water. Dehydration can lead to headaches and exhaustion, especially if your brain is already under stress from the rigors of the test. Particularly if your test is a long one, drink water during the breaks. And if possible, take an energy-boosting snack to eat between sections.

Along with sleep and diet, a third important part of physical health is exercise. Maintaining a steady workout schedule is helpful, but even taking 5-minute study breaks to walk can help get your blood pumping faster and clear your head. Exercise also releases endorphins, which contribute to a positive feeling and can help combat test anxiety.

When you nurture your physical health, you are also contributing to your mental health. If your body is healthy, your mind is much more likely to be healthy as well. So take time to rest, nourish your body with healthy food and water, and get moving as much as possible. Taking these physical steps will make you stronger and more able to take the mental steps necessary to overcome test anxiety.

Copyright © Mometrix Media. You have been licensed one copy of this document for personal use only. Any other reproduction or redistribution is strictly prohibited. All rights reserved.
This content is provided for test preparation purposes only and does not imply an endorsement by Mometrix of any particular political, scientific, or religious point of view.

Mental Steps for Beating Test Anxiety

Working on the mental side of test anxiety can be more challenging, but as with the physical side, there are clear steps you can take to overcome it. As mentioned earlier, test anxiety often stems from lack of preparation, so the obvious solution is to prepare for the test. Effective studying may be the most important weapon you have for beating test anxiety, but you can and should employ several other mental tools to combat fear.

First, boost your confidence by reminding yourself of past success—tests or projects that you aced. If you're putting as much effort into preparing for this test as you did for those, there's no reason you should expect to fail here. Work hard to prepare; then trust your preparation.

Second, surround yourself with encouraging people. It can be helpful to find a study group, but be sure that the people you're around will encourage a positive attitude. If you spend time with others who are anxious or cynical, this will only contribute to your own anxiety. Look for others who are motivated to study hard from a desire to succeed, not from a fear of failure.

Third, reward yourself. A test is physically and mentally tiring, even without anxiety, and it can be helpful to have something to look forward to. Plan an activity following the test, regardless of the outcome, such as going to a movie or getting ice cream.

When you are taking the test, if you find yourself beginning to feel anxious, remind yourself that you know the material. Visualize successfully completing the test. Then take a few deep, relaxing breaths and return to it. Work through the questions carefully but with confidence, knowing that you are capable of succeeding.

Developing a healthy mental approach to test taking will also aid in other areas of life. Test anxiety affects more than just the actual test—it can be damaging to your mental health and even contribute to depression. It's important to beat test anxiety before it becomes a problem for more than testing.

Study Strategy

Being prepared for the test is necessary to combat anxiety, but what does being prepared look like? You may study for hours on end and still not feel prepared. What you need is a strategy for test prep. The next few pages outline our recommended steps to help you plan out and conquer the challenge of preparation.

Step 1: Scope Out the Test

Learn everything you can about the format (multiple choice, essay, etc.) and what will be on the test. Gather any study materials, course outlines, or sample exams that may be available. Not only will this help you to prepare, but knowing what to expect can help to alleviate test anxiety.

Step 2: Map Out the Material

Look through the textbook or study guide and make note of how many chapters or sections it has. Then divide these over the time you have. For example, if a book has 15 chapters and you have five days to study, you need to cover three chapters each day. Even better, if you have the time, leave an extra day at the end for overall review after you have gone through the material in depth.

If time is limited, you may need to prioritize the material. Look through it and make note of which sections you think you already have a good grasp on, and which need review. While you are studying, skim quickly through the familiar sections and take more time on the challenging parts.

Copyright © Mometrix Media. You have been licensed one copy of this document for personal use only. Any other reproduction or redistribution is strictly prohibited. All rights reserved.
This content is provided for test preparation purposes only and does not imply an endorsement by Mometrix of any particular political, scientific, or religious point of view.

Write out your plan so you don't get lost as you go. Having a written plan also helps you feel more in control of the study, so anxiety is less likely to arise from feeling overwhelmed at the amount to cover.

Step 3: Gather Your Tools

Decide what study method works best for you. Do you prefer to highlight in the book as you study and then go back over the highlighted portions? Or do you type out notes of the important information? Or is it helpful to make flashcards that you can carry with you? Assemble the pens, index cards, highlighters, post-it notes, and any other materials you may need so you won't be distracted by getting up to find things while you study.

If you're having a hard time retaining the information or organizing your notes, experiment with different methods. For example, try color-coding by subject with colored pens, highlighters, or post-it notes. If you learn better by hearing, try recording yourself reading your notes so you can listen while in the car, working out, or simply sitting at your desk. Ask a friend to quiz you from your flashcards, or try teaching someone the material to solidify it in your mind.

Step 4: Create Your Environment

It's important to avoid distractions while you study. This includes both the obvious distractions like visitors and the subtle distractions like an uncomfortable chair (or a too-comfortable couch that makes you want to fall asleep). Set up the best study environment possible: good lighting and a comfortable work area. If background music helps you focus, you may want to turn it on, but otherwise keep the room quiet. If you are using a computer to take notes, be sure you don't have any other windows open, especially applications like social media, games, or anything else that could distract you. Silence your phone and turn off notifications. Be sure to keep water close by so you stay hydrated while you study (but avoid unhealthy drinks and snacks).

Also, take into account the best time of day to study. Are you freshest first thing in the morning? Try to set aside some time then to work through the material. Is your mind clearer in the afternoon or evening? Schedule your study session then. Another method is to study at the same time of day that you will take the test, so that your brain gets used to working on the material at that time and will be ready to focus at test time.

Step 5: Study!

Once you have done all the study preparation, it's time to settle into the actual studying. Sit down, take a few moments to settle your mind so you can focus, and begin to follow your study plan. Don't give in to distractions or let yourself procrastinate. This is your time to prepare so you'll be ready to fearlessly approach the test. Make the most of the time and stay focused.

Of course, you don't want to burn out. If you study too long you may find that you're not retaining the information very well. Take regular study breaks. For example, taking five minutes out of every hour to walk briskly, breathing deeply and swinging your arms, can help your mind stay fresh.

As you get to the end of each chapter or section, it's a good idea to do a quick review. Remind yourself of what you learned and work on any difficult parts. When you feel that you've mastered the material, move on to the next part. At the end of your study session, briefly skim through your notes again.

But while review is helpful, cramming last minute is NOT. If at all possible, work ahead so that you won't need to fit all your study into the last day. Cramming overloads your brain with more information than it can process and retain, and your tired mind may struggle to recall even

Copyright © Mometrix Media. You have been licensed one copy of this document for personal use only. Any other reproduction or redistribution is strictly prohibited. All rights reserved.
This content is provided for test preparation purposes only and does not imply an endorsement by Mometrix of any particular political, scientific, or religious point of view.

previously learned information when it is overwhelmed with last-minute study. Also, the urgent nature of cramming and the stress placed on your brain contribute to anxiety. You'll be more likely to go to the test feeling unprepared and having trouble thinking clearly.

So don't cram, and don't stay up late before the test, even just to review your notes at a leisurely pace. Your brain needs rest more than it needs to go over the information again. In fact, plan to finish your studies by noon or early afternoon the day before the test. Give your brain the rest of the day to relax or focus on other things, and get a good night's sleep. Then you will be fresh for the test and better able to recall what you've studied.

Step 6: Take a Practice Test

Many courses offer sample tests, either online or in the study materials. This is an excellent resource to check whether you have mastered the material, as well as to prepare for the test format and environment.

Check the test format ahead of time: the number of questions, the type (multiple choice, free response, etc.), and the time limit. Then create a plan for working through them. For example, if you have 30 minutes to take a 60-question test, your limit is 30 seconds per question. Spend less time on the questions you know well so that you can take more time on the difficult ones.

If you have time to take several practice tests, take the first one open book, with no time limit. Work through the questions at your own pace and make sure you fully understand them. Gradually work up to taking a test under test conditions: sit at a desk with all study materials put away and set a timer. Pace yourself to make sure you finish the test with time to spare and go back to check your answers if you have time.

After each test, check your answers. On the questions you missed, be sure you understand why you missed them. Did you misread the question (tests can use tricky wording)? Did you forget the information? Or was it something you hadn't learned? Go back and study any shaky areas that the practice tests reveal.

Taking these tests not only helps with your grade, but also aids in combating test anxiety. If you're already used to the test conditions, you're less likely to worry about it, and working through tests until you're scoring well gives you a confidence boost. Go through the practice tests until you feel comfortable, and then you can go into the test knowing that you're ready for it.

Test Tips

On test day, you should be confident, knowing that you've prepared well and are ready to answer the questions. But aside from preparation, there are several test day strategies you can employ to maximize your performance.

First, as stated before, get a good night's sleep the night before the test (and for several nights before that, if possible). Go into the test with a fresh, alert mind rather than staying up late to study.

Try not to change too much about your normal routine on the day of the test. It's important to eat a nutritious breakfast, but if you normally don't eat breakfast at all, consider eating just a protein bar. If you're a coffee drinker, go ahead and have your normal coffee. Just make sure you time it so that the caffeine doesn't wear off right in the middle of your test. Avoid sugary beverages, and drink enough water to stay hydrated but not so much that you need a restroom break 10 minutes into the

Copyright © Mometrix Media. You have been licensed one copy of this document for personal use only. Any other reproduction or redistribution is strictly prohibited. All rights reserved.
This content is provided for test preparation purposes only and does not imply an endorsement by Mometrix of any particular political, scientific, or religious point of view.

test. If your test isn't first thing in the morning, consider going for a walk or doing a light workout before the test to get your blood flowing.

Allow yourself enough time to get ready, and leave for the test with plenty of time to spare so you won't have the anxiety of scrambling to arrive in time. Another reason to be early is to select a good seat. It's helpful to sit away from doors and windows, which can be distracting. Find a good seat, get out your supplies, and settle your mind before the test begins.

When the test begins, start by going over the instructions carefully, even if you already know what to expect. Make sure you avoid any careless mistakes by following the directions.

Then begin working through the questions, pacing yourself as you've practiced. If you're not sure on an answer, don't spend too much time on it, and don't let it shake your confidence. Either skip it and come back later, or eliminate as many wrong answers as possible and guess among the remaining ones. Don't dwell on these questions as you continue—put them out of your mind and focus on what lies ahead.

Be sure to read all of the answer choices, even if you're sure the first one is the right answer. Sometimes you'll find a better one if you keep reading. But don't second-guess yourself if you do immediately know the answer. Your gut instinct is usually right. Don't let test anxiety rob you of the information you know.

If you have time at the end of the test (and if the test format allows), go back and review your answers. Be cautious about changing any, since your first instinct tends to be correct, but make sure you didn't misread any of the questions or accidentally mark the wrong answer choice. Look over any you skipped and make an educated guess.

At the end, leave the test feeling confident. You've done your best, so don't waste time worrying about your performance or wishing you could change anything. Instead, celebrate the successful completion of this test. And finally, use this test to learn how to deal with anxiety even better next time.

Review Video: Test Anxiety
Visit mometrix.com/academy and enter code: 100340

Important Qualification

Not all anxiety is created equal. If your test anxiety is causing major issues in your life beyond the classroom or testing center, or if you are experiencing troubling physical symptoms related to your anxiety, it may be a sign of a serious physiological or psychological condition. If this sounds like your situation, we strongly encourage you to seek professional help.

Copyright © Mometrix Media. You have been licensed one copy of this document for personal use only. Any other reproduction or redistribution is strictly prohibited. All rights reserved.
This content is provided for test preparation purposes only and does not imply an endorsement by Mometrix of any particular political, scientific, or religious point of view.

Online Resources

Due to our efforts to try to keep this book to a manageable length, we've created a link that will give you access to all of your online resources:

mometrix.com/resources719/priispedtssli

It's Your Moment, Let's Celebrate It!

Share your story @mometrixtestpreparation

Copyright © Mometrix Media. You have been licensed one copy of this document for personal use only. Any other reproduction or redistribution is strictly prohibited. All rights reserved.
This content is provided for test preparation purposes only and does not imply an endorsement by Mometrix of any particular political, scientific, or religious point of view.